NN08001282 Theo £55.00

INSPIRING FAITH IN SCHOOLS

Inspiring Faith in Schools addresses the privileging of secularism that appears to affect RE in countries influenced by modern western thought. The authors argue that a more engaging form of RE would emerge if religious life were to inhabit centre stage. Currently religious faith is made to hover in the wings awaiting the call to face the inquisitorial challenge of the modern day enquirer. The consequent relationship between pupil and the Divine as the purpose of study is then already intrinsically irreligious, as indicated in the Book of Job by putting God in the dock, whereas it is the pupil who should be (cross-)examining his or her life. What are the ways of exciting and engaging the young so that they begin to entertain the possibility of religious life as a genuine option for themselves? Leading scholars in philosophy and theology from the UK, Australia, Canada and the USA come together to address these questions together with RE experts. Marius Felderhof writes an Afterword summing up the challenges faced by such a re-visioning of RE.

Explorations in Practical, Pastoral and Empirical Theology

Series Editors: Leslie J. Francis, University of Wales, Bangor, UK
and Jeff Astley, Director of the North of England
Institute for Christian Education, UK

Theological reflection on the church's practice is now recognised as a significant element in theological studies in the academy and seminary. Ashgate's new series in practical, pastoral and empirical theology seeks to foster this resurgence of interest and encourage new developments in practical and applied aspects of theology worldwide. This timely series draws together a wide range of disciplinary approaches and empirical studies to embrace contemporary developments including: the expansion of research in empirical theology, psychological theology, ministry studies, public theology, Christian education and faith development; key issues of contemporary society such as health, ethics and the environment; and more traditional areas of concern such as pastoral care and counselling.

Other titles in the series include:

The Bible and Lay People
An Empirical Approach to Ordinary Hermeneutics
Andrew Village
978-0-7546-5801-6

Deaf Liberation Theology
Hannah Lewis
978-0-7546-5524-4

Theological Reflection and Education for Ministry
The Search for Integration in Theology
John E. Paver
978-0-7546-5754-5

Renewing Pastoral Practice
Trinitarian Perspectives on Pastoral Care and Counselling
Neil Pembroke
978-0-7546-5565-7

Engaging with Contemporary Culture
Christianity, Theology and the Concrete Church
Martyn Percy
978-0-7546-3259-7

Inspiring Faith in Schools
Studies in Religious Education

Edited by

MARIUS FELDERHOF
University of Birmingham, UK

PENNY THOMPSON
Freelance Writer and Researcher in Religious Education

DAVID TOREVELL
Liverpool Hope University, UK

ASHGATE

Published by
Ashgate Publishing Limited
Gower House
Croft Road
Aldershot
Hampshire GU11 3HR
England

Ashgate Publishing Company
Suite 420
101 Cherry Street
Burlington, VT 05401-4405
USA

Ashgate website: http://www.ashgate.com

British Library Cataloguing in Publication Data
Inspiring faith in schools : studies in religious education. – (Explorations in practical, pastoral and empirical theology)
   1. Religious education 2. Religious education – Teaching methods
   I. Felderhof, M. C. II. Torevell, David III. Thompson, Penny
   200.7'1

Library of Congress Cataloging-in-Publication Data
Inspiring faith in schools : studies in religious education / [edited by] Marius Felderhof, David Torevell, and Penny Thompson.
      p. cm. – (Explorations in practical, pastoral, and empirical theology)
   ISBN 978-0-7546-6031-6 (hardcover : alk. paper) 1. Religious education. I. Felderhof, M. C. II. Torevell, David. III. Thompson, Penny.

   BL42.I57 2007
   207'.5–dc22

2006103257

ISBN 978-0-7546-6031-6

Printed and bound in Great Britain by MPG Books Ltd, Bodmin, Cornwall.

For Terry McLaughlin

Contents

List of Figures

List of Contributors

Dr M.C. Felderhof
Department of Theology and Religious Studies
University of Birmingham
Elmfield House
Selly Oak
Birmingham B29 6LG
m.c.felderhof@bham.ac.uk

Mrs Penny Thompson
14 Chestnut Avenue
Crosby
Liverpool L23 2SZ
Merseyside
penelopethompson@btinternet.com

Dr David Torevell
School of Theology, Philosophy and Religion
Liverpool Hope University
Hope Park
Liverpool L16 9JD
torved@hope.ac.uk

Revd Professor Jeff Astley
8 Vicarage Court
Heighington Village
Newton Aycliffe
Co Durham DL5 6SD
Jeff.Astley@durham.ac.uk

Dr Philip Barnes
Department of Education and Professional Studies
King's College London
University of London
Franklin Wilkins Building (Waterloo Bridge Wing)
Waterloo Road
London SE1 9NH
philip.barnes@kcl.ac.uk

Professor David Carr
Dept of Educational Theory and Practice
Moray House Institute
Charteris Land
Edinburgh EH8 8AQ
davidc@education.ed.ac.uk

Dr G.P. (Joe) Fleming
6 Keating Court
Highton
Victoria 3216
Australia
flemingg@pipeline.com.au

Professor Joe Houston
103 Balshagray Avenue
Glasgow G11 7EG
joseph.houston@hotmail.com

Revd Dr William K. Kay
Centre for Pentecostal and Charismatic Studies
Department of Theology and Religious Studies
University of Wales
Bangor
Gwynedd LL57 2DG
w.kay@bangor.ac.uk

Dr Ieuan Lloyd
16 St. Oswald's Close
Upper Tything
Worcester WR1 1HR
rarebooks@worcester74.freeserve.co.uk

Dr Grant Maple
Anglican Education Commission
Diocese of Sydney
PO Box A 287
Sydney South 1235
Australia
grantm@aec.edu.au

Professor John Sullivan
School of Theology, Philosophy and Religion
Liverpool Hope University
Hope Park
Liverpool L16 9JD
sullivj@hope.ac.uk

Professor Elmer Thiessen
305 Bushview Crescent
Waterloo, Ontario
N2V 2A6
Canada
ejthiessen@sympatico.ca

Dr Brenda Watson
Wyke House
Croft Bank
West Malvern
Worcestershire WR14 4BP
bgwykehouse@ukonline.co.uk

Dr Andrew Wright
Centre for Theology, Religion and Culture
King's College
Franklin-Wilkins Building
Waterloo Road
London SE1 9NN
andrew.wright@kcl.ac.uk

Professor Iris M. Yob
Walden University
Home Office:
2252 Cape Cod Dr East
Bloomington IN, 47401
Mailing Address:
P.O. Box 6595
Bloomington, IN 47407
USA
Iris.Yob@waldenu.edu

Foreword

This book has emerged from a series of colloquia held at St Deiniol's Library, Hawarden near Chester between 2003 and 2006. The purpose of these colloquia was to bring together professionals in the field of Religious Education (RE) with theologians and philosophers to debate some of the fundamental questions and challenges facing the subject at the start of the twenty-first century. Observations, insights and recommendations were exchanged between those with experience of teaching the subject and those primarily concerned with the theological and philosophical implications of the debate. While it has not been possible to include all the major voices in the field, it is hoped that the chapters will reflect something of the range of views and positions held and do justice to clarifying central issues facing RE, not only in England and Wales, but throughout the world at the present time.

The chapters, therefore, confront a number of central issues about the trajectory RE has taken over recent decades and, in the light of this history, offer suggestions and possibilities for a critical review of the subject in the early years of the twenty-first century. Such questions include the extent to which secular agenda continue to influence and drive the philosophy, practice and policy-making of RE. In a culture that has witnessed methodological atheism and secular approaches to education – which seem to win hands down in both the humanities and sciences – what might be the appropriate (and urgent) response of religious educators to this *zeitgeist*? Have religious educators taken some wrong turns over recent years in attempting to reflect, and engage too readily with, a culture which seems hostile, if not contemptuous, of religion's deeply-held claims about truth, meaning and purpose? Are the difficult questions of truth and commitment overlooked in RE? Is religious faith really appreciated and understood? What might it mean to begin from faith rather than doubt, from inspiration rather than agnosticism?

Ignoring such questions is a disservice to the integrity of the discipline itself. Indeed, some of the claims made in the book suggest that narrow and limited conceptions of religion do persist and are having a damaging effect on pupils' religious formation. The secularist view of religion has for decades governed the approach to RE in state schools; the time has come for a fuller, more sympathetic account of religion, allowing sensitive reference to how flourishing and dynamic faith communities understand their lives, mission, spirituality and purpose. This not only promotes and shares the excitement of RE with pupils and teachers but also does justice to the integrity of the religious quest. Any such realignment would not, of course, ignore the trickier, more philosophical, indeed negative, aspects of religion, but would begin to emphasise systematically more rounded notions of what being religious might entail, including debate about respect for God, truth, meaning and beauty and the radical difference religious commitment makes to understanding the world and the self.

Allied to such concerns, some contributors argue that many of the approaches to RE over the past thirty years have not been helpful in presenting to pupils a solid and well-rounded understanding of Christianity or, indeed, other world faiths. The ongoing practice of giving equal weight to a variety of spiritual expressions, of marginalising truth claims and devaluing the experience of faith, both individual and communal, have had a major influence on the philosophy and teaching of the subject, with the consequence that many pupils are left confused in their understanding of what religion is essentially *about* and *for.* Old questions start to re-emerge with renewed vigour in the light of such appraisals: Has the personal commitment of the teacher no longer any function in the classroom? Is faith a dangerous and loaded word, never to be uttered confidently within the school? How far might the religious commitment of teachers themselves influence curriculum development, methodology and policy in RE? Has the time come to explore more fully the dialectical relationship between faith and reason, described by Pope John Paul II as the 'two wings, on which the human spirit rises to the contemplation of truth' (1988, p. 3). Such questions remain urgent and global; indeed, many of the contributions have significant implications for RE outside England and Wales.

Of course, no one working in the world of RE can sensibly deny the impact that secular liberalism and pluralism have had on society and self-identity. All the writers recognise this cultural shift and are sensitive towards those contemporary Western thinkers who are suspicious of the imposition of the Christian religion on non-Christian pupils. The public understanding of the role and nature of RE has moved on, as pluralism, diversity and multiculturalism take root in new soil; clearly, religious educators must tailor their methodological cloth according to this new landscape; the safeguarding of human dignity is essential and must be promoted within schools. Narrowly conceived authoritarian, sectarian and fundamentalist claims to truth and morality must be challenged and debated. Rightly, a 'hermeneutics of suspicion' operates within the educational world, especially in relation to theological and religious claims. Religious educators have a duty to be cognisant of, and at times sympathetic towards, this position.

But while there has undeniably emerged a more tolerant attitude towards others in RE, the authors outline numerous ways in which it remains problematic. The challenges and opportunities about how the subject might operate effectively in an increasingly pluralist and secular society are addressed in this book. How, some ask, are religious educators going to critique the secular agenda and yet at the same time operate with fairness, integrity and impact within it? If a narrow form of secularism has dominated recent discussions about RE, how is the balance to be redressed effectively? If pupils are beginning to view religion as being marginal to their own hopes, aspirations, concerns and lives, what needs to be done? How might a realist view of religion be best expressed by teachers? A common thread throughout these pages is that many external forces are unsympathetic to religious metanarratives. Even if a battle for the soul of the subject were to commence, it is unlikely that a clear consensus would emerge. What then, is the most effective way forward?

It is for these reasons that some contributors suggest that a pragmatic rather than an idealistic approach needs to be taken: the liberal secular paradigm has proved to work coherently for numerous democracies, and has had important success in upholding freedom and been highly supportive of diversity (to the point of protection by law), especially with regard to minority groups. RE has to find a way of working and operating meaningfully within such a context. The art of humility needs to be exercised and honed in order to achieve what is possible in such circumstances. An honest, humble engagement with the liberal worldview is the answer. For others, what is essential is a far more bullish and aggressive stance towards secularism. Religious educators have a responsibility to highlight the historically short-lived and flawed nature of secularism's foundations by pointing to those things it can never possibly deliver without recourse to the transcendent and the eternal. The natural and supernatural cannot be divorced without grave consequences. RE must seek to offer pupils an appreciation of how the whole of human life and creation are to be understood with constant reference to the transcendent and the divine. Any such critique of liberalism would point to its association with capitalism and to its overriding legacy of fostering a vague relativism – the result, some scholars argue, has been the emergence of a valueless people for a valueless society.

The contributors also offer important insights about a future model of RE relevant to the twenty-first century. Issues about different types of nurture inevitably surface in relation to state schools and how these might be at variance with the distinctive kind of nurture religious educators want to promote. Discussion about tolerance and the inclusion of atheism into the RE curriculum are also assessed. Imagine asking historians to debate with pupils whether there was any such thing as the past, writes one contributor. Presenting religion as simply one hypothesis among many and asking pupils to choose their favourite belief-system (or none whatsoever), undermines the integrity of the subject itself and blocks the lifeblood that religious traditions offer pupils.

The stance taken by the teacher is, of course, always crucial in such discussions about the future of RE. Although it is now generally agreed that more liberal, secular attitudes towards religion have been helpful in countering misplaced authoritarian approaches towards the subject, the dominant phenomenological approach has not been adequate in addressing some of the fundamental issues of truth and commitment at stake in RE. How is it possible to have a concern for truth *and* be tolerant, to be committed *and* searching, to practise *and* objectively observe religion, to have empathy *and* exercise judgement, to be anchored in a tradition *and* open to others? How might teachers be more proficient in their use of theological language to enable pupils to appreciate how spiritual, moral and aesthetic discourse is grounded in reality and how it operates within religious forms of life?

Inevitably, part of the ensuing discussion focuses on those elements of a more confessional approach which might be worth retrieving for the future; such stances might well have the potential to reflect more accurately a 'religious' understanding of religion, far more than phenomenological perspectives. How these approaches differ in church and state schools also becomes crucial for the future of the subject. Clearly, in church schools, where a strong commitment towards Christian nurture is openly advocated, the debate about confessional approaches would be less problematic. But what about schools, which, in UK parlance, do not 'have a religious character'? What kind of confessional approach is possible here, if at all, in the present climate? Would more truth-sensitive and truth-directed approaches, which offer pupils opportunities for prayer and religious nurture, be the way forward?

All the contributors accept that the existing status and perennial pressures of pluralism and secularism call for a reappraisal of the directions RE might take in the future. Their reflections emerge from their close attention to what has been happening in the subject over many years. The authors are keen to take stock of the history of recent developments in RE and to offer safeguards, suggestions and hopeful possibilities, as more appropriate models come into focus which might serve the subject and pupils better in these times of international uncertainty and spiritual challenge.

Reference

Pope John Paul II (1988) *Fides et Ratio (Reason and Faith). Encyclical Letter of Pope John Paul II.* London, Catholic Truth Society.

Acknowledgements

The editors gratefully acknowledge the support of Liverpool Hope University in the development of this book. The Department of Theology and Religious Studies sponsored both the first and second Hope Colloquium that brought together the authors of this volume (and others) in 2005 and 2006. The university has also supported the editing of the book financially. Thanks to Professor Kenneth Newport for the interest and encouragement he has given to the project. Special thanks to William Kay who has acted as editorial adviser and to Jeff Astley who has given invaluable advice. We would like to thank all the contributors for their patience and willingness to make changes as we have tried to fashion a coherent piece of work. A longer version of David Carr's chapter 'On the Grammar of Religious Discourse' appeared in German in *Zeitschrift fur Erziehungswissenschaft* (ZfE), Heft 3, pp. 380–93 (2004). Ieuan Lloyd's chapter is a revised and updated version of 'Confession and Reason' first published in the *British Journal of Religious Education*, 8 (3), pp. 140–45 (1986). The Foreword was written by David Torevell. Marius Felderhof contributed the Afterword and Penny Thompson wrote the introductions to the three parts.

International readers need to know that Religious Education in Britain's schools is not uniform. Schools in England and Wales operate under one legal system (see pp. 63–5) while Scotland and Northern Ireland have their own separate institutional arrangements. Nonetheless, there is a commonality of concerns and this book contains contributions from Scotland, Northern Ireland and (south of the border!) England. Contributions from Canada, the United States and Australia indicate that these concerns are also live issues further afield.

PART 1

Introduction

The chapters in Part 1 raise important issues about the place of truth and reasoning in Religious Education (RE). Why has it become so difficult to discuss the truth of religious claims in RE and, if we must accept that such matters are not at the heart of RE, what place in an *educational* setting could possibly be claimed for a subject so patently lacking in forms of rational dialogue? It might be countered that syllabuses regularly require the pupils to 'rationally evaluate' the truth or otherwise of what they are learning. But one looks in vain for exemplars to set before pupils as happens routinely in other subjects (primary and secondary evidence in history for example). One answer as to why truth is sidelined regularly in RE is that the secularist judgement upon religion is allowed to go by default (a point taken up in chapter 1) and the subject serves merely to establish the uncertainty of religious claims in the minds of pupils. If so, something is seriously wrong with RE and concerted action is needed. Chapter 4 takes up the theme and argues that what is needed is an expansion of religiously based schools where it is possible for pupils to be introduced to forms of reasoning and evaluation that undergird and develop religious faith. Here the tables are turned in favour of religious life while the emphasis on rationality and openness to other points of view means that the canons of a liberal education are fully respected. But, lest we think that such an endeavour is a simple solution, chapter 5 suggests that even where the possibility for proper RE pertains, subtle pressures may undermine the attempt to inspire faith.

Chapter 1

Secularism, Schools and Religious Education

Brenda Watson

Abstract

A secularist outlook has been privileged in schools resulting in a form of confessionalism as controversial as more well-recognised religious forms. The educational vision of delivering a fair and balanced curriculum calls for a twofold approach: firstly, to articulate an alternative basis for the curriculum as a whole, which acknowledges the possible validity of both religion and secularism; secondly, to establish a Religious Education (RE) which is truth-focused and capable of challenging the assumptions of a deeply secularised society.

All education is founded on certain beliefs and has particular aims in mind. In this sense all teaching is confessional, whatever the subject, in that it conveys certain values and not others. Challengeable assumptions about the nature of the world, who or what human-beings are and the purpose of life, are inextricably involved in all decision-making.

We may deplore this unavoidable confessionalism because it seems to offend against the search for openness, pupil autonomy and reliance on what can be established by reason. Nevertheless, as no value-free education is possible, the question actually becomes, what is the appropriate confession; what values and beliefs are, or should be, put across?

The Prevalence of Secularism

It is the contention of the writers of this book that in Britain the values and beliefs conveyed in schools are, and have been for a long time, mainly secularist, that is, assuming that there is no God and that the world is explainable in principle without reference to anything that transcends it. Such secularism is shown particularly clearly in attitudes to RE. The dominant way in which religion has been portrayed is as a cultural phenomenon in which any claim to truth becomes privatised as subjective. This viewpoint implies that central religious beliefs are no more than human constructs invented for cultural usefulness.

Unlike the clearly confessional approach to RE of the pre-1960s era, most of the approaches currently in favour, such as the phenomenological, the experiential and the ethnographic, lend themselves readily to acceptance within a secularist framework. This is because the focus of their concern is religious believers as people who do and believe certain things. The truth or otherwise of what they believe tends to be left in the air, as though bracketed out of the equation.

As other chapters in this book explain, this is at variance with how religious people themselves see their faith. The view of religion as basically cultural or purely personal is a possible way of looking at religion because of the longevity of religions and their incorporation within societies. It is fundamentally, however, an outsider's view, not what is at the heart of religion.

Religion revolves around belief in Spiritual Reality, named in most religions as God. Take that away, and religion becomes, however valuable it may be for an individual or community, an empty husk with external features such as rituals, buildings, dress, doctrine. These features are detachable and applicable to any ideology or way of life. In this sense football or consumerism can become a religion, as well as obvious ideological movements, such as communism and fascism.

It is only fair to add that such secularisation of RE has been aided and abetted by many religious people themselves who have frequently overemphasised the part played by external rituals, creeds and institutions. Without mostly realising it, they have gone along with the assumption that religion is to do with membership of completely separate communities, one called Christianity, another Islam, another Hinduism, and so on, each subdivided into smaller almost self-contained units. The analogy of boxes suggests itself. Outside them all – from the point of view of the secularist – is the beautifully open area inhabited by that section of humanity that has thrown off the chains of religion and escaped from tutelage within the boxes.

Such a view of religion has led to the extraordinary irony of a subject that purports to teach understanding of religion doing so often from a position fundamentally unlike how the saints and scholars of the great religions themselves understand religion. For them truth is supremely important. Thus for Muslims, Islam matters supremely because they are sure that Allah actually exists, and Christianity is a response to what is believed to be the truth about Jesus. The same can be said of all major religions; but the secularist confession sees it the other way round.

The Fact/Belief Divide: Intellectual Apartheid

A major reason why the secularist agenda has engulfed education and RE is the powerful impact of positivism in Higher Education for the past two centuries. This has influenced the intellectual leadership of society as a whole, and still does in so many ways despite the rise of postmodernism. The extraordinary overemphasis on assessment in education is just one example that betrays the presence of positivism.

Positivism holds that only empirically determined areas of study, such as the sciences or quasi-sciences, can claim the label of knowledge. It thus sets up what may be termed a 'fact/belief divide'. This presumes that subjects like the arts, ethics, politics, metaphysics and religion are – from a truth angle – meaningless and merely subjective. Thus, in discussing the arts today, it is hard today even to mention the word 'beauty', and morality has become reduced for many to what can be negotiated and embodied within rules and laws for the benefit of society.

The impact on religion is clear. Religions can be described as phenomena in acceptable academic terms, but no adjudication regarding levels of truth within them is deemed possible. Individuals may practise such adjudication, but what they think has no universal validation: it is no more than just what they happen to think. Deeply felt awareness of the Divine has thus been reinterpreted in psychological or sociological terms, even in biological terms.

Besides promoting a false either/or attitude, this divide has also helped to de-power several generations from the capacity to think intelligently and sensitively about issues on the belief side of the divide. The extreme concentration of intellectual energy on empirical and pragmatic matters has produced an increasingly secularised society where, even though talk of the spiritual may be retained, it is regarded largely as a private domain governed by emotional reactions. This has both made it hard for secularists to understand religion, and deprived religious people of that proper open and respectful debate which they also urgently need. The rise of religious fundamentalism owes much to the intellectual apartheid created by the liberal West.

Secularist Indoctrination?

In an important book, *Indoctrination, Education and God*, Terence Copley (2005) argues that what has happened amounts to secularist indoctrination. Beginning pointedly with the question 'If we were being indoctrinated now, at this minute, would we know?' he asks: 'What if young people are never in a real position to choose between a religious way of life and a non-religious way of life? What if they irresistibly acquire a non-religious world-view in the same way they acquire a taste for jeans, logo trainers and pop music?' (Copley 2005, pp. xi and viii).

After a wide-ranging survey of both media and education, he concludes that our society has seen 'the surrender of mind to an uncritical secular world-view' (Copley 2005, p. 150). He considers that education has been complicit in producing such an effect:

> Education is visibly preserving the discourse of religion but sometimes, rather like a fish that has been filleted. God, the backbone of religion, has too often been neatly excised from the presentation. (Copley 2005, p. 148)

In a thoughtful and provocative review Stephen Burwood (2006) considers that Copley has not made his case. He concludes that 'something like the current approach offers the best safeguard of children's freedom to discuss and question' (2006, p. 107). In the course of his argument, however, Burwood makes some damaging concessions. Thus he notes that 'all education reflects the biases and prevalent values of the society in which it takes place' (2006, p. 106). But we may ask whether there is no more to education than that? Should schools not challenge society as well as reflect it? What has happened to the notion of passing on knowledge in the pursuit of truth? Notably this still appears to be important in other areas of the curriculum. Thus scientists are currently trying to ban the teaching of Creationism in schools because it is false.[1] If truth matters for science, then who has decided that it doesn't matter for religion? Isn't the pursuit of knowledge and truth, independent of the bias of any particular culture or society, part of what the word 'educate' properly means?

Secondly, he quotes the interesting phrase of Max Weber that our society is 'religiously unmusical'. Can we be satisfied with such an education? The philosopher Bryan Magee thinks it an advantage that he came from a home where God's existence was never considered: 'By sheer chance I had the good fortune to grow up in a family in which religion was never mentioned' (Magee 1997, p. 8). Would he, however, say the same about the arts: music, theatre, poetry etc.? Elsewhere he notes that 'he had the good luck to be born into a family that took an active interest in them' (Magee 1997, p. 25). Discussing philosophy, science and the arts, he writes: 'all three confront the mystery of the world's existence, and our existence as human beings, and try to achieve a deeper understanding of it … and a fully rounded human being will find himself becoming naturally interested in all three' (Magee 1998, p. 9). Prior to this quotation, he had commented on and excluded religion as irrelevant. This seems a particularly clear example of secularism at work!

On the one hand the educational rhetoric wants to educate pupils for choice; on the other hand highly educated and cultured people like Magee imply that it doesn't matter if people are ignorant in religion. Yet ignorance is a poor basis for choice, as Daniel Barenboim remarked in his first Reith Lecture. Faced with a comment that schools should not push music on the young so as not to infringe their free will, he replied, 'Ignorance has not yet for me acquired the category of free will decision. First you have to know about it'.[2]

Thirdly Burwood admits that there is no 'value-neutral position' and that secularism is 'as ideological and value-laden as any other'. He sees no problem, however, regarding the dominance of secularism because he associates it with freethinking, promoting notions of openness, tolerance and perhaps even criticality. Such secularism cannot be considered as an attempt to indoctrinate, as the 'wholesale pumping'[3] of secular values into children.

The problem is that by themselves these values are inadequate as the basis for education. It is impossible to be open all the time; and the appropriateness of tolerating the intolerant is increasingly seen today to carry immense problematic consequences. Furthermore, the use of reason does not easily lead to agreement, as philosophers constantly demonstrate. Commitment to such virtues is therefore no guarantee that they are pursued in practice. To take but one example, the openness of the secularist is often strangely selective – it appears to exclude openness to religion! Most philosophy, both academic and popular, has largely privileged secularism and looked with great suspicion upon the possibility of religious faith.

Finally, Burwood defends the status quo on the grounds that it is not just the responsibility of schools to teach understanding of religion: the home and religious

---

1   See for example, *The Independent*, 22 June 2006.

2   D. Barenboim (2006) responding to comment by Willard White at BBC Radio Reith Lecture 1, London, 7 April.

3   Copley's phrase.

institutions are crucial. This, however, misses the point of Copley's argument which is that it is through the secularist assumptions operating in schools, *and* outside them especially through the media, that children are effectively indoctrinated into secularism and against religion. Those from religious homes may receive nurture in religion. It is the majority who do not about whom Copley is concerned, and whom education in schools should be helping.

Fundamentally I believe that Copley's thesis concerning the power of secularism in our society is correct. But because the term *indoctrination* is highly emotive, one which moreover tends to imply *deliberate* conscious imposition of beliefs, the term is perhaps too strong to describe what has happened. It is not however overstating the case to speak of the serious *over-influencing* of the young in a secularist direction. By avoiding unnecessary controversy about the use of the term, we can avoid distracting attention from Copley's main point that the educational language of openness, accessibility and choice becomes meaningless regarding religion unless people have proper and fair exposure to the *possibility* of religious belief. In our society widespread ignorance and prejudice are operating against this. There is a clear need therefore for a truth-focused RE to counteract this situation.

Truth-Focused RE without Illicit Confessionalism?

But it is possible that some may still be inclined to see such an approach to RE which seeks to address secularism, such as is argued for in this book, as an attempt to establish an educationally illicit religious neo-confessionalism. The following section seeks to reassure readers that this is not so.

Such a charge would imply an unacceptably one-sided use of the term 'confessional' as:

1. appropriate only for religion;
2. acceptable to religious people because drawing attention to the crucial *faith* element in religion;
3. inevitably involving an attempted religious take-over if the teacher tries to communicate the truth of religion.

All these points need reassessing.

1. *Appropriate only for Religion*

The 'only' is false. Confession in the form of challengeable beliefs, assumptions, world-views, faith, lies behind all action, reaction and judgement-making and not just behind religion. This is a point brought out, for example, in John Gray's book *Straw Dogs: Thoughts on Humans and Other Animals* (2002). His fierce dismissal of Humanism indicates that the Humanist stance in particular is not as unassailable as its advocates tend to imply.

Whereas religion openly affirms and celebrates, thus making itself vulnerable to the charge of confessionalism, secularists argue that they are not instilling any belief about God, but just allowing people to think what they want; by not teaching about

God it is presumed that a tolerant, neutral, flat playing-field is achieved. Secularism, however, is not neutral in its understanding of reality. It rests on the belief that there is no God and that the world can be adequately – as fully explained as is possible or necessary – in wholly molecular terms.

The denial has positive effect despite its faith-position being often masked by not being voiced as such. A chance example I have just come across occurs in *What Good are the Arts?* by John Carey. He specifically notes: 'I shall assume a secular viewpoint in what follows ... not out of disrespect for religion, but because the assumption of a religious faith would alter the terms of the discussion fundamentally and unpredictably' (Carey 2005, p. 3). This implies a secularist stance because he does not consider it important to lay before the reader the alternative understanding of the arts which religion might give.

The problem is further complicated in that not bringing God in can easily slide into alternative belief concerning the nature of the world and the purpose or non-purpose of human life. I mean by 'slide' accepting views not as a result of thinking about them but largely by default, by not thinking. So the secularist position is not the value-free neutral ground it pretends to be.

The fact that secularists are normally reluctant to admit that they operate from a faith basis enables the myth of their neutrality to continue flourishing. The issue has at least been raised recently in the philosophy journal *Think* around the question 'Is atheism a faith-position?' and has prompted some debate (Watson 2005 and 2006).[4]

2.   Religion concerns Faith

A misleading either/or can easily be read out of this. Whilst faith is crucial for religion and raised to a special place, this should not imply that reason and experience are unrelated to that faith, or that faith is somehow an alternative to reason. This is partly what lies behind the easy separation of religion from anything associated with philosophy. Thus Bryan Magee omits religion from his discussion of the value of philosophy, science and art already quoted, on the grounds that philosophical enquiry operates 'without making it a question of religious faith, or appealing to the say-so of an authority' (Magee 1998, p. 7). In other words, the assumption here is that faith is blind and unrelated to reason.

Religious people have often unknowingly supported this false dichotomy by under-playing the cognitive element in faith and over-playing the emotional. Indeed the presumed split between cognitive and affective states is one of the manifestations of the fact/belief divide discussed above.

3.   Inevitably a Religious Take-Over?

The word to be questioned here is 'inevitably'. There have been many forms of religious, as of secularist, indoctrination. But it is as possible to teach a religious viewpoint as it is a secularist viewpoint without trying to pressurise conformity. The

---

4   Following comments by Brendan Larvor and Marilyn Mason.

understanding of RE expressed in this book takes for granted how crucial it is to avoid any hint of bullying.

All communication with the young, in home or school, conditions – and indeed indoctrinates – to some extent. It is well known that assumptions gathered in childhood exercise a very great hold over the adult mind. Immature minds are necessarily affected, in a way that they cannot at that time critique, by what the adults in their environment believe and regard as important and true. A measure of confessionalism is part of all upbringing and all education, not just regarding religion.

This is why I consider that the current debate about faith schools and community schools is unhelpfully supporting this misunderstanding. It implies that only religious schools are driven by faith when, in community schools, a secularist faith has been privileged over religious faith.

What is needed in *all* schools is space for pupils as persons to reflect on what is presented to them, so that they become capable of discerning for themselves insight from oversight, and understanding from misunderstanding.

The Educational Requirement

Regarding the secularist/religious controversy all educationalists, not just RE teachers, face a dilemma: how to educate without indoctrinating. For at base there are two very fundamental, conflicting faith-positions: *either* the world is the blind product of molecular evolution *or* it is the work of some Power outside it which in most religions is termed God.

Both these positions are challengeable. There is no rational proof for the view that there is no more to the world than its empirical reality, any more than there is rational proof for the existence of God, if by reason is meant a logical, absolutely objective demonstration of truth. For the theist and atheist positions both start from assumptions which people arrive at through reflection on life as a whole – using imagination, empathy, intuition, and many other aspects of cognitive and emotional activity.

The educational requirement must permit real choice based on knowledge, attentiveness and civilised debate. Education should enable pupils to grapple with this possibility. Not to share it with them is tantamount to over-influencing in one direction or another.

Education, as opposed to mere training, should seek to pass on to future generations what is important and help them to think about it for themselves. It is obviously absurd to equate all teaching with indoctrination, in that selection is inevitable. But faith in God or in a God-less world is a matter of such potential moment that failure to present the possibility of God may be seen as unwarranted conditioning. Legitimate specialist interests, or what is appropriate for hobbies, may be considered ripe for non-inclusion in an over-crowded curriculum. But the argument is not so persuasive when matters of potentially great moment are involved.

What is involved regarding belief in God is fundamental; it alters every aspect of a person's assessment of life, as the quotation from John Carey above implies.

The theologian John Magee put it like this: 'Every society is based on a conviction concerning the ultimate nature of things.' As a religious person he quotes T.S. Eliot,

> What life have you if you have not life together?
> There is no life that is not in community
> And no community not lived in praise of God.

He goes on:

> Modern efforts to build a purely secular society are in futile opposition to this principle of moral and spiritual togetherness in the community. When secularism has at last divorced man from his ultimate meanings, pulled him up by the roots and let him wither above the life-nourishing ground, then the frantic efforts to create an artificial community begin. These efforts produce at last the compulsory social collectives of modern history. (Magee, 1957, pp. 1–2)

The secularist will tend to dismiss this viewpoint on the grounds that it is partial and prejudiced. But the point is that the religious person can reply in like manner. What crucially needs to be presented in schools is that *both* religious and secularist convictions are faith-commitments that are challengeable.

How to meet this situation? I believe that two approaches are needed:

A. An Alternative Values-Basis for Schools

There needs to be widespread acknowledgement, right across the curriculum and affecting the whole ethos of the school, of the values needed to support education. In a time of marked uncertainty and changing values it is particularly important to be clear about this. Such clarity can give some kind of stability and coherence and act as a reference point in the life and organisation of the school.

In a specifically religious faith school, such as a Catholic or a Muslim school, the values in the school are presumed to flow from faith in God as perceived within those traditions. This is in effect a hierarchical top-down model. In community schools a different hierarchical model is presumed appropriate: one in which human values such as autonomy, openness and tolerance take precedence, and God is an option somewhere down the system. This is the solution adopted in Britain in the attempt over the last two centuries to include religion within an overall liberal approach to education – unlike in the USA, for example, where religion is generally absent from schools.

The problem with this is twofold. Firstly, there is a certain incoherence surrounding these general human values; they are unable to sustain the weight placed on them, as we have seen. They are not absolutes in their own right, for their validity is dependent on a variety of other deeper considerations. Secondly, to treat God as an optional or exotic extra is already to have lost touch with all the religions which see God as THE reality upon which all the rest is dependent. The apparent carrot of allowing toleration of religions merely underlines that the secularist view is on top and controlling the exercise.

The basic structure of core values for schools needs to incorporate a common approach agreeable to all which nevertheless does not compromise other beliefs held. The 'human values' solution will not do. But neither will the religious hierarchical solution which sees God as the *raison d'être* for education, for this is offensive to secularists who do not believe in God. It is important that integrity is safeguarded for all.

The following is an attempt to draw up a statement of core values permitting a school to function as a conscious unity whilst nevertheless doing justice to what is deeply controversial, that is, to satisfy both secularist and religious convictions. It is set out in two figures. Figure 1 sees a six-fold valuing as the basis of education: it depicts the need for balance, together with a commitment to trying to see things whole and not fragmented. Over-attention to one aspect needs correcting by being mindful of the rest (see, e.g.,Watson and Thompson 2007, ch. 1).

Figure 2 expresses the possibilities of interpreting this six-fold valuing using the metaphors of a circle and an orb. What for non-religious people may appear to be a two-dimensional surface can be seen by religious people to constitute an essential and true aspect of a three-dimensional orb.

On the basis of this, both secularism and RE can operate in schools as consciously legitimate options, not one alone controlling the agenda.

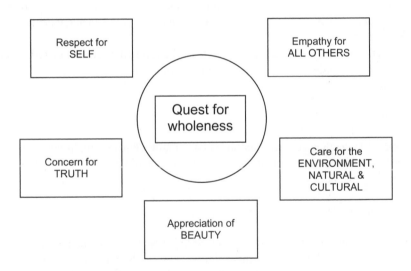

Fig 1   A six-fold approach to valuing, capable of being shared by all

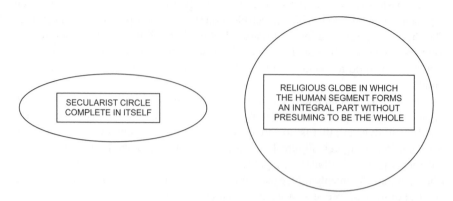

Fig 2   The circle and the orb, permitting the six-fold approach to valuing to be seen from a secularist or a religious perspective without loss of integrity

B.   Truth-Focused RE

The second essential for creating a fair and balanced curriculum is for RE to be given a proper and respected place in the curriculum and be allowed to challenge the secularism of society.

Such truth-focused RE should exhibit at least the following four characteristics, whatever else is included, or whatever syllabus is followed:

It needs to

1. be primarily God-centred;
2. incorporate strong emphasis on thinking skills;
3. acknowledge the necessarily controversial nature of all assumptions;
4. encourage a growing capacity for discernment regarding the nature of religion and its possible counterfeits.

1.   RE Should be Primarily God-Centred

This means opening up for pupils the *possibility* that the fundamental focus of religion on a Reality that transcends this empirical world is true. RE needs to be God-centred because no one can come to intelligent faith in God, nor intelligently deny the existence of God, unless they have acquired some developed understanding of this key concept. We can and should use names such as Ultimate Reality or Spiritual Reality or Transcendent Power to indicate something of that Mystery to which the word 'God' points.

This is a kind of RE which is not just descriptive of the externals of religion but which takes seriously the truth-claims of religion. RE must be aware of how easily in our society teaching about religious people and what is meaningful to them can promote a secularist view. Conveying factual knowledge about external procedures such as the Five Pillars of Islam, without promoting real understanding of the underlying principles of religion, is unhelpful. The origins of Islam lie in the blinding vision of reality which Muhammad had. He became utterly convinced that Allah is the ruling principle behind the whole of reality to whom everyone is responsible and to whom submission is due. The central question which RE should enable pupils to reflect upon is: was he right? By failing to encourage pupils to wrestle with such gigantic truth-claims, RE can by default teach externalism.

2. RE Should Teach Thinking Skills

The assumptions which have led to such massive secularisation have had an unchallenged field day for far too long. RE should help pupils challenge those assumptions. The intellectual difficulties with the secularist case against religion need to be communicated.

.We need specifically to move beyond the normal approach of the *Teaching Thinking Skills* movement.[5] This has been on the whole secularly orientated, focusing on developing logical skills and problem-solving. There is an urgent need for RE to enter this field. I well recall the comment by one experienced primary school teacher attending a Teaching Thinking conference: on hearing that I taught RE he remarked as he walked away: 'Oh you're the folk who believe the moon is made of green cheese!' RE should help even young children to see through that one!

Such work on thinking skills does not mean capitulating to a purely cognitive approach. Rather, RE needs to empower pupils/students to think and reflect in a way that engages their whole personality. It has been a serious weakness of much RE that it has tended to undervalue and underplay thinking. It has suffered from stereotypes derived from Piaget and Goldman, themselves dependent on the fact/belief divide already discussed. I believe that the time has come for reversing this suspicion of thinking and, joined to a more generous understanding of what thinking comprises, allow it to take centre-stage along with other ways of knowing.

3. RE Should Openly Acknowledge the Controversial Nature of Religious Belief

RE needs to accept fully the element of challengeability in all human knowledge and invite pupils into the debate. Neither intellectual nor emotional pressure should be placed on pupils to accept a controversial commitment as though it were not controversial.

We need to remember that the case against believing in God remains possible, and something that must be wrestled with. This is one reason why Rowan Williams has supported the inclusion of Philip Pullmann's atheistic material in RE (2004). We must be honest about disagreements concerning the reality of God when we are dealing with children in schools. By trying to give the impression to them that there is no doubt about God, teachers are making it more difficult for pupils to understand and come to have a real knowledge and love for God; for even young children become

---

5   Associated with de Bono, Lipman, Buzan and many others. See, e.g., Lipman, Sharp and Oscanyan (1980) and Fisher (1990).

aware that many people do not believe in God. The capacity of young children tends to be consistently underrated, as Olivera Petrovich's research shows (1989).

Teaching even young children, therefore, that belief in God is controversial will not result in their indifference provided that they are also taught that *not* believing in God is controversial too. They should be helped to see signs of the secularist bias of our society, especially in the media, and invited to question what is there presented to them.

The underpinning understanding of knowledge which the teacher needs, whatever age-group is being addressed, is one midway between positivism and postmodernism – one which does justice to the human situation, accepting the partial and provisional status of all our knowledge, and therefore, open always to the possibility of fresh evidence based on a range of ways of knowing.

4. *RE Should Seek to Develop Discernment Enabling an Honest Evaluation of Religion*

Real belief in God becomes impossible for those who do not learn to distinguish between genuine faith and the many counterfeits of the real thing which are possible. These may be due to such factors as superstition, hypocrisy and the operation of a power syndrome whereby those in authority try to keep others ensnared. RE should include a radical critique of what passes as religion. What indeed does it mean to be religious? Is a person a Christian or a Muslim just because they say so?

It will not do to try to give the impression that if everybody were religious then the world would be lovely. Unfortunately the damage which religion misunderstood and abused can do is only too apparent. Much anger with religion has a great deal of well-founded experience to support it, and it is a major reason put forward for secularism. Religion can work up strong emotions capable of use for good or ill. With religion we must never imagine that we are dealing with a tame lapdog of a subject; rather it is a potentially ferocious wolf.

Viruses present in almost all religions need to be openly spotted and corrected – racism for example. The peace of the world may depend upon learning to appreciate that any concept of God or Allah as an ethnic cleanser contradicts the fundamental perception in Judaism, Christianity and Islam of God as love, Allah as compassionate. Promoting discernment about the abuse of religion is especially necessary, and will link up with the teaching of thinking skills already mentioned.

Teachers are often fearful of introducing this awareness of negativity in the classroom. I think they do not need to be, provided they genuinely want to encourage children's thinking and involvement in the debate. For such matters lie close to questions almost everyone asks about religion. The usefulness of the virus metaphor moreover does allow religion to be seen in a positive way without pretending that all is well with religion throughout. The point needs to be made that the sternest critics of religion have often been religious people themselves, people like St Francis of Assisi. Such people see the need for reform from within, and work towards it.

Conclusion

RE which features such components as the four just discussed can supply the anti-indoctrinatory feature of the curriculum necessary to help counter the prevailing secularism of society and of much that is taught in schools. RE should appear on the curriculum in schools precisely because belief in God cannot thus easily be disproved. Such belief is a crucial question, completely unsettling attitudes to every other aspect of life, and therefore it is important that children and students have the opportunity to think about it and make decisions about it intelligently and sensitively for themselves on the basis of knowledge and understanding instead of ignorance or prejudice.

References

Burwood, S. (2006) Review of T. Copley, *Indoctrination, Education and God. British Journal of Educational Studies*, March, pp. 105–107.

Carey, J. (2005) *What Good are the Arts?* London, Faber & Faber.

Copley, T. (2005) *Indoctrination, Education and God*. London, SPCK.

Fisher, R. (1990) *Teaching Children to Think*. Oxford, Basil Blackwell.

Gray, J. (2002) *Straw Dogs: Thoughts on Humans and Other Animals*. London, Granta Books.

Lipman, M., Sharp, A.M. and Oscanyan, F.S. (1980) *Philosophy in the Classroom.* Philadelphia, Temple University Press.

Magee, B. (1997) *Confessions of a Philosopher.* London, Phoenix.

—— (1998) *The Story of Philosophy*. London, Dorling Kindersley.

Magee, J. (1957) *Reality and Prayer: A Guide to the Meaning and Practice of Prayer.* London, Hodder & Stoughton.

Petrovich, O. (1989) 'An Examination of Piaget's Theory of Childhood Artificialism', unpublished PhD thesis. University of Oxford.

Watson, B. (2005) 'Should Philosophy Replace RE?' *Think*, 9, 7–11.

—— (2006) 'Is Atheism a Faith-Position?' *Think*, 12, 43–8.

—— and Thompson, P. (2007) *The Effective Teaching of Religious Education*. London, Pearson Prentice Hall, ch. 1.

Williams, R. (2004) *Belief, Unbelief and Religious Education*. Downing Street Paper 8, March.

Chapter 2

Understanding, Belief and Truth

Joe Houston

Abstract

To achieve worthwhile understanding of a religion, we will, at least, be greatly assisted by a grasp both of the beliefs of its adherents, and of their reasons for believing. This is insufficiently reflected in current Religious Education. Moreover, failure to treat religious beliefs as properly subject to a serious rational assessment of their truth leads to indifference about religion, and deprives pupils of critical skills which RE could and (now more than ever) should be well placed to foster. Renewed attention to the critical and the evaluative in relation to a necessarily selective range of religions is needed to rectify these deficiencies.

Gaining some understanding of a religion is, surely, a proper aim of RE in anyone's view. Less generally agreed (though long advocated, and still held by reasonable people) is the dictum that unless you believe you will not understand. For reasons that I shall indicate I do not accept the latter, though I can (I think) see why it may have been asserted. What I do want to argue here is, firstly, that if there is to be more than a very superficial understanding of a religion, attention to, and understanding of, its beliefs is needed; and for that is required, among other things, attention to and understanding of the reasons religiously committed people will give for believing as they do.

Secondly, I contend that the adequate satisfying of that desideratum can go a long way towards dealing with a major concern and dissatisfaction which many properly feel over RE, namely that it fails to equip pupils to develop and exercise powers of perception, discrimination and evaluation in respect of religion's claims. Of course, it has become common, even usual, for pupils to be encouraged to make a 'response' to the religious phenomena presented to them. But while this response may be 'educated', in that the pupil is enabled, say, to recognise parallels or similarities, or differences, between some phenomena and others, education in assessing what is good, and in reckoning what is likely to be true, in a religion, is too little in evidence. (That group of pupils who proceed to A-level study, it is true, are required to engage in some evaluative work; but even there, concerns about truth or other sorts of goodness do not run through all parts of the curriculum.)

This lack (to expand on the issue of the previous paragraph) tends to have these consequences:

1. It removes one of the distinctive educational potential merits of RE: that of educating people in careful critical reflection and discussion of important,

often emotionally highly charged and deeply felt issues. Relatedly,

2. It reduces the capacity of pupils (compared to what that might have been) and perhaps in due time that of their religious communities, to resolve differences both within and between these communities by rational discussion and debate. It will not be in respect only of religious differences that this loss will be felt.

3. It gives pupils the impression that reasonable assessment of religious contentions, what religions apparently assert to be true about the world, is either (a) inappropriate, (b) impossible, or (c) inconclusive.

   a) Rational evaluation may be thought inappropriate, because religions, as distinct from affirmations of truths, are adopted attitudes toward the world, poetic visions of the world, or emotional responses to the world, and are not to be treated as *truth*-claims. (Even on that view, or to the extent that it has a point in holding that religions do often involve attitudes to the world, poetry, and emotional responses, it may well be urged that something more could/should be provided to enable evaluation: of attitudes, and visions, and emotional responses.)

   b) It may be thought impossible because no one can come to know the truth in the matters about which religions try to inform us; human cognitive powers are not up to the job. (The positivist will support (a), and the sceptic/agnostic (b); though on some versions of each, both (a) and (b) can be held. Hume seems to have held both. Among professional philosophers there are few positivists now. Agnostics present the greater contemporary challenge, most usually to be met by challenging 'scientism', of which more anon.)

   c) It may be thought inconclusive and probably pointless because when it is attempted (or the motions are gone through), this is commonly done by considering (the allegedly) 'traditional' arguments for the existence of God. These arguments are taken in the versions presented and then routinely opposed, by counter arguments now routinely treated as decisive; this against a background where people (including some religious believers) confidently assert that God's existence cannot be 'proved'. The 'tradition' is that of a selective religious scepticism (ignoring, to take one example only, the version of the design argument found in Paley and more recently revived by Swinburne (1979, pp. 133–51) based on the prevalence of laws of nature, while attending to versions, also in Paley, held to have been undermined by Hume and Darwin); the work of, say, Adams (1987), Mitchell (1973), Plantinga (2000), or Swinburne (1979) is not reflected. The idea that religious belief is, or may be, or can be, rational is in this manner discounted. The impression that discussion of the truth of religion is not much worth engaging in conveys the corollary that religion is not about realities that we (may) have to reckon with, and breeds not robust agnosticism but indifference, indifferentism.

There are several likely contributory reasons for the prevalence of this state of affairs:

1. There is an obvious need in an RE programme, which is given limited time, to supply pupils with basic uncontroversial information about religions. It is worthwhile for pupils to gain that information not only for its own sake and for what it can contribute to understanding of neighbours but also and at least as much for what it can open up in further understanding of the religions. Unhappily too little progress is made beyond basic information even where that sort of information is adequately provided. If more time can be found, that will help. Perhaps a narrower range of information could be attempted to allow for greater understanding in that range – as at least an example of what greater understanding could be.

2. Some secularist supporters of RE intend (or half hope) that when the variety of religions is set before pupils with little attempt made to engage in assessment (and spectres of 'indoctrination' can be excluded most easily if no determination of truth is involved – though reading Mitchell's insufficiently reckoned-with paper (1970) on the subject would be a much better way of coping with 'indoctrination'), it will seem obvious to all, as it seems to them, that no one knows anything about the realities with which religion purports to deal. Others, who do not think of themselves as secularists are not exercised over whether religions do make claims to say the truth or over whether, if a religion does make such a claim, that religion does speak the truth. Sometimes, incredibly, teachers do not treat these issues as of importance. Such people are happy just to describe, it seems.

3. The sensitivity of evaluative questions in relation to religions is, of course, enormous especially in religiously mixed communities. Rather than bringing out a truth-claiming character of religious discourse with the exclusiveness that that may (and often does) entail, it is easier to rest at the level of description and leave alone the hornets' nests and sleeping dogs. If, however, we leave it at that we shall precisely deprive pupils of the opportunity to acquire the skills in liberal debate over matters that affect us most deeply, skills which are the best hope of our bridging and resolving deep differences satisfactorily. If we do not equip people to debate deep differences, they only have other undesirable ways of dealing with them. A secularist may harbour the thought that the best hope of communal peace is to persuade the next generations that, indeed, nobody knows anything about the *supposed* realities *supposedly* dealt with by religions. But that thought cannot be a basis for public policy because it is deeply partisan, in favour of secularist scepticism about religion, a contentious and contended issue. Further, even if that secularist approach *is* adopted, a consequence may well be that people will see the claim of their religion on them as not a claim in the name of rationality, truth or goodness, but a claim of tribal, national, ethnic or racial loyalty!

4. Where a 'postmodern' account is approved (more often tacitly than explicitly), that is an account of evaluative standards (in epistemic as well as moral matters) as serving and as relative to the interests or wishes of those who hold power, calls to encourage and enable rational assessments in religion are likely to fall on deaf ears. Since one consequence of adopting a postmodern view here will be that debate between religions will be impossible except as

attempts to exert power, and religious groups can only see the claim of their religion on them as being that of race and tribe, with the hopeless divisiveness thus entailed, it will be best (precisely on post-modern assumptions) if those who exert power in our society can impose a belief in liberal rationality: that way relative peace will be possible as different groups *try* to debate, acknowledging reasonableness as having a claim. Postmodernism in this way (as in others) seems to undermine itself.

5. The high status of science leads people to think of it as a paradigm for rational enquiry and as providing *the* sort of justifications which reasonable beliefs need. Attempts to formulate standards for rational investigation in religion of the sort we find in science have been made. Many of the most influential (e.g. the requirement that a contention be in principle falsifiable by some possible experience) have been rejected as simplistic. Even if a more adequate formulation can be provided, it may be that the particular *way* in which science, for example, typically depends on evidence will be different from the ways in which other incontestably rational procedures appeal to evidence. I have in mind such as those in the law courts, or those of historians, or interpreters of ancient texts. Scientism tries to impose the standards allegedly proper to science on any kind of enquiry or body of assertion that lays claim to being rational; and religion is often disparaged by this means. But even if the science-generated standards imposed are not crudely inadequate as applied even to science, the existence of other sorts of incontestably rational discourse that religions may more closely resemble, undercuts scientism. According to some of the best regarded recent theories of knowledge or belief (Moser 1989; Haack 1993), and contrary to simplistic scientism, there is in fact little difference between the bases for the claims of 'religion' and those of 'science' on our acceptance of them.

6. The obvious plurality of mutually incompatible religions and the seeming failure of rational debate over centuries to resolve differences of view inclines people to think that rational debate, assessment for truth or goodness, are impossible or futile. But why should that conclusion be arrived at when we do not treat other long-standing and difficult-to-resolve issues in that way? Nobody treats Goldbach's conjecture (that every even number greater than two is the sum of two prime numbers) as beyond rational assessment even though long effort has not determined its truth or falsehood; still less do we raise a question over the rationality of mathematics for that reason. Fermat's last theorem has only recently been proved after centuries of mathematical work on it; nobody treated that example, during these centuries, as justifying despair about mathematical reasoning. The strength of the Whig or progressivist view of history is likewise a dispute of centuries, with no one for *that* reason treating historians' work as non-rational. Religious disagreements of great age and difficulty do not call for us to treat religions as beyond reasonable evaluation. (And, of course, we do, sometimes, reckon some religions as utterly unreasonable, nutty, as we do apply rational criteria to them.)

7. The widespread adoption of so-called 'phenomenological' approaches in religious studies, in the last third of the twentieth century, was often

(notwithstanding some contrary guidance) taken to omit evaluative concerns. The original phenomenologists' philosophical programme required the careful scrutiny of appearances, phenomena, simply as they appear to the subject, with the subject's beliefs, values and attitudes to life set aside, bracketed off. Phenomenological approaches in RE could be wider or narrower, but the effect was to give primacy to the descriptive, and to offer descriptions of what was observed in religions, in terms minimally theory laden. On this last point, of course, variations in what was acceptably minimal were to be found. Although the heyday of this range of approaches has passed, it encouraged people to think that evaluation of believers' beliefs and/or their grounds for believing were problematic either because evaluation would be entailed or because theory-ladenness would inevitably encroach. Effects of that heyday are still with us in attitudes and curricula. I have two comments: (i) quite without engaging in evaluations, a wider phenomenology could have described believers' beliefs and the grounds they had, and even the objections they faced. Without engaging in evaluation, that could have helped pupils to engage in due course in *their* evaluations, and sometimes this did happen. Hence (ii), a better approach to RE, better assisting pupils in their evaluations *need* not itself be evaluative. (Of course, it may *be* all the better for being evaluative, even prescriptive.)

Now I return to the matters indicated in the first paragraph of this chapter, concerning the understanding of a religion.

In 1998 a group of (mainly English) tourists was receiving a brief introduction to a small town in the (Italian) Dolomites, their holiday base for the next week or two. The guide had pointed out the chairlifts, walkers' routes, notable shops, and was indicating the approach up to the church at the centre of the place. Just then the beginning of a procession came into view. There were canopies, clerics and others in vestments, and people moving along singing quietly or praying earnestly, dressed as for church. The devotion was demonstrative, intense on people's faces. It seemed that several hundred people were processing, perhaps half of the population. Perhaps more than half. It was the feast of Corpus Christi. As they passed, one of the English tourists said, 'It's like watching the antics of some remote tribe; superstitious magic.' I came to know him and others during the next days. He was a commonsensical secular person from south-east England, rather than a zealot for a Protestant cause.

How might he have been able to grasp better what it was like to be a devout member of the procession, to feel and think as these people did?

a) The information that such a procession takes place every year and that, traditionally, it takes this route and most townspeople take part would help a bit. But he'd probably guessed that; and the respects in which these facts touch the minds or hearts of the devout are, surely, pretty superficial.

b) Suppose he knew, roughly, what Christian doctrines say – as for instance that somehow Jesus Christ was/is both divine and human, and that he had inaugurated a peculiar practice of eating bread that he designated as his own body. The attitudes, actions and feelings of the devout would then be more intelligible to the onlooker not only in that he grasps something of how they come to be, but also in that he can rather more fully enter in to the desires, emotions and beliefs of the devout by sympathetic imagination.

c) It can help him in these respects still more if he can see not only causes of the beliefs given under (b), but the believers' *reasons* for them; and to the extent that he can see these reasons to have force he will be able even better to see them as reasons he could have for believing and having the attitudes which share in the conative, emotive and cognitive components of the believers' faith. (Even where he cannot accept the beliefs, his being able to see how someone could more or less reasonably hold them can lead to better imaginative sharing in the believers' wishes, actions and feelings.)

It is an exaggeration to say that no sort of understanding of religious life is possible without a grasp of the rationale of the religious beliefs of the religions; but (at least it can be said) valuable, non-superficial types of understanding of religion certainly are opened up by that sort of grasp: many emotions, and attitudes of kinds important in religion, involve beliefs; and although we can have some understanding of a person's belief without our knowing what are their grounds for it, it will, characteristically, help us to understand their belief and their believing of it better if we do know what their reasons for the belief or the believing are. Often an individual's reason for believing will presuppose their trust in their community and its knowledge and wisdom, received by the community as it may be through reflection on the events of the past or from the insights of sages. An individual devotee may have the sketchiest grasp of the community's reasons, but it can help the student of religion to understand the religion being studied if the student has a good grasp of the community's standard reasons, and also (which may not be the same) the best reasons it could have, its best case for its worldview.

To say this is not to argue (as has been said) that unless you believe you will not understand. As I have acknowledged, *some* (albeit shallow) understanding of a religion is possible for observers or students who have no knowledge of, or interest in, or acceptance of the beliefs of people practising that religion. More than that, it is possible for a person to acquire a sophisticated mastery of a belief system and the reasonings that have underpinned it; and that comprehension of the belief system, its supposed grounds, past arguments about it and within it, its various relations with the cultures in which it has been placed, can constitute a deep understanding without that person being a believer. Indeed, an insightful person whose understanding of a particular religious belief system was deep and wide in these ways might also see how believers' attitudes, emotions and dispositions can inform and be informed by those beliefs of theirs, and this, still, without the insightful person having to be a believer. Authors such as P. Brown on Augustine (1967), or A. Kenny on Aquinas (1980) are notable examples. (On a strongly platonic view of faith, such as Augustine's, a better case can be made for 'unless you believe …'.)

Even though it is not necessary to believe in order to understand, in religious studies, awareness of and attention to, the beliefs of the religions is important (so I insist) for understanding their religion. Even where a religion seems much more a matter of practice than doctrine, dogma or belief (whether belief is construed as trust or, as a propositional attitude), beliefs, the assenting to or presupposing of propositions will be involved – even, it may be, second-order meta-beliefs about the absence of first-order beliefs. And prescriptions for action or contemplation will presuppose beliefs about the world, what it contains, how it works, who has rights in respect of it.

In the assertion of the importance of propositional belief, I do not intend to exclude or play down belief-as-trust. For many religions, trust, for example in God, is central to faith. But there can be no trust without there being believed propositions: to trust God, or, say, the universe, a person must have *some* propositional beliefs about God, or the universe in order to have a sufficient notion of whatever that person trusts in for it to be said that their trust is reposed – in some particular way, or in some thing/ person. And to understand that trust, the student of religion needs to know what the propositional beliefs are.

Reflection on the tourists in the Dolomites, and the limited extent of the understanding where there is little or no awareness of the procession's beliefs or the basis for the beliefs, suggests that a move beyond superficiality in understanding a religion calls for attention to be given to beliefs and their basis. Take another case: the musical *Fiddler on the Roof* stresses the importance of tradition in Jewish community life. So feasts and rituals and songs are those passed on by tradition. But it is a superficial conception of Jewish life and practice which has no grasp of the *beliefs* handed on and vouched for in the tradition, and what grounds the tradition puts forward (further beliefs) as grounds for the former beliefs and for the authority of the tradition. And indeed the musical does offer such a superficial conception. No doubt a musical sets out to appeal to popular sentimentality rather than to risk seriousness. RE curricula which aim to enable understanding of religion, and equip pupils to engage in more worthwhile assessment and evaluation of religious claims and forms of religious life, both for their own benefit and for that of wider community life, cannot settle for mere reference only to overt and more striking, distinctive or colourful aspects of religious life.

Certainly we may not wish to begin in RE, with younger pupils, simply discussing propositional beliefs. Especially as individual particular beliefs of other faith communities than the pupil's own will, when taken initially and on their own, seem difficult. There is an obvious case for focusing on the more immediately accessible: stories, practices, religiously significant objects and occasions, songs, prayers ... A grasp of belief-in-context is then implicitly, and possibly in due course explicitly, opened up as pupils are taken beyond the introductory features of religions. The worry is that where this 'taking beyond' is inadequate, understanding is weak and pupils ill-equipped to deal with religions.

Older credal and catechetical teaching began with beliefs; such beliefs could be contextualised in discussion, and in relation to prominent features of religious life. But it began with concise statements of belief, crafted to convey *something* to pupils, yet saying things about which understanding could grow, saying things that constituted a systematic coherent body of beliefs. Creeds and catechisms have been likened to structures, like capacious houses, to be occupied room by room as people appropriate more and more of this which they may make their home. Those creeds and catechisms had drawbacks – the sequence of the topics was determined more by logical/thematic than pedagogical considerations – but in the limited time available for RE then as now, they provided something that pupils could grow into rather than grow out of.

Limitations on time make it impossible to provide the worthwhile understanding, of the sort argued for here, of several major religions. *Selection* must be introduced to enable worthwhile understanding and the fostering of capacities for appreciation and assessment in relation to a restricted range of religions.

None of the foregoing will be a matter of indifference to people of conviction about religion, whether they are believers or unbelievers. In the absence of much discussion of beliefs and their grounds there is no sufficient reason set before students to treat any as having better claims on our allegiance than any others. So the attitude is fostered that most religious standpoints are little better or worse than any other – and it is not clear that anyone should take any of this seriously as having a claim on us. If this is the view of religions currently fostered (as I maintain that it is), it is sharply at odds with the view of their religion held by mainstream believers in the various faith communities (but is congenial to secularists). That RE as currently practised leaves a false impression of religion as religious people see it, is reason enough for re-thinking. Whatever value that point may have, the points about shallowness of understanding, and the failure to nurture appreciation/evaluation skills, cry out.

References

Adams, R.M. (1987) *The Virtue of Faith*. New York and Oxford, Oxford University Press.

Brown, P. (1967) *Augustine of Hippo*. London, Faber & Faber.

Haack, S. (1993) *Evidence and Inquiry*. Oxford, Blackwell.

Kenny, A. (1980) *Aquinas*. Oxford, Oxford University Press.

Mitchell, B.G. (1970) 'Indoctrination'. In A. Wedderspoon (ed.) *The Fourth R*, London, SPCK, pp. 353–8.

——— (1973) *The Justification of Religious Belief*. London, Macmillan.

Moser, P.K. (1989) *Knowledge and Evidence*. New York, Cambridge University Press.

Plantinga, A. (2000) *Warranted Christian Belief*. Oxford, Oxford University Press.

Swinburne, R.G. (1979) *The Existence of God*. Oxford, Clarendon Press.

Chapter 3

Confession and Reason

Ieuan Lloyd

Abstract

Religious educationists are likely to recoil at the word 'confession' and even at the word 'commitment'. They want to be on the side of 'reason', as are their colleagues in other subjects. However they should not be embarrassed by confession or commitment, as those colleagues also have fundamental beliefs for which they have no reason. There are differences between religion and other subjects, as there are between morality and other subjects, but those differences must be tackled after first recognising, that in the end, fundamental beliefs in all areas of human understanding are non-rational.

The Desire to be Rational

There is one feature above all others that is characteristic of philosophy of education in recent times. It is the desire to justify every belief and every action. The word that is most commonly used to express that desire is 'rational'. So we have rational thought, rational behaviour, rational policies and the rational curriculum. We must offer rational arguments and encourage children to develop rationality. A more recent expression that has crept into the vocabulary is 'critically reflect'.

This desire for a justification for one's beliefs and actions seems unexceptional. We do not want people to believe the first thing that comes into their heads, or to behave impulsively. We want them to believe and do what is right, and philosophy more than any other subject has encouraged that. Socrates paid the penalty of death for encouraging those he taught to challenge the conventional beliefs of his society. The educated person is the thoughtful person, who distances himself or herself from the immediate so that they can be critical of it. But this practice has gone too far. In almost every sphere of education, people are encouraged to be rational or reflective, by which is meant the giving of reasons and arguments for even the most basic of their beliefs. This is especially true in morality and religion. Yet those who are challenged to find such reasons are nervous and often at a loss as to what to say. Those who challenge seem to have the upper hand. They speak with confidence, but it is a confidence that springs from ignorance, if not arrogance. It is a confidence reminiscent of the positivistic Ayer. It is the language of the abstract not tempered by example or an understanding of the past. The language has a life of its own, so unfamiliar to those in the field that the practitioner feels their work is undermined by such erudition. I have tried to show elsewhere how this is prevalent in psychology (Lloyd 1976).

One reason why the desire to be rational is so attractive is that it has a liberating ring about it. It is believed that such an approach enables us to put the past behind us and start all over again. We can see ourselves, perhaps for the first time, as choosers of our own destiny. Sociologists like Michael Young (1971), Peter Berger and Thomas Luckmann (1966) were much taken with these ideas in the 1960s, and their influence has remained. The challenge to our existing condition will unsettle us enough to look beyond our class-ridden society to new possibilities, free from the evils that are either perceived or hidden in our own. Philosophers of education, on the other hand, have not been so concerned with the political as with the individual application of rationality. They see rationality as a means of becoming autonomous. Let us look at one example from this area.

J.P. White and Rational Choice

J.P. White has been a major figure in wanting to promote an education that will lead to the autonomy of pupils. Although his book *Towards a Compulsory Curriculum* (1973) was published some time ago, his subsequent writings are consistent with those expressed in this book. In it, he wants to maximise the choices of pupils. He divides the curriculum, which is the instrument for achieving this end, into two main areas. The first area is made up of 'subjects and activities', and the second of 'ways of life'. Subjects include the traditional subjects such as mathematics, and activities like mountaineering. 'ways of life' include a life devoted to the altruistic life, the ascetic life, a life devoted to the acquisition of goods. He lists fourteen of these 'ways'. The introduction of both of these areas is made manageable by dividing them into two further categories: those that can only be understood by engaging in them, and those for which a description or demonstration will suffice.

The first area, subjects and activities, is largely consistent with Paul Hirst's 'forms of knowledge' where each form, such as science, is unique and therefore not reducible to further description. Engagement in the subject is essential. It is worth noticing that when it comes to the second area, ways of life, White does not use the distinction of the two categories. This is puzzling, for ways of life are even less accessible by description than subjects or activities, because here we are speaking not about a subject within a system but about whole systems of belief and practice. He makes this illogical mistake because he is in a dilemma. He wants children to be free to choose a way of life, but realises that they will only understand them if they engage in them. But in so doing, they will be changed by that experience. So he opts for description alone, but that does not enable children to understand the alternative ways of life sufficient to extend their horizons and equip them to make choices. His inadequate alternative, at best is the offering of 'glimpses' of these ways of life. But there are serious difficulties with this view, as there are when religious educationists give 'glimpses' of other faiths.

Difficulties in White's View

First, any attempt to expose a child to a variety of lifestyles adequately could mean that the child is progressively changed by those experiences. He or she will not be the same as he was before. It is not like choosing a holiday by inspecting a number of brochures, where the person as well as the criteria is independent of the object.

Second, the presentation of alternatives may unsettle a child. But educationists are driven on by a belief that seems to have for them an a priori status, namely, that the more alternatives you offer, the better.

Third, little is ever said about what constitutes an adequate understanding of other lifestyles that would enable a child to be sufficiently competent to make a choice. Talk about increasing one's life-chances can roll off the tongue easily, but there is a point in acquiring knowledge when some knowledge is worse than none. There are worse things than ignorance, for example, stupidity. Yet we blindly offer children other conceptions of life without seeing whether they are illuminating or confusing. In fact, the number of ways of life that is offered is determined more by some mistaken democratic principle (don't leave anything out) than it is by what the pupils can digest.

Fourth, we are never told in the literature how teachers who teach alternative ways of life are to judge whether they are successful or not: or, how teachers are to recognise one of these rational choices when it is made. One of the reasons why this important question is not asked, is the reluctance of curriculum planners to tackle the question of truth and value in relation to these cosmic alternatives. This is to abdicate intellectual responsibility rather than to embrace it. The teaching posture is called neutrality (often confused with impartiality). But we are not told how we can recognise what makes it the *pupil's* choice, rather than the teacher's or parents'. But an even more sceptical question one should ask is whether the notion of choice in relation to these alternatives is appropriate; which ever way you look at it, we have a strange picture of Religious Education (RE). Teachers have commitments they cannot reveal, offer alternatives of massive proportions, none of which is presented in any order of preference of value or truth, and who justify the surrendering of their own responsibility by saying 'The child must make up its own mind.' An analysis of this important notion of what it is to 'make up one's mind' is rarely carried out.

Unshakeable Beliefs and the Confessional Approach

Many religious educationists agree with White's approach to education. Almost universally, they are against a confessional approach to RE. Their grounds are practical and moral. They claim that the UK is no longer a Christian country and there are children with other cultural backgrounds which make it impracticable to teach Christianity. The moral reasons are of two sorts. There are those that relate to the freedom of the parents and their wishes for their children. And there are those that relate to the obligation teachers have towards the 'autonomy' of their pupils.

The wishes of the parents must be respected, and there is legislation to ensure that. But is there anything wrong in principle with the confessional approach, such that it offends the autonomy of the child? It is thought that the reason why the confessional approach is an offence is because it inculcates unshakeable beliefs. It is seen as a form of indoctrination – a much-overused word.

But what is wrong with inculcating in children unshakeable beliefs? The issue is not that we have unshakeable beliefs, but *which* beliefs are unshakeable. In many cases, the more unshakeable they are, the better. This point is not to be confused with the beliefs that philosophers are concerned with. They ask such questions as whether there is an external world, or whether objects are still in the drawer when no one is looking at them, and the like. But this doubt is philosophical doubt, not ordinary doubt. Philosophers agree that no one in his right mind will ever challenge certain beliefs we have. The point here is that many of our beliefs must be secure. Other beliefs revolve around the axes of fixed beliefs. All subjects must have a core, base or centre, without which other beliefs could not find their location. We refer to those basic beliefs when we do offer reasons. We do not offer reasons for those beliefs. Such basic beliefs include beliefs in the external world, in our own identity, that events are caused, that the sun will rise tomorrow, that one cannot walk through walls, and so on. Few if any of these beliefs are taught explicitly. As Wittgenstein says (1969, p. 21 para. 143) a child 'swallows down' these basic beliefs. Sometimes there will be changes in the location of these beliefs, but this is a further refinement of his view that does not immediately concern us here. The main point is that the possibility of questioning certain beliefs requires that some of our beliefs are not questioned. You cannot doubt where you stand. If you do, it is because you already regard other beliefs as more fundamental. Otherwise why invoke them? So confession (of basic beliefs) is not to be set against reason. Rather, there is a proper place for reason and it should not overreach itself. There is a point where reasoning comes to an end.

Not to recognise this will lead one into an infinite regress. To make the point more strongly, fundamental beliefs are part of our experience but not deduced from it. For example, we do not carry out experiments to prove that every event has a cause. That is something we assume. Nor do we establish the uniformity of nature by any form of testing. We are sure that night will follow day, that the anatomy of human beings is the same though relatively few have been studied. The principle of induction is itself something that is neither analytic nor empirical. It is a foundational belief on which our perceptions of the world depend.

The Confessional Approach in Moral Education

It is a useful exercise to substitute in the writings of religious educationists 'moral education' for 'RE' in order to see how uncomfortable one would be with the same point of view. It appears that moral educationists do not blush at introducing what is a confessional approach in the teaching of morality. For example, various approaches introduce morality into the curriculum. Earlier the Social Morality Council and latterly, the orders for Personal, Social and Health Education, advocate that we as teachers should get children to have due regard for other human beings and for animals; that we should be fair in the appraisal of the views of others; that we should consider the motives of people, and where possible try and see things from other people's points of view.

All these are taken as beliefs that should be taken for granted – in my terms, they are unshakeable beliefs. Both at home and at school this requires getting children to act in certain ways, just as we do when as infants they are learning about the physical world. Action is at the heart of their learning. So in moral learning we get them to care for their brothers and sisters, for their hamsters and for their earthworms. There is no question that this might not be the best thing to do, or that these principles are tentative. We praise them if they do the right thing and rebuke them if they do wrong. They see us praising generosity and disapproving of meanness. If we are ever challenged as to why these values have the position in our lives that they have, we are lost for words. This is not because we are speechless, but because there are no words that are required. It is like being asked to define the words we have already used in a definition, or like being asked if the ruler is the right length. Reasoning must stop somewhere. This is not a logical deficiency but a logical necessity. We certainly do not ask children to 'critically reflect' on the principle that one should not cause gratuitous pain to other live beings. So if a bully asks why he should not hurt someone, there are no more reasons we can give. If he cannot see that it is wrong to hurt someone, we can only continue to point to situations that illustrate kindness. If this has no effect on him we may have to speak of him as morally blind and not that he lacks intelligence.

There is, therefore, no reason to speak of the inculcation of these moral beliefs as being indoctrination. One has to learn the infrastructure. Without it there is no distinction between the important and the unimportant, the central and the peripheral, the secure and the insecure, the moral and the immoral and what counts as a good or a bad reason. There is, of course, such a thing as indoctrination. That is the inculcation of beliefs where, inter alia, we are able to challenge the views of someone by showing how unreasonable they are, but we normally do that by reference to beliefs we do not challenge.

Lurking behind the rational approach is the mistaken assumption that in the end, those who employ reason will come to the same answer. Yet hardheaded scientists will differ even though both employ reason. Opposing barristers will present reasonable cases, but one will be mistaken. Two perfectly moral persons will both employ reason but may reach a point of irresolvable disagreement.

The Confessional Approach in Religious Education

If all this is true both of our understanding of the physical world and of morality, then may it not also be true of religion? For any religion, like the other dimensions of experience, has its foundations, its principles and its superstructure. Yet it sometimes seems as if we are being asked to put all our beliefs into the melting pot as if all our beliefs have the same logical status. It is not surprising that some religious educationists are of no fixed abode. They are nervous of settling down anywhere. Their firm beliefs have been replaced by a pseudo-rationality, where it seems they are prepared to claim that whole systems of beliefs can be judged to be rational or not. This is difficult to make sense of. Something similar has occurred in Ethics. It is sometimes taught as if moral principles were just a matter of choice. The consequence of this is to make moral relativists of one's students. The same happens in RE. To be that open, especially with children, is to be intellectually irresponsible. Could it be that some teachers who have no religious commitment, have taken refuge in a relativistic approach so that they do not have to show their own hand?

It would be a mistake if one were not to recognise that there are problems which face the religious educator which are not present in the teaching of, say, morality or science. The problems of other faiths complicate matters. There are questions of truth and meaning, and questions concerning the depth and shallowness of religions. There is the unique phenomenon of the loss of faith. But it does not help matters if one does not start with asking the questions in the correct order.

What has brought about this approach to teaching in recent times has been the presence of other faiths. If the UK was a uniformly Christian country, would we be saying the same things about other faiths that we are now saying? If we were in a country of one religion would we want to say that one could never truly be a religious person unless one had to make a rational choice amongst alternatives? Would it mean we would have to artificially introduce children to other faiths via the syllabus? What, then, would we say of Abraham, David, Isaiah, Paul, Augustine, St Francis, Father Damien and Mother Teresa? Do we have to say that if they have not chosen their faith on rational grounds and rejected others that they were not religiously educated? And what of the millions of unknown believers who followed their faith simply but devoutly? Are we to conclude that their lives were inadequate in some way? I have yet to read the literature on indoctrination in religion that Samuel was indoctrinated. There is no evidence that he knew about other religions, and we can assume Eli initiated him into his faith. Yet God spoke to him. Take Billy Bray, a Cornish man who was a devout and simple evangelist. I am not sure I want to ask whether he was a rational man. He proclaimed his faith. His reply to the sceptic was his life. And what do we say about Jesus? He does not fit the description of a rational educator. His Sermon on the Mount is prescriptive and frequently adopts the imperative mode – Do good to them that hate you (Matthew 5:44). This would have prevented him today from taking assembly in most schools.

The onus then is on the rationalist to say what is seriously deficient with someone whose confession of a faith has been brought about in an educational institution. Teachers of other subjects are not so nervous about what they teach, so that we rarely ask questions about their confessional approach. Religious educationists sometimes get round their problem by conceding that the confessional approach is permissible in the home but prefer to call it nurture rather than education. But the sceptic will rightly say that if religion is epistemologically unsound in school, it is unsound anywhere. If it limits the autonomy of a child in school, it must limit the child at home. Is nurture the same as education? It is true that being initiated into beliefs in religion and the examining of matters of difference and dispute in those areas comes later. But that is inevitable in the learning of anything. To say that the one is education and the other not, matters little as long as the difference between the two is recognised. The distinction is present in moral education. In the early stages moral education is involved, as has already been pointed out, in getting children to hold particular beliefs and to behave in particular ways. It will be later that different moral points of view and the controversies that surround them will be introduced. It seems that in the case of RE, we are recommended to go straight into the second stage. But even at that stage it is unclear whether what is being recommended is RE, anthropology or theology. (It is worth considering the difference between the kind of reasoning that goes on in a theological college and what goes on in a department of theology.)

Much of this confusion arises because reason and faith are seen to be in opposition. If I am right, then reason requires faith. Reason without faith is like a cogwheel that does not engage. It has potential but requires something of substance on which to work. So reason is not sufficient. Admittedly, we live in a world where all kinds of issues arise, say in morality and religion that were not present in the world of our forebears. We are able to say of someone that their faith was deep, their life honourable, without having anything like the kind of reasoning we employ. One may be devout without ever worrying about free will, natural and revealed religion, the ontological argument, theodicies and the like.

Religious Education and Compulsion

One way in which the problem of the status of religion arises is over the question of whether RE should be compulsory or not. It appears to be the most insecure subject with the most secure position. John Hull (1975), a highly influential figure in RE, argued against school worship in his book *School Worship: An Obituary,* on the grounds that one cannot compel a child to worship. He says that it is as impossible to achieve as attempting to make someone love you by threatening them. Now the point that love is not under voluntary control has to be accepted. Marriages that break up would have been rescued if it were up to the wills of the partners concerned. But love is not a matter of volition. It can only be hoped for. Why then is RE singled out to make this point? For what John Hull says about worship is true of all subjects. No subject in the early years is optional. Children have to attend lessons in maths, history and English, whether they like it or not. They could not have been allowed to choose these subjects, since, if they had enough knowledge to choose, it would mean that they had already learned the subject. Hence, even Mill, a libertarian in educational matters, admits that children have to be forced to be free. What he means is that children have to be taught a subject before they can react to it. They may come to love or hate it. The whole of compulsory schooling is based on this belief, not just RE. Here again is another example of religious educationists being harder on themselves than they are with others. A distinction that may help here is that between formal and actual compulsion. A child may formally be compelled to attend school, but he does not actually feel compelled. He does not feel coerced. He is in school because others think he should be there, yet his arousal of love and desire, his enjoyment and spontaneity are consistent with that arrangement.

One could go a stage further. Even if a child does resist something initially, a change of heart is possible, simply because the child may have been resistant to something he or she knew little about. Tortelier was made to play the cello. He hated it at first, especially on those occasions when he wanted to join other children at play. Nevertheless, what grew out of that experience was a life-long devotion to music. It would be unwise to infer from this example some general rule. It is only offered to illustrate that one must be aware of the range of human reactions there are to similar circumstances, such that generalising can be a hazardous business. Rarely can one make a tight causal connection between conditions and reactions when discussing human beings. In regard to circumstances that are thought to limit our freedom, it is worth remembering that the circumstances that affect us most are ones we could not have chosen – to be born, our parents, when we were born, or where we were born. Yet the freedom we enjoy is compatible with those facts. It is a matter of delicate judgement how far we press on with teaching something of which the child disapproves. Compulsion can alienate a child. But the general point is that compulsion and the generation of interest and desire are not necessarily incompatible.

Religious Education: A Diversity

One final point: RE can mean many things. It can mean initiation into a particular faith. It can mean the study of religion, its origins, its theology, its psychology, its sociology and so on. It would just be arbitrary legislation to say that it is only one thing. Sometimes we confuse what the forms education can take with the education of which we approve. It would be confused to say that only the kind of education one agrees with is really education. That would be like saying that the only morality that exists is the one that I adopt. There is a difference between what counts as morality and the morality of which one approves.

Conclusion

What I have tried to do in this chapter is to confront the religious educationist with the question 'What is wrong with a confessional approach?' The history of post-war thinking on RE, as Penny Thompson (2004) has shown so vividly, has been bedevilled by contrary, and sometimes contradictory, views on which curricula have been based. It has been a muddle. Unless one begins with the question concerning the basis upon which we teach religion and Christianity in particular, all the other questions, such as the rights of parents, the problems of other faiths, will never be resolved. I have tried to do this by suggesting that we should press the same questions on other areas of the curriculum. In so doing it will assist us in seeing that we have wrongly made an exception of religion. It may be true that a confessional approach today is both inadvisable and impracticable. The same may be increasingly true of morality. But it is deeply confused and irresponsible to pass on the task of deciding whether a religion has any truth to a child.

References

Berger, P. and Luckmann T. (1966) *The Social Construction of Reality.* London, Allen Lane The Penguin Press.

Hull, J.M. (1975) *School Worship: An Obituary.* London, SCM Press.

Lloyd, D.I. (1976) 'Theory and Practice', *Proceedings of the Philosophy of Education Society of Great Britain*, 10, 98–113.

Thompson, P. (2004) *Whatever Happened to Religious Education?* Cambridge, Lutterworth Press.

White J.P. (1973) *Towards a Compulsory Curriculum.* London, Routledge and Kegan Paul.

——(1995) 'Education and Personal Well-Being in a Secular Universe': an inaugural lecture delivered at the Institute of Education University of London,16 November 1994.

Wittgenstein, L. (1969) *On Certainty.* Oxford, Blackwell.

Young, M.F.D. (1971) *Knowledge and Control.* London, Collier-Macmillan.

Chapter 4

Religious Education and Committed Openness

Elmer Thiessen

Abstract

There may be something wrong with the way in which Religious Education is generally practised in the common state schools of the Western world but both the way in which the problem is conceived and the solutions to it vary considerably. There is a deeper problem – a failure to address the context in which RE is offered. Reform of RE in the direction of taking religion more seriously is not possible in a state maintained system of education. Genuine RE that teaches from commitment and for committed openness can only occur within the context of religious schools.

The overriding theme of this book is the need for reform in RE in community schools of Great Britain. Penny Thompson has traced the changes in RE in Great Britain in her earlier work, provocatively entitled *Whatever Happened to Religious Education?* (2004). In this book, Thompson provides a helpful analysis of the history and tradition of RE in England and Wales through a study of government reports. The 1988 Swann Report is seen as crucial in marking a shift in policies regarding RE. But the shift in practice and in professional literature happened earlier. Various approaches were and have been advocated since the 1970s. What they had (and still have) in common is a rejection of a confessional approach to RE, a rejection of teaching a particular faith (i.e. the Christian faith), and a shift to a neutral and more pluralistic study about religions. I will use the expressions 'multi-faith RE' or 'teaching about religion' to identify post-Swann RE in its various forms.

These trends in RE are not restricted to England and Wales. Lois Sweet examines 'the controversial issue of religion in Canada's schools' in her book, *God in the Classroom* (1997). Though herself a secularist, Sweet expresses concern that Canadian society has lost sight of the spiritual dimension to life. This extends also to our schools, she maintains, where religion is denied and/or ignored (pp. 6, 239). Sweet describes her son, now at university, discovering for the first time that Western civilisation was rooted in religion. 'Nothing in his previous thirteen years of study had given him an inkling of that,' Sweet writes (p. 213). A tragedy, indeed, and somewhat odd, given that schooling in Canada, as in Great Britain, evolved from decidedly Christian origins, as Sweet shows in Chapter 2.

Elsewhere I have suggested three broadly distinguishable approaches to RE in state-supported schools in Canada and other Western countries (Thiessen 1993, pp. 10–18).

In the past RE was overtly Christian. Its aim was to nurture children into the Christian faith. Today we use the words 'Christian nurture' or 'confessional RE' to describe this approach. There has been a widespread rejection of this approach to RE in Canada, resulting eventually in no religion being taught in our schools. Though perhaps never completely actualised, this approach has been, and for many people is still seen as the ideal. It is this second approach that Lois Sweet is reacting against, and in its place, she advocates teaching about religion(s) in our schools. What Sweet does not perhaps acknowledge sufficiently in her book is the implementation of this third approach in Canadian schools over the last 30 years, though not to the extent achieved in the United Kingdom. This approach has emerged in part due to the growing realisation that religion is not dead or even dying. A more significant factor is the growing awareness of the pluralistic nature of Canadian and other Western societies. Instead of fostering Christian faith, what is needed, it is felt, is an open, descriptive, critical, enquiring study of world religions.

The Problem of RE

Clearly, there are things to be said for a multi-faith approach to RE, especially within the context of secularised and pluralistic society. Students need to achieve religious literacy. Students need to understand and appreciate the various religious commitments held by people within their society and the wider world. Students also need to appreciate the religious way of life as an alternative to the rampant secularism that exists in our societies.

But this 'teaching about religion' approach does not and cannot do justice to an authentic and fully rounded RE. Such RE must include nurture within a particular religious tradition. I like to describe such RE in terms of teaching from and for commitment. Drawing on some classic descriptions of education as initiation, such RE can also be described in terms of a systematic initiation of students into a particular religious tradition. Christian nurture, for example, will then be defined as the initiation of a person (a child or an adult) into a Christian heritage, an inheritance of Christian sentiments, beliefs, imaginings, understandings and activities (cf. Oakeshott 1972; Peters 1966, ch. 2). The same can be said for Muslim nurture or Jewish nurture. Teaching *about* the Christian or Muslim or Jewish religion is simply not enough. Now there is more to RE than just initiation, but I want to postpone a treatment of this additional component until later.

We recognise the importance of initiation or nurture or teaching from and for commitment in other subjects. We don't just want students to learn *about* history or mathematics. We want them to become historians and mathematicians. We want to cultivate in students a love for history and mathematics. More generally, we want to initiate students into the forms of knowledge. We want to give them a first-hand feel of what it means to think within each form of knowledge. We want them to care about the valuable things involved in each form of knowledge. Hence R.S. Peters' observation, 'We would not call a man "educated" who knew about science but cared nothing for truth' (1965, p. 96). Initiation that leads to knowledge 'must involve the kind of commitment which comes through being on the inside of a form of thought and awareness' (Peters 1967, p. 8). The teacher, functioning as master in his/her field, guides the apprentice students into a particular discipline.

More than that, the teacher as master guides students into a particular way of thinking within a discipline. He or she is a person committed to certain ideas in history or social studies or even mathematics. Similarly with regard to the teaching of religion. It is not enough to introduce students to a general form of religious knowledge or to initiate them into a vague spirituality. Students need to be initiated into a particular kind of religious knowledge or spirituality or way of life. Again, more on this later. My central point here is that an RE that merely teaches about religion and does so from an allegedly neutral standpoint is simply not enough and is perhaps not as neutral as is being assumed.

I believe this is part of what some authors are objecting to when they criticise the kind of RE that has evolved since the 1970s. However, I suspect that these same writers will be uncomfortable with the language that I use to describe the problem. While they will agree that it is not enough to teach about religion, they will be troubled by the use of words like 'initiation' or 'nurture' into a particular religious tradition. This discomfort is found, for example, in Lois Sweet's treatment of the neglect of religion in Canadian schools. Her primary worry about such initiation is that it is narrow, that it involves indoctrination or sectarianism, and that it will lead to intolerance (Sweet 1997, pp. 13, 17, 33, 53). The purpose of genuine education is not to make people distinct, Sweet argues (p. 49). Fostering a particular faith and helping students to continue within a particular faith is not an educational objective that is worthy of public support in state schools (p. 173). Genuine education, including genuine RE, involves critical thinking, autonomous thinking and behaving, tolerance of dissent, and the celebration of diversity (pp. 102, 159).

The basic problem with Sweet's worry and that of other writers who might be concerned about the narrowness of initiation, is that it fails to do justice to the fact that nurture into a particular tradition is a necessary foundation for growth toward autonomy. Narrowness necessarily precedes openness. Critical thinking can only occur if we have first been given something to be critical about. More generally, the worries about initiation and nurture rest on a misguided and one-sided paradigm of liberal education. A healthy liberal education includes both initiation and liberation (see Thiessen 1993, ch. 8). I will have more to say about the liberation component of liberal education later.

There is one other dimension of the 'problem' of RE that needs to be explored briefly. There is talk about secularism or secularist attitudes that pervade post-Swann and contemporary RE – for example, talk about the 'privileging of secularism' in RE, the 'secularist' assumptions underlying the approach to RE, or the use of 'alien secular categories' that ultimately misrepresent RE.

There are some classic statements on education and RE to illustrate this aspect of the problem. In a chapter entitled 'The Secularisation of Education', Paul Hirst gives an account of 'a secularised concept of autonomous education', and concludes that a rational society will necessarily have its 'thoroughly secular schools' (1974, pp. 85, 90). Hirst goes on to apply this secularised account of autonomous education to the area of RE. Interestingly he advocates a kind of 'secular religious education' (p. 89). For Hirst, the latter involves an objective study of religion that is autonomous in the sense that it does not itself rest on any particular religious commitments. We see here the basis of the 'teaching about religion' approach that is so predominant in schools today. Different versions of this approach have emerged, but the core remains the same. For example, John Hull argues for 'an open, secular, critical view of religious education', and he too does this in the light of the secularisation of society and the need for a secular education (1984, pp. 206, 40, 260, 263; cf. 1987). Interestingly, Lois Sweet draws on an interview she had with Hull in order to defend her solution to the approach to RE being taken in Canada (1997, pp. 224–8).

Both Hirst and Hull describe the process of secularisation as something to be accepted, not critiqued; hence old-fashioned approaches to RE involving nurture and initiation into the Christian faith are viewed in a negative light and even described as 'primitive' and 'simple' (Hirst 1974, p. 80; Hull 1987). These assessments are in keeping with the widely held liberal assumption that man's search for identity and meaning in his particular ethnic, cultural, and religious heritage is part of man's primal, primitive, and pre-rational past out of which he is evolving (Berger 1974; 1977). Thus also Charles Bailey's description of liberal education in a book entitled, *Beyond the Present and the Particular*: 'A general liberal education is characterized most centrally by its liberating aspect indicated by the word "liberal" … What it liberates the person from is the limitations of the present and the particular' (1984, p. 20).

There is an obvious common theme in the writers quoted in the previous paragraph. Particularity is viewed as primitive and simple. Humankind is evolving from a primitive state where humans define themselves in terms of particular ethnic or cultural or religious identities to a more sophisticated state where identities are universal and inclusivist. But empirical evidence seems to refute this liberal assumption. Particular identities seem to be growing in importance in our day. We need to learn to live with the importance of particular identities.

Bailey's description of liberal education as liberation from the limitations of the present and the particular is also problematic. The word 'limitations' is important. A commitment to the present and the particular is viewed as a limitation from which one must be liberated. But I would argue that this negative view of a narrow upbringing is entirely unwarranted. Indeed, as various authors have argued, a 'primary culture' is essential to becoming an individual, and it is also essential as a foundation for growth towards autonomy (McLaughlin 1984; Watson 1987, pp. 58–9). Bailey also fails to address, adequately, the question as to how we acquire that from which we need to be liberated. It should be obvious that children must first of all be initiated into a particular home, a particular language, a particular culture, a particular set of beliefs, and so on, before they can begin to expand their horizons beyond the present and the particular. So here again, we are back to the importance of initiation as an essential component in a balanced ideal of liberal education.

But, what about Hirst's and Hull's call for a secular approach to RE? The very notion of a 'secular RE' sounds contradictory. Perhaps a better label might be a 'neutral' approach to RE, because Hirst describes his approach in terms of an objective study of religion which does not itself rest on any particular religious commitments. The problem here is that there is no such a thing as a neutral objective study of anything. Thankfully, this is generally accepted today, given significant

developments in the field of epistemology that have called into question tl
of objectivity and the idea of one universal rationality. Indeed, the idea of a u..
and neutral rationality is now recognised to be itself an expression of a particular
narrative, an Enlightenment narrative that is generally seen to be problematic.
Indeed, Hirst, in his more recent writings has expressed dissatisfaction with the idea
of a universal, secular rationality that underlies his earlier analysis of the forms of
knowledge (1993).

It is no doubt considerations such as these that lie behind the concern of various
writers about the secular nature of RE in the common schools of Great Britain
today. I agree entirely with this concern. Education cannot help but be confessional.
However, does the teaching about religion approach to RE entail the teaching of
secularism or secular humanism as a philosophy? Here I am not so sure. It must
be conceded that at least religion is not being ignored when schools offer courses
that teach about religion. This is what is at the heart of Sweet's concerns about
Canadian schools where religion is denied and/or ignored. Schools that include
various approaches to teaching about religion are at least acknowledging the place
and importance of religion in societies today.

Solutions to the Problem

In the previous section, my focus has been primarily on the problem that needs
to be addressed. Multi-faith approaches to RE that have emerged since the 1970s
are thought to undermine religion. They fail to address questions of truth and
commitment. Indeed, for some, such approaches to RE lead to a 'privileging of
secularism'.

What then is the solution to the problem? There is a general consensus that
we need a kind of RE that takes religion seriously. It is not enough to teach about
religions. It is not enough to treat religion objectively and from a distance. We need
to help children to understand and appreciate the religious life. But I want to suggest
that difficulties emerge when describing what should replace the old RE. There are a
variety of positions on the solution being proposed. Indeed, there would seem to be
some confusion as to how we go about reforming RE. While there is some sympathy
with the idea of initiating children into the religious way of life, there is a hesitation
to include initiating children into a *particular* religious way of life. The spectre of
indoctrination raises its head again and again. Some of the solutions being proposed
also sound very much like the 'teaching about religion' approach that in the main is
seen as problematic.

Here let me provide one example of the difficulties and inconsistencies that I find
in proposals to reform RE. Andrew Wright has for quite some time been expressing
concerns about current practices in RE. In his most recent work he objects to both
modernist and postmodernist assumptions underlying RE (Wright 2004). Wright
worries about the failure to take seriously the particularity of religious traditions.
He is also unhappy with the standard liberal responses to religious differences that
favour the privatisation and domestication of religious claims, thus tending to sweep
under the carpet the resulting tensions between people offering conflicting accounts

of ultimate reality. Following David Hay, Wright wants to overcome modernist and postmodernist suspicions about the spiritual. He wants a transformative RE that exposes children to the realm of the transcendent (Wright 2004, pp. 212–14). But is it helpful to talk about a general sort of spirituality? Such talk further conflicts with Wright's laudable attempt to do justice to the particularity of religious traditions. He correctly applies the postmodernist critique of a neutral epistemology to RE, arguing that we need to be open and honest about the faith commitments of the teacher and the pupil (p. 216). We need, in addition, to be open to alternate ways of understanding reality. But such openness, Wright argues, does not preclude rejecting the commitments of others, though this must be done in a spirit of humility, 'grounded in a mutual recognition of the Otherness of contrasting positions' (p. 218). I fully endorse this ideal of humble committed openness. But there is something strange about the postmodern expression, 'the Otherness of contrasting positions', an ambiguity that runs through much of Wright's book concerning postmodern openness. Openness to the contrasting positions of *other people* is simply not the same as openness to the *transcendent Other*, except of course, in a humanistic religion.

Furthermore, while Wright wants to do justice to religious particularity, he expresses doubt as to whether a particularistic RE can be critical and open. For example, when he goes on to examine the context of RE, Wright expresses doubts as to whether confessional schools will really be able to accept his critical RE (2004, p. 229). But why not? In fact, Wright is not entirely consistent on this matter. In an earlier chapter on critical pedagogy, he admits that his argument would appear to favour structural pluralism (p. 175). But again, he worries about the dangers inherent in sectarian schools. Wright, it would seem, is not willing to go where his argument carries him.

Wright's examination of the context of RE raises for me another question concerning the difficulties in describing how to reform RE. Might there be a deeper problem that Wright and various other writers are trying to address?

Context of RE

I want to suggest that the difficulties surrounding attempts to provide a solution to RE are rooted in a deeper failure to address the question as to the appropriate context in which students can be given a proper RE. The authors are assuming a context of common state-supported schools. They are trying to describe an approach to RE which would be appropriate for common schools where students come from a variety of religious traditions. But, they want to move beyond an objective and descriptive approach to teaching about religions. Though cautious, they are trying to move in the direction of confessional RE. My question is, is this possible within the context of a common school where students have a plurality of religious commitments?

Elsewhere I have outlined some of the difficulties common schools have in doing justice to the particularity of RE (Thiessen 2001, ch. 13). I maintain that attempts to reform RE within the context of the common school will ultimately fail because they cannot do justice to the particularity of religious commitments and the need to educate and initiate children into a particular religious tradition. Thus, despite the efforts of various critics to move towards an approach which takes religious commitment more seriously and moves us closer to teaching from and for commitment, in the end these calls for reform invariably slide towards the very approach that they are rejecting.

Why? Because the very culture of the common school is universalist in nature, stressing that which students have in common. Hence common schools cannot take religious particularity seriously. Multi-faith programmes cannot help but trivialise religious commitments. Instead of treating them as serious life-consuming commitments, 'rival creeds are cast together in a common educational environment, and religious scruples and practices are celebrated as so many charming ornaments of ethnicity' (Callan 2000, p. 57). The culture of common schools also includes some basic values of the traditional concept of liberal education with its emphasis on liberation from the present and the particular. I have already cited claims (made by some) that the purpose of genuine education is not to make people distinct. Thus again, the difficulty of doing justice to religious particularity. We must also not forget that the liberal ideal of neutrality undergirds state-maintained common schools. But, this culture of neutrality will invariably cause RE to slide towards a teaching about religion approach. Even if the common school were to give up the ideal of neutrality, there is still the very practical difficulty of trying to accommodate all of the cultural and religious traditions in a typical state school. There are simply too many particularities to be accommodated.

I believe that it is only a system of educational pluralism that can do justice to cultural and religious plurality within a society. It is only in the context of religious schools that the new RE being proposed by various authors in this book can be appropriately and fully realised. While common schools cannot do justice to religious particularity, religious schools can do justice to both religious particularity and the universal values that are necessary for life in a democracy. Contrary to Lois Sweet, religious schools can and do foster social harmony and tolerance. Sweet herself tells a moving story to illustrate this point. Esther Enkin, a Toronto Jewish mother explains why she sends her daughter to a Hebrew Day School. 'I'm giving her a sense of herself and her people.' Enkin says she knows how important it is to teach children about living together. 'And here I am, educating my child separately. But there's a paradox,' she says. 'The more I teach her who she is, then the better she can live with others' (Sweet 1997, p. 112).

There is another contextual issue that needs to be dealt with, and here I am dealing specifically with the fact that this book has its origins in the United Kingdom and that many of the authors are British. In dealing with the various dimensions of the problem being addressed as well as the proposed solutions being offered, there is an assumption that needs to be brought to the fore. In the Introduction to this book, the question is asked: 'What might it mean to begin from faith rather than doubt, from inspiration rather than agnosticism?' But from what faith do we begin? The answer to this question, I'm sure, is the Christian faith. After all, Great Britain is a Christian country. The Church of England is the established church in England where the monarch is the head of the Church of England and is crowned king or queen of the countries of the United Kingdom by the Archbishop of Canterbury. At the very least,

.ssumed that Christianity has played a key role in the history of Great Britain and still plays a role that is culturally and legally decisive.

Before I address this contextual issue, some autobiographical comments might be in order. I am a Christian who belongs to the 'free church' tradition. I understand the church as a voluntary association of people with like-minded religious beliefs. I am also a Canadian. Although Canadians have not historically accepted the American principle of the strict separation of church and state, we implicitly accept the basic assumption underlying this principle. Although some would describe Canada and the USA as Christian countries, others would dispute this. But all would agree that we need to avoid the privileging of any particular church. There is no established church in either country. All of this has led to a fairly widespread acceptance of the secularisation of our state-maintained schools. There are, of course, some who still argue for the privileging of the Christian faith in our common schools, but I think this view is held by a minority in both Canada and the USA.

Given my background, it will probably not come as a surprise that I have some problems with the contextual assumptions underlying various proposals to reform RE. Some British writers are quite comfortable with the idea that the approach to teaching the Christian faith in schools should be different from the approach to teaching other religions. Schools can and should give students some knowledge about other religions. But, with regard to the Christian faith, more can and should be done. In fact, what various authors are now objecting to is that the Christian faith is not given a preferred status in schools. Students learn about the Christian faith, in the same way that they learn about the other major world religions. What various authors are calling for is an approach that not only 'privileges the religious life' but one that privileges the Christian way of life.

But I believe such an approach to RE is wrongheaded. It fails to take into account the pluralistic nature of England and Wales. Common schools must by their very nature be common, open to all, and they must treat all students, including their deeply cherished beliefs, fairly. To use a state-maintained system of education to privilege the Christian religion is simply wrong. It violates the basic principle of the freedom of religion. It involves coercion of religious belief.

But there is still something very right about the concerns being raised about current approaches to RE. Teaching students *about* the religions of the world is not enough. This alone does not satisfy the religious needs of students. This approach fosters life without commitment. Contemporary political and liberal writer, William Galston describes the problem in this way: 'The greatest threat to children in modern liberal societies is not that they will believe in something too deeply, but that they will believe in nothing very deeply at all' (Galston 1991, p. 255). Students need to be inspired to be religious. But this cannot be done in the abstract. I believe that students also need to be nourished within a particular religious tradition. Thus, we also need a confessional form of RE. We need to teach from and for commitment. But, how can this be done, given the pluralistic nature of a society and given that there will be several religions represented in the typical classroom of a common school? I have already argued that the common school is ill suited to teach from and for faith. It is inappropriate and impossible, in our common schools, to do justice to the initiation or confessional component of a fully rounded approach to RE. I would suggest that multi-faith teaching about religion is in fact the only approach that is suitable for the common school.

The only context in which a confessional approach to RE is appropriate is in religious schools. The only way to do justice to a fully rounded approach to RE which includes both the teaching of a particular religion and the teaching about religions is to have a pluralistic system of education (Thiessen 2001, chs 12 & 13). Only in this context can one teach from faith and for faith. Each particular school must of course also teach about the other religions. And here the approach will in part be similar to that being advocated in post-Swann RE. But in a pluralistic system of education students will be initiated into a particular faith, with no excuses made for doing so.

Teaching for Critical Openness

Let me explore the central thrust of my solution a little more carefully. Here it should be noted that my description of RE will in fact be very close to that of contemporary authors calling for reform in RE, except with regard to the question of context. I agree with much of what these writers are saying, except that I am applying their recommendations to religious schools which are the only appropriate context for confessional RE.

I have used the language of teaching from and for commitment as a way to describe what we should be doing in RE. I am drawing on the ordinary sense of the term 'commitment' which is referred to in any good dictionary. 'Commitment' refers to the binding or pledging of oneself. One can be committed to a person, a community, a belief system, or to a certain kind of behaviour or lifestyle. Of course, some of these elements are often inter-related – commitment to a belief system often entails commitment to a certain lifestyle, and also to a community that seeks to abide by this lifestyle. Teaching for commitment with regard to the Christian faith, therefore involves committed teachers seeking to inspire students to be similarly committed to Christ, to Christ's way of life, and to the Christian community, and doing this both by example and in their teaching. Neutrality is given up as an ideal in such teaching. So is an overemphasis on the cognitive dimension of RE.

Here let me make one important qualification. The main title of my first book is *Teaching for Commitment* (Thiessen 1993). If I were able to re-title this book, I would call it 'Teaching for Committed Openness'. It is not that I didn't deal with the theme of critical openness in my book (see ch. 6). But I think that combining the notions of commitment and openness better conveys what we should be doing in RE. This is what I meant when earlier I referred to a well-rounded notion of RE. It includes both initiation into a particular religious tradition and, with the gradual maturing of students, an exposure to other religious traditions including a more critical examination of the religious tradition into which a student has been initiated.

Now I'm sure that for many, the very notion of 'committed openness' will be viewed as an oxymoron, but this is not the case. These two concepts do not contradict each other. In fact they need each other (see Mitchell 1994). Committed openness describes what it means to be a healthy human being. It also describes the healthy academic mind, including that of the scientist. Scientists are often portrayed as being objective and open-minded. But, as Karl Popper has argued, a degree of closed-mindedness is necessary for a good scientist (1970, p. 55). Scientists should not give up a theory too soon in the face of contrary evidence. Of course, eventually the evidence becomes overwhelming and then one must be prepared to give up a theory. That is what 'committed openness' means. This same balance is also required in the area of religion. A well rounded RE includes both the teaching of a particular religion and the teaching about other religions. RE teachers should seek to display and encourage commitment with openness.

The need for this balance is reinforced by the dangers of religious terrorism. I write these words shortly after Canada experienced its own 9/11, though fortunately we were spared the horrors of an actual terrorist attack with the arrest of 12 men and 5 boys who were allegedly planning a series of attacks on Canadian soil. All of us today, wherever we live, worry about terrorism that is sadly often connected with religious fanaticism. Indeed, it is precisely these images of religious fanaticism, threats of terrorism, and schools that are training religious fanatics and terrorists that lead many to conclude that religion itself is the problem. And these same images also lead many to reject any calls for confessional approaches to RE. Surely it is dangerous to teach from and for religious commitment. We need to face these concerns head on (see Thiessen 1996; 2001, ch. 11). I confess that it seems foolhardy to defend teaching for religious commitment in times like these. But the key here is to distinguish between teaching for healthy religious commitment and teaching for religious fanaticism. And the key to avoiding teaching for religious fanaticism is to combine teaching for commitment with teaching for critical openness.

This is, of course, part of the agenda of multi-faith RE, and I concur with this agenda. But, I believe that this agenda can and should be a component of the new RE that teaches from and for commitment. Only in this way will we be able to avoid the dangers of religion becoming evil (Kimball 2002) and achieve healthy religious commitment. We need to combine pre-Swann and post-Swann RE, but we need to do this within the context of faith-based schools.

This combination is also the key to answering the worry that any move towards confessional RE opens the door to indoctrination. There is nothing indoctrinative about confessionalism *per se*, or even naïve confessionalism or the teaching of doctrine. Teaching doctrine may not be a particularly effective way to teach the young. But that is another issue. We need to boldly initiate the young into the content of the Christian faith, including its stories. That is at the heart of much current concern about RE. But RE must also include a broadening of horizons, teaching about other religions and even teaching students to think critically about the faith into which they are being initiated. It is only if we fail to combine a confessional approach to RE with a liberating approach to RE that we can be charged with indoctrination.

The two approaches to RE should therefore not be seen as mutually exclusive. If we adopt a system of educational pluralism such as I advocate in this chapter, then each school would boldly teach from and for commitment with regard to the religious or (irreligious) faith represented by that school. But at the same time, there would be a broadening of students' horizons, and as students mature, increasing exposure to other religions (including the religion of secularism), and a critical examination of their own religious commitments. Only in this way will we help our students to acquire a healthy religious commitment.

References

Bailey, C. (1984) *Beyond the Present and the Particular: A Theory of Liberal Education*. London, Routledge & Kegan Paul.

Berger, P.L. (1974) *Pyramids of Sacrifice: Political Ethics & Social Change*. New York, Penguin Books.

—— (1977) *Facing up to Modernity: Excursions in Society, Politics & Religion*. New York, Penguin Books.

Callan, E. (2000) 'Discrimination and Religious Schooling'. In W. Kymlicka and W. Norman (eds) *Citizenship in Diverse Societies*. New York, Oxford University Press, pp. 43–67.

Galston, W.A. (1991) *Liberal Purposes: Goods, Virtues and Diversity in the Liberal State*. NewYork, Cambridge University Press.

Hirst, P.H. (1974) *Moral Education in a Secular Society*. London, University of London Press.

—— (1993) 'Education, Knowledge and Practices'. In R. Barrow and P. White (eds) *Beyond Liberal Education*. London, Routledge, pp. 184–99.

Hull, J. (1984) *Studies in Religion and Education*. London, Falmer Press.

—— (1987) 'Religious Education and Modernity'. *British Journal of Religious Education*, 9 (3), 117–23.

Kimball, C. (2002) *When Religion Becomes Evil*. New York, HarperSanFrancisco.

McLaughlin, T.H. (1984) 'Parental Rights and the Religious Upbringing of Children'. *Journal of Philosophy of Education*, 18 (1), 75–83.

Mitchell, B. (1994) *Faith and Criticism*. Oxford, Clarendon Press.

Oakeshott, M. (1972) 'Education: The Engagement and its Frustration'. In R.F. Dearden, P.H. Hirst and R.S. Peters (eds) *Education and the Development of Reason*. London, Routledge & Kegan Paul, pp. 19–49.

Peters, R.S. (1965) 'Education as Initiation'. In R.D. Archambault (ed.) *Philosophical Analysis and Education*. London, Routledge & Kegan Paul, pp. 87–111.

—— (1966) *Ethics and Education*. London, George Allen and Unwin.

—— (1967) 'What is an Educational Process?' In R.S. Peters (ed.) *The Concept of Education*. London, Routledge & Kegan Paul, pp. 1–23.

Popper, K. (1970) 'Normal Science and its Dangers'. In I. Lakatos and A. Musgrove (eds) *Criticism and the Growth of Knowledge*. Cambridge, Cambridge University Press, pp. 51–8.

Sweet, L. (1997) *God in the Classroom: The Controversial Issue of Religion in Canada's Schools*. Toronto, McClelland and Stewart.

Thiessen, E.J. (1993) *Teaching for Commitment: Liberal Education, Indoctrination and Christian Nurture*. Montreal, McGill-Queen's University Press; and Leominster, Gracewing.

—— (1996) 'Fanaticism and Christian Liberal Education: A Response to Ben Spiecker's Commitment to Liberal Education'. *Studies in Philosophy and Education*, 15 (3), 293–300.

—— (2001) *In Defence of Religious Schools and Colleges*. Montreal and Kingston, McGill-Queen's University Press.

Thompson, P. (2004) *Whatever Happened to Religious Education?* Cambridge, Lutterworth Press.

Watson, B. (1987) *Education and Belief*. Oxford, Blackwell.

Wright, A. (2004) *Religion, Education and Post-modernity*. London and New York, RoutledgeFalmer.

Chapter 5

Religious Education in Australia and New Zealand

Grant Maple

Abstract

Religious Education in some English-speaking countries is surprisingly similar to that in England, yet dissimilar in a number of less obvious but important ways. Despite the opportunity for it to be different, Australian and New Zealand RE has clung closely to the theories and patterns prevailing in the United Kingdom. Reasons for this are put forward along with an overview of how RE has developed in these countries. A number of the major weaknesses of the present situation are examined and some suggestions offered as to what is required for more effective programmes.

Separation of Church and State and its Impact on Religious Education

The years between the establishment of the British penal colony at Sydney in 1788 and the annexation of New Zealand following the Treaty of Waitangi in 1840 were years of remarkable change during which Georgian complacency gave way first to political reform then to Victorian improvement. The dominant colonial ideology was a form of political and economic liberalism based on Locke's view of natural rights as applied to life, liberty and property. In fashioning these settler societies, colonists fought against the wholesale transfer of the English establishment, yet sought to reproduce English institutions in such a way as to preserve individual rights in a more egalitarian society. Churches and schools fit within this mosaic.

From that time RE passed through five distinct phases. The first phase in Australia may be described as one of Anglican quasi-establishment. Although an Anglican chaplain was sent with the first fleet, many of those who made up this settler society were not Anglicans. The assumption was that the chaplain would minister to all colonists, bond and free, and ordained clergy from other churches were not welcome, despite the fact that Irish Roman Catholics made up almost a third of the population (Breward 1993, pp. 12–23).

Little thought was given to the education of children born to these early colonists partly because of the huge imbalance of five males to every female among transported convicts. It was some time before there were sufficient numbers of free settlers to prompt colonial administrators to address the issue. In 1819 a recommendation for the adoption of the Canadian model of land endowment and an

Anglican ecclesiastical structure and school system was accepted by the Imperial parliament. This arrangement came under immediate criticism from landowners, from Nonconformists and Roman Catholics, and from political liberals (Judd and Cable 1987, p. 9). Meanwhile satellite penal settlements had been formed at Norfolk Island (1789), Van Diemen's Land (Tasmania, 1803) and Moreton Bay (Queensland, 1824). Samuel Marsden had begun missionary outreach to New Zealand and Polynesia in 1814, one of a number of factors leading to the establishment of the British Crown colony there.

The second phase was one of stagnation while successive governors sought a workable solution to the many issues facing the NSW colony. The early assumption that the Church of England would be established was put to rest during Anglo-Irish Sir Richard Bourke's administration (1831–37). Against the background of Westminster's removal of disabilities for Dissenters (1828) and Catholics (1829) and the extension of the franchise (1832), in New South Wales there was a progressive separation of church and state in an attempt to make peace between English, Scots and Irish Protestants and Catholics, liberals and conservatives. Bourke wound up the Church and Schools Lands Corporation and proposed to the Colonial Office that direct financial aid should be given to the Churches of England, Scotland and Rome (later extended also to the Wesleyan Methodists) for the payment of clergy and the erection of buildings and that the Irish National Model of schools should be adopted (Bourke, 1833). Anglicans successfully lobbied against these proposals. So at a time of booming population and colonial wealth, little could be done to address the educational needs of the colony's children. The 1844 report to the NSW Legislative Council revealed that 13,000 of the 25,626 school-aged children were receiving no instruction (Legislative Council, NSW 1844, pp. 1–2). It also recommended the adoption of the Irish National system. Meanwhile new colonies had been established at Swan River (Perth, 1828) and Adelaide (1836).

The third phase saw the introduction in 1848 of a dual system of education. A National Schools Board established schools for those who were not receiving any education while a Denominational Schools Board distributed state funds to the various denominational schools that were already involved in the task. With the separation from NSW of Victoria (1853) and Queensland (1859) and the granting of self-government in 1853, the limitation of funds, the poor standards in many denominational schools and the perception of wasteful duplication all led to the passage of amending legislation in each colony. Starting with the Queensland Primary Education Act 1860 followed by Victoria's 1862 Common Schools Act and the 1866 NSW Public Schools Act, denominational schools were brought into the National system with uniform standards and a 'common Christianity' was made the basis of public schools (Austin 1961, pp. 133–65). The NSW Act granted the right of access to clergy to the Council's schools to give one hour of religious instruction a day to children of their faith (Judd and Cable 1987, pp. 97–9). In South Australia E.G. Wakefield's 'voluntary principle', that undergirded the settlement, led to a system of public education with 'good secular instruction, based on the Christian religion'. No public funding was given to non-government schools (Austin 1961, p. 101).

The fourth phase, following the passage of the 1870 Forster Act in England, saw the enactment of 'free, compulsory and secular' universal schooling in each colony and the withdrawal of government funding from denominational schools. At this time religious plurality was construed purely in Christian terms, since over 80% of enrolments were comprised of Anglican, Methodist and Presbyterian students. None of the Protestant leaders was unduly concerned for the position of minority groups who were disadvantaged by the common Christianity assumptions.

The provision of RE was handled differently by each of the legislatures. In New South Wales a compromise was reached between secularists, who favoured non-sectarian General RE (GRE) taught by the class teacher, and Evangelical denominationalists, who wanted Special RE (SRE) taught by visiting clergy or their representatives. They legislated in 1880 for both forms of RE and the withdrawal of state funding from faith-based schools. Elsewhere the majority took the view that dogmatic religious teaching was the province of the church and the home but that a form of common Christianity and morality should be taught in state schools. In Victoria, where secular liberalism was stronger, the 1872 legislation withdrew state aid from church schools and banned religious teaching from public schools. However the morality taught in the latter was a blend of the Mosaic law, the Sermon on the Mount, the golden rule and British patriotism. A concession was made that school buildings could be used for other forms of religious instruction outside school hours (Grundy 1972). South Australia was characterised by a far greater proportion of free settlers from Dissenting backgrounds. Its 1875 Education Act permitted clergy to use schools for at least a quarter of an hour before the fixed time for secular instruction to read portions of Scripture from the Authorised or Douay versions. Queensland (1875), Tasmania (1885) and Western Australia (1895) adopted compromises that were similar to NSW. This was effectively the adoption of the Irish system: general religious instruction in the school curriculum (using the Irish First and Second Books of Lessons) and special religious instruction by visiting clergy (Langdon 1991, pp. 29–46).

The New Zealand pattern was similar. Initially provincial governments undertook the provision and support of all schools. With the abolition of this level of government in 1876, the central government enacted 'free, secular and compulsory' primary education the following year with the provision for religious instruction by visiting clergy. Maori children were provided for in the 1867 Native Schools Act.

There had been a failure to discern the different climate that was developing in the Roman Catholic Church following the publication of the *Syllabus of Errors* in 1864 and its accompanying encyclical *Quanta cura*, which attacked modern liberalism. Along with Lutherans and some Presbyterians and High Church Anglicans, Roman Catholics believed that the non-sectarian common Christianity approach of government schools was as bad as no education at all (Breward 1993, pp. 68–9). In each self-governing colony, the Roman Catholic Church decided to continue providing denominational schools, staffed mainly by French, Irish or local religious orders. Some Presbyterians and High Church Anglicans also persevered with alternate fee-charging faith-based schools after colonial government funding ceased.

The fifth phase from 1945 to the present has seen Australia and New Zealand moving in different directions. In Australia the separation of church and state has never been as complete as it has been in the United States. At the formation of the

Commonwealth of Australia in 1901, the six colonies became federated states of the Commonwealth. Education remained a responsibility of the state governments. However, by the early 1960s burgeoning population, strained resources and falling standards in many non-government schools, led the Commonwealth to consider its role in remedying this situation. The ceding of income taxing powers by the states in 1942 had created a fiscal imbalance where the state governments were increasingly unable to fund public works and services to meet population growth. Furthermore, the Commonwealth government emerged from the Second World War convinced that post-war reconstruction demanded heavier investment in education, especially secondary and tertiary education. During the 1970s the Commonwealth accepted responsibility for providing financial aid to the non-government school sector in the form of per capita funding of student places on a sliding scale according to changing measures of need. Most state governments have subsequently provided some per capita funding of non-government schools. These schools on average now receive almost 55 per cent of the recurrent costs of educating a student in a government school from the public purse (70 per cent of this from the Commonwealth and 30 per cent from the relevant state government). This has stimulated the establishment of Anglican, Lutheran, Seventh Day Adventist and non-denominational Protestant fee-paying schools. As a result of this generous funding regime, there has been a significant shift in school population from government to non-government schools. In 2004, of the 3.358 million Australian school students just over 67 per cent attended government schools, approximately 19 per cent were at Catholic schools and nearly 14 per cent in a range of other faith-based and a small number of other independent schools (Australian Bureau of Statistics 2004, p. 15). Although such schools are required to be registered by state authorities for government funding, and are inspected to ensure curriculum compliance in order to present students for public examinations, this does not extend to the RE component of the curriculum. Greater freedom in governance, employment practice and RE curriculum development exists in Australian non-government schools than in the English maintained school sector.

Like Australia, New Zealand experienced a population boom from 1945 to 1961 that put pressure on schools (King 2003, pp. 233–4). The government response differed from that of Australia; financial incentives favoured home schooling as an alternative to public schools rather than the establishment of schools by faith communities, although a moderate number of these exist.

Some contradictory trends have emerged in Australia. A greater percentage of students are currently receiving RE in faith-based schools, yet a higher proportion of Roman Catholic students are now being educated in government schools than ever before. This, along with an immigrant intake from Asian Muslim, Hindu and Buddhist countries, has dramatically changed the composition of government schools in most urban areas.

While the provision of SRE in state schools has flourished in some states, it has been in severe decline in others. In NSW the distinction between SRE (taught by visiting members of the religious persuasions) and GRE (taught by the regular class teacher) has been maintained, yet GRE is neglected in many state primary schools without question from public authorities. In junior secondary years GRE has suffered from competition in an overcrowded curriculum at the hands of advocates for traditional disciplines such as History and Geography. At the same time, the Higher School Certificate courses in Studies of Religion are very popular in many Catholic and some state schools, yet eschewed by most Protestant schools because of their perceived inadequacies with respect to teaching about Christian beliefs and practices. In no small measure this also has to do with teacher training, which has largely been the province of secular universities.

In other states there has been a blurring of the SRE / GRE distinction and a growing expectation that all RE will be taught by volunteers drawn mainly from the Christian churches, but that it will contain teaching about other major religions to meet the needs of an increasingly multi-faith society. Thus in these public schools a compatibilist form of RE predominates, while in other states that make the SRE / GRE distinction a transformationalist approach is more common, even when SRE is taught by joint-denominational groups. Christian schools in the Reformed tradition embrace a reconstructionalist approach (Cooling 1994, pp. 127–30) while longstanding denominational schools have retained an older form of civic Protestantism that focuses on moral outcomes. In New Zealand and Victoria there has been a progressive devolution of authority to the local school community which can determine whether any RE will be taught in the school and, if so, what type.

At a time when the two Roman Catholic universities in Australia have provided RE courses to train lay teachers now that most religious orders have withdrawn from Catholic schools, Protestants have not given the training of RE teachers the same priority. In contrast, secular universities in South Australia, Western Australia and New Zealand have offered training courses for both professional and, in certain cases, volunteer teachers.

Factors Affecting RE in Australia and New Zealand Schools

A key to understanding this complex situation is to recognise the low importance RE has in the curriculum in Australian and New Zealand schools. It is seen as belonging to the 'Culture' subset of the Studies of Society and Environment curriculum in Australia, and the 'Culture' and 'Social Organisation' sections of the Social Studies curriculum in New Zealand, which means its role is restricted to describing the customs and practices of groups within the broader society in order to serve the social goal of community harmony. Because of its narrow role, there are few incentives for educational theorists and theologians to be concerned about RE. Instead of developing a coherent theory and practice suited to local conditions, most have been content with an eclectic borrowing of philosophies and models for RE teaching drawn mainly from the United Kingdom in the case of government and denominational schools. Some Christian schools have adopted the Kuyperian model from Holland and North America (Wolterstorff 2004, pp. 64–86) and some denominational schools have adopted Peter Vardy's (1997) five-strand model. The main exceptions are to be found in the work of local theorists such as Moore and Habel (1982), Crawford and Rossiter (1985; 1988), Lovat (1989), Ryan and Malone (1996), Hobson and Edwards (1999), and Hill (2004). It is significant that many of the latter are Roman Catholic educators.

As well, a number of more general contemporary social and political concerns affect the way RE is being taught.

Human Rights

Controversy over the specification and assignment of rights affects RE in Australian and New Zealand schools. Government schools increasingly find themselves under pressure to deny the right of students to receive RE because minority groups claim the right to be free from such teaching. This has made an impact on the schools' willingness to introduce SRE where it is not already in operation and to provide a programme of GRE in the core curriculum of primary schools. In some cases, fear of offending non-Christian minorities has led to a banning of Christmas and Easter celebrations that have any Christian content.

Whilst current legislation recognises the rights of parents to determine the form of RE given to their children, with specific provisions for withdrawal, there are advocates for law reform who want to remove these provisions because they see them as infringing the rights of the child (for the reasons advanced by Marples 2005). It is unlikely that they will succeed because of the force of international treaties to which Australia is a signatory.

Of more immediate seriousness are calls from activists for the removal of exemptions for educational institutions from the application of anti-discrimination laws. At present faith-based schools are free to employ teachers who are in sympathy with the nature and mission of the school. Roman Catholic schools have a general requirement that applicants for teaching positions have formal qualifications from a Catholic university to teach RE. Christian schools in the Reformed and Baptist traditions and diocesan Anglican schools have similar expectations, although they do not necessarily insist on formal qualifications.

Schools are also free to set their own enrolment policies, although there are requirements for those in receipt of public funding that they provide for students with special needs. Denominational schools have tended to have open enrolment policies whereas some of the Christian parent-controlled and individual church-controlled schools have more restrictive requirements. Jewish, Muslim, Greek and Coptic Orthodox, Assyrian Catholic and Armenian Apostolic schools tend only to enrol students of their respective faiths. State education advocates oppose funding to schools with restrictive enrolment policies and regularly call for greater accountability, particularly with respect to special needs provisions.

Underlying these rights debates is the belief of secularists, especially in militant government school teachers' unions and parent associations, that there ought to be complete separation of church and state and that public funds should not be used to support private choice. Some go so far as to deny that religion has a place in state education. However, the most recent survey research suggests that 62 per cent of all Australians still favour the teaching of religion in government schools (Roy Morgan Research, 2005), although the number has declined by about 12 per cent in the last 25 years.

The Role of the School

Different political philosophies also give rise to different views on the nature and purpose of schooling. The broad divide affecting RE is between humanists, who emphasise the nurture of individuals, and instrumentalists, who are concerned with the outcomes for society. Rapid change has favoured the instrumentalists, regardless of their political affiliation, who want either work-ready graduates for economic growth and competitiveness, or socially aware graduates, who will enhance the community's social capital. Clearly RE does not feature highly in the agendas of either side of this debate.

The strongly unionised teaching force in Australia has resisted public scrutiny of educational outcomes and standards in government schools, not least in RE with its weak syllabus requirements. On the other hand state school advocates have successfully called for greater accountability from schools in the non-government sector. For this reason, cross-sectoral comparison such as that undertaken by John Marks in England (Marks 2001, pp. 5–36) is not possible in Australia.

The place of religion in Australian cultural heritage is largely unrecognised owing to the widely accepted interpretive paradigm advanced by Manning Clark that 'within three generations [of European settlement] the Protestant ascendancy was crumbling to its ruins, and the dream of the brotherhood of man was taking possession of men's minds' (Clark 1962, p. 380). His many followers have demonstrated a complete blind spot to the contribution of religion to the fabric of Australian society. This lack of vision has flowed through into the curriculum designed to promote civic education (Curriculum Corporation, 1999). In particular, the Christian churches suffer in this portrayal and there is a resultant lack of confidence among teachers in the public sector in presenting these aspects of GRE.

Another significant concern has been whether religion can be taught descriptively without making it normative (Judge 1964, pp. 106–115). Wariness among teachers in state schools has reinforced the idea that it is not safe to venture into such domains. This is in spite of carefully argued cases against such misgivings (such as Thiessen 1993; Hill 2004). On the other hand, more care about the presumptive use of language and enforced compliance in religious observance needs to be taken by some schools in the non-government sector.

Competing Religious Truth Claims

The question of how rival truth claims can be handled in school curricula must be addressed if the integrity of the religion in question is to be respected. This problem is not peculiar to Australia and New Zealand (see Cooling 1994, pp. 88–93).

The elevation of tolerance to being a, if not *the*, primary value of democratic society presents serious problems to orthodox Christians. Strong religious truth claims do not sit comfortably with the spirit of toleration. Instead of allowing these claims into the public arena for examination and discussion, modern democracies have followed the American model of allowing each religious persuasion 'in the words of Rabbi Arthur Hertzberg "to remain the one true revealed faith for itself and in private, but each must *behave in the public arena as if* its truth were as tentative as an aesthetic opinion or a scientific theory"' (Mouw and Griffioen 1993, p. 6). Civility requires conviction to be sacrificed. It is small wonder that Muslims in the West are most reluctant to comply. Conservative Australian Christians consider it shameful that their more liberal counterparts have allowed themselves to become part of this complicity.

Many Christian educators are also concerned that, in the absence of an a-historical universal source of knowledge, namely God's self-revelation through the Scriptures, contemporary students are denied what their forebears had. But their situation is further complicated by the assault of postmodern philosophers such as Derrida and Foucault on the text of Scripture itself, which disallows any definitive interpretation. Jesus' claim to be 'the way, the truth and the life' (John 14:6), which he grounded in the unity of the Father and Son and their commonality of purpose (John 14:9–10), is no longer allowed to stand as the way of access to God and to ultimate truth. It has been relativised and tamed. The same treatment is given to the notion that Christianity is absolutely true for everyone, everywhere and at all times because it accords with transcendental reality as well as the reality we experience (Wells 2005, p. 87). An increasing number of conservatives from various faith traditions are beginning to argue that, because rival truth claims are simply relativised and disempowered by the way RE is currently taught, there is a need to provide students with the analytical tools for adjudicating between such claims. It is to be expected that, as they develop more sophisticated arguments, their voice will be heard in academic journals.

The Contemporary Study of Religion

The way in which religion is conceptualised has changed. RE now faces the post-modern claim that all metanarratives are to be treated with suspicion because they advance someone's interests and contribute to their power over others. Modernity brought with it an intense awareness of pluralities; postmodernity has introduced the reign of subjectivity. As a consequence RE as part of the school curriculum is floundering. It lacks a coherent philosophical and theological rationale for it to prosper, despite the work of Brian Hill over many decades culminating in his recent call for RE to become a national priority (Hill 2004).

Part of the problem lies in the secular academy. Atheists such as Richard Dawkins consider religion to be discredited and not worthy of a place in the university curriculum. On the other hand, some maintain that it is possible to undertake a scientific, objective and rational study of religion, but not of theology (Wiebe 1998). Australian universities were reluctant to permit the teaching of theology in the first place and, where they did, this has subsequently been replaced by Religious Studies with a couple of notable exceptions. As a consequence, theological teaching has become the province of a range of denominational colleges that work in isolation from mainstream academic endeavour. At best, advances in Christian theology gain delayed acceptance into the academic study of religion; at worst they are disregarded. Calls for a revision of this dysfunctional relationship are not welcomed by academics committed to the status quo, either because they seek to perpetuate the modernist view that their enterprise is objective and impartial, untainted by belief, or the postmodernist view that Christian theological reflection is but one view among many with no claim for particular consideration (see Vanhoozer 2003; Webster 2003).

More recently, the questionable assumption that you can study religion objectively from a neutral, external standpoint has come under fire from a number of quarters (Hauerwas 1988; Milbank 1990; MacIntyre 1990). So too has the rejection of theology as part of the Enlightenment objection to foundationalism: Plantinga and Wolterstorff (1983, pp. 16–93, 135–86) have argued that God can legitimately be taken as the starting point of human thought. There is little evidence for the impact of these arguments on the thinking of Australian RE academics.

Since many of the theoretical models of RE have not served Christians well, there are a growing number of calls from Christian religious educators for a paradigm shift, although not all are in agreement as to the direction (so, for example, Cooling 1994; Thompson 2004; Murphy 2004).

In Australia and New Zealand the method of argumentation has been conducted largely within the modernist framework. Here, as elsewhere, the philosophic naturalism of the social sciences, liberal humanistic assumptions and rationalistic reductionism have predisposed these thinkers to overlook the complexities and diversities of and within religious faiths.

Teacher Supply, Training and Recruitment

The consequence is that most graduating teachers from public universities have very limited understanding of religious belief systems, of the foundational nature of Christianity for Western democracy and human rights, or of the nature of the human person as a spiritual being. Catholic universities, to their credit, have tried to address this deficiency. However, as Murphy has shown, the leading Catholic educational theorists, Gabriel Moran, Thomas Groome and Mary Boys, are fully immersed in the modernist paradigm (Murphy 2004, pp. 29–94). Curiously, it is in the Australian states where Religious Education is in decline in state schools that public universities have offered courses in RE content and methods, presumably in the hope that trained teachers will be engaged to take over where volunteers have failed. But these suffer from many of the same shortcomings because of their positivist approach.

Elsewhere, the churches and the educational arms of the other religious persuasions have maintained a strong programme for the recruitment and training of volunteers to teach RE in state schools but they have generally trusted to luck in finding suitably equipped teachers for denominational schools. Faith-based schools have teachers with a well-developed personal faith but they are not always equipped to reflect theologically and philosophically on their professional practice. To address this, two of the non-denominational Christian school groups have set up postgraduate professional development programmes and Anglicans in at least two Australian states are developing teacher education programmes that reflect regional distinctives.

The Learner

Hill, rightly in the author's view, maintains there is a contemporary lack of an integrating vision of what it is to be an educated person (Hill 2004, p. 44). However his approach remains anchored in the liberal humanist framework with its emphasis on the individual and the function of RE being seen as assisting 'students to pursue their personal quest for meaning and spiritual affirmation by introducing them to the resources of major religious traditions and equipping them to evaluate these traditions critically' (Hill 2004, p. 181). It has been argued elsewhere that Hill has too optimistic a view of the human learner and the power of human rationality to make informed choices on the basis of the evidence. From a Christian perspective he fails to give sufficient weight to the constraints on one's power to choose (Maple 2005, pp. 52–3). There is also the question of the basis for such a choice to be made if the student has only the data from such a limited study of religion as is provided by most Australian state schools. More realistic are Thiessen's arguments for instruction in a primary culture in which growth can occur before choices need to be made, particularly where there is limited or no knowledge of basic beliefs that could once be taken for granted (Thiessen 2001, p. 41).

Suggestions for Effective RE Programmes

Hill (2004) is justified in his call for RE to be given a much higher place on the national agenda. The first issue must be how to afford RE a more significant place in the school curriculum. This will require relinquishing the notion that unity can only be achieved by asking people to privatise their beliefs that they hold as universal and non-negotiable (Cooling 1994, p. 10). The twenty-first century world in which we live demands that students have an understanding not only of the basis and content of their own belief system (however unorthodox it may be), but also of the major world religions and of the diversity that exists within each of them. Without this understanding, an empathetic appreciation of another faith's personal meaning and purpose for its adherents is unlikely. It is necessary to have this depth of appreciation for informed citizenship in a democratic society. The relative failure of most families and religious groups to provide a sufficiently detailed understanding means that the school is the most appropriate avenue for providing it.

This in turn raises the question of whether it is desirable to have a national or state RE curriculum, or whether this is a decision best left to the school because of the diverse and specific nature of the student population of a school and the student needs that stem from this. Past experience suggests that, if the status of RE in Australia and New Zealand is to be improved, it will be most likely achieved through a central curriculum either at the state or the national level. However, in view of Thiessen's comments above, it is desirable for a central curriculum to be sufficiently flexible to enable all students to be well grounded in their own faith before undertaking critical engagement with others. It will also mean clearing sufficient space in an already overcrowded curriculum to enable this to happen.

Thirdly, to improve the status of RE will require that teachers be adequately prepared to teach this part of the curriculum and to have a compelling rationale for doing so. This will entail incorporating into teacher training programmes a more robust treatment of the philosophy, contents and methods of RE teaching.

Fourthly, it will also require a better understanding of the spiritual, intellectual and moral development of students than many teachers now have. These need to be open to theological insights from the various traditions about the nature of the learner and what is to be learnt.

Fifthly, attention must be given to the truth claims of the religions that are studied. Students need to be equipped with the intellectual tools to adjudicate between rival claims. In doing this, care must also be taken not to distort the religions that are taught by imposing external frames of reference on them (Maple 2005, p. 48).

These requirements apply equally to government and non-government schools. In non-government faith-based schools, there may need to be a broadening of what is currently undertaken so that there is sufficient space given in the early years to the faith traditions of all those represented in the class (especially for schools having open enrolment policies), even though the major emphasis will be on the faith tradition (or subset of it) to which the school belongs. Progressively what is taught should challenge the students' own understanding, beliefs, what is valued and how these affect the way they live, so that any faith commitment becomes an owned one. The outcomes of the RE programme should be within reach of all students, not just those whose beliefs are congruent with the school's faith position. On the other hand, nurture of believers should be primarily the task of voluntary groups and not an explicit outcome of the curriculum.

In government schools where SRE is also taught, the visiting teacher from the faith group would therefore become an added resource for students from families that claim allegiance to that faith. The two types of RE should be complementary and mutually reinforcing. Those visiting teachers who lack professional teacher training need to be much better trained to teach effectively without placing on them the modernist constraints that currently exist with respect to RE. Finally, it is high time for schools to drop the expectation that these representatives of particular faith traditions will shoulder the responsibility for teaching about other religions.

References

Austin, A.G. (1961) *Australian Education 1788–1900: Church, State and Public Education in Colonial Australia*. Melbourne, Pitman & Sons.

Australian Bureau of Statistics (2004) *Schools Australia*. 4221.0

Bourke to Stanley, 30 September 1833 and Bourke to Glenelg, 8 August 1836, *Historical Records of Australia*, 1 XVII, pp. 224–9 and XVIII, p. 466.

Breward, Ian (1993) *A History of the Australian Churches*. St Leonards, NSW, Allen & Unwin.

Clark, C.M.H. (1962) *A History of Australia: Vol. 1 From the Earliest Times to the Age of Macquarie*. Melbourne, Melbourne University Press.

Cooling, T. (1994) *A Christian Vision for State Education: Reflections on the Theology of Education*. London, SPCK.

Crawford, M. and Rossiter, G. (1985) *Teaching Religion in the Secondary School: Theory and Practice*. Sydney, Province Resource Group, Christian Brothers.

—— (1988) *Missionaries to a Teenage Culture: Religious Education in a Time of Rapid Change*. Sydney, Province Resource Group, Christian Brothers.

Curriculum Corporation (1999) *Australian Readers, Discovering Democracy*. Carlton South, Curriculum Corporation.

Grundy, D. (1972) *Secular, Compulsory and Free: The Education Act of 1872*. Carlton, Melbourne University Press.

Hauerwas, Stanley (1988) *Christian Existence Today*. Durham, NC, Labyrinth Press.

Hill, B. (2004) *Exploring Religion in School: A National Priority*. Adelaide, Open Book.

Hobson, P.R. and Edwards, J.S. (1999) *Religious Education in a Pluralist Society: The Key Philosophical Issues*. London, Woburn Press.

Judd, S. and Cable, K. (1987) *Sydney Anglicans: A History of the Diocese*. Sydney, Anglican Information Office.

Judge, E. (1964) 'Problems of General Religious Teaching'. *Journal of Christian Education*, 7 (2 & 3), 106–115.

King, M. (2003) *The Penguin History of New Zealand*. Auckland, Penguin.

Langdon, A. (1991) 'Religious Education in the Public (Government) Schools of New South Wales: Part 1: General Religious Education'. *Journal of Christian Education*, Papers 101, June, pp. 29–46.

Legislative Council, NSW (1844) Report of the Select Committee on Education *Votes and Proceedings*, Vol. 2, p. 2.

Lovat, T.J. (1989) *What is This Thing Called Religious Education? Summary, Critique and a New Proposal*. Wentworth Falls, Social Science Press.

MacIntyre, Alasdair (1990) *Three Rival Versions of Moral Enquiry: Encyclopaedia, Genealogy and Tradition*. Notre Dame, IN, University of Notre Dame Press.

Maple, G. (2005), 'Exploring Religion in School: An Anglican Response'. *Journal of Christian Education*, 48 (2), 43–58.

Marks J. (2001) 'Standards in Church of England, Roman Catholic and LEA Schools in England'. In John Burn *et al. Faith in Education. The Role of the Churches in Education: A Response to the Dearing Report on Church Schools in the Third Millennium*. London, Civitas, pp. 5–36.

Marples, R. (2005) 'Against Faith Schools: A Philosophical Argument for Children's Rights'. *International Journal of Children's Spirituality*, 10 (2), 133–47.

Milbank, John (1990) *Theology and Social Theory: Beyond Secular Reason*. Oxford, Blackwell.

Moore, B.S. and Habel, N. (1982) *When Religion Goes to School: Typology of Religion for the Classroom*. Adelaide, South Australian College of Advanced Education.

Mouw, R.J. and Griffioen, S. (1993) *Pluralisms and Horizons*. Grand Rapids, Eerdmans.

Murphy, D.D. (2004) *Teaching That Transforms: Worship as the Heart of Christian Education.* Grand Rapids, Eerdmans.

Plantinga, Alvin and Wolterstorff, Nicholas (eds) (1983), *Faith and Rationality: Reason and Belief in God.* Notre Dame, IN, University of Notre Dame Press, pp. 16–93, 135–86.

Roy Morgan Research (2005) *Reduced Majority of Australians Favour Teaching Religion in Government Schools.* Article No. 387 – 17 May.

Ryan, M. and Malone, P. (1996) *Exploring Religion in the Classroom: A Guidebook for Catholic Schools.* Wentworth Falls, Social Science Press.

Thiessen, E. (1993) *Teaching for Commitment: Liberal Education, Indoctrination and Christian Nurture.* Montreal, McGill-Queens University Press.

—— (2001) *In Defence of Religious Schools and Colleges.* Montreal, McGill-Queens University Press.

Thompson, P. (2004) *Whatever Happened to Religious Education?* Cambridge, Lutterworth Press.

Vanhoozer, K.J. (2003) 'Theology and the Condition of Postmodernity: A Report on Knowledge (of God)'. In K.J. Vanhoozer (ed) *The Cambridge Companion to Postmodern Theology.* Cambridge, Cambridge University Press, pp. 149–69.

Vardy, P. (1997) *Towards a New Approach to Religious Education.* Jolimont, VIC, IARTV.

Webster, John (2003) 'The Human Person'. In K.J. Vanhoozer (ed.) *The Cambridge Companion to Postmodern Theology.* Cambridge, Cambridge University Press, pp. 219–34.

Wells, David (2005) *Above All Earthly Pow'rs: Christ in a Postmodern World.* Grand Rapids, Eerdmans.

Wiebe, D. (1998) *The Politics of Religious Studies: The Continuing Conflict with Theology in the Academy.* New York, St Martin's Press.

Wolterstorff, N. (2004) *Educating for Shalom: Essays on Christian Higher Education.* Grand Rapids, Eerdmans.

PART 2

Introduction

The chapters here, all written by scholars in the field of Religious Education (RE), raise further uncomfortable questions about RE. Has modern British RE become so ill at ease with the conflicting truth claims of the different religions that it prefers to present religions to children as 'really the same'? Such an accommodation gains strength from the conviction that it engenders social cohesion, but, as chapter 7 argues, it may have the opposite effect, founded as it is on a deep mistrust of religions. Once it was thought to be of the essence of the task to guide children into an understanding and appreciation of Christianity (although there has always been provision for the syllabus to meet the religious needs of children from other faiths) because the faith was thought to furnish something of infinite value. Is this no longer the case? Then why, as chapter 6 argues, has this tradition come under constant fire at least since the Swann Report? That there are practical difficulties with maintaining such a tradition goes without saying. But we need to find a way of presenting religious life to children in a way that does not implicitly undermine it. The introduction of atheism (see chapter 8) into a RE syllabus might be thought ill advised in this regard. While forms of 'protest atheism' could illuminate the need for reform within a religious context and something of the power of religious ideas, to teach atheism as a form of religious life seems counter-intuitive. Is the religious educator therefore involved in an unwitting deception? Chapter 9 reflects upon the language of skills in RE and suggests that while such language may make the subject appear modern and professional, on close inspection it is difficult to see what help it offers to the teacher and it could be distracting. Is there in fact, asks chapter 10, anything religious about RE any more?

Chapter 6

Religious Education from Spens to Swann

Penny Thompson

Abstract

A brief history of Religious Education in England and Wales is given, followed by a study of selected government reports into the teaching of the subject, beginning with the Spens Report of 1938 and ending with the Swann Report of 1985. It is suggested that the latter broke with tradition and introduced patterns of teaching which distance children from religious life. There is a need to find ways of teaching which avoid such pitfalls and the 1988 Education Reform Act legislated for just this.

A Brief History of RE

Nineteenth Century

For most of the nineteenth century free education was provided by the churches. The National Society offered general education with Anglican instruction and the British and Foreign Schools Society general education alongside Nonconformist instruction. Both societies received state grants. In 1870 the Forster Education Act provided for 'board schools' in those areas where the churches could not cope with the numbers of children. Many Anglicans fought for religious instruction based on Anglican principles in those schools, a solution doggedly opposed by Nonconformists. In the end a compromise solution was arrived at by means of the Cowper Temple clause, still in force today (in modified form). It stated that teaching must not include any denominational formulary or catechism.

The Origin of the Agreed Syllabus

In the 1920s groups of teachers and representatives of the churches met together to agree syllabuses for the boards to allay concerns about what could, and could not, be taught and to raise the standard of teaching. Here is the origin of the phrase 'agreed syllabus'.

The 1944 Education Act

The Butler Act built on and extended existing practice. It became compulsory for local education authorities (LEAs) to set up agreed syllabus conferences (ASCs) to write local syllabuses. Four committees (three in Wales where the Church in Wales was not established) were to form the conferences. These committees (still in force today) were:

A – religious denominations other than the Church of England
B – the Church of England
C – the teachers' unions
D – the local authority.

At the same time permission was given to LEAs to set up standing advisory councils for RE (SACREs) as advisory bodies. Schools had to provide Religious Instruction and Collective Worship, with conscience clauses in the law allowing parents to withdraw their children, and teachers not to teach religious instruction or take part in worship. Provision was made for more than one syllabus to be adopted so that children for whom a Christian syllabus was inappropriate (mainly Jewish children) could have one suited to their needs.

The 1988 Education Reform Act (ERA)

The Baker Act similarly built on and extended existing practice. SACREs were made compulsory and schools were required to teach by means of the agreed syllabus. A later education act legislated for syllabuses to be reviewed every five years by a newly appointed ASC. The Cowper Temple clause was re-worded to make it clear that teaching *about* denominational formularies could take place alongside teaching that was agreed upon by the ASC. It was made clear that religions other than Christianity could be represented on Committee A of the SACRE and ASC. Representation on these bodies has to be proportionate to numbers of adherents in the area and humanists[1] may not be appointed to Committee A (on the grounds that humanism is not a religion). The right for religions other than Christianity to have their beliefs taken into account was enshrined in the phrase that a syllabus must '[take] account of the beliefs and practices of the principal religious traditions represented in Great Britain'. This was intended to signal the need to make provision for pupils from non-Christian religions (as did the 1944 Act), but has been widely interpreted to require the inclusion of the (unnamed) principal religions on every syllabus, without taking account of the presence of children from these faiths (see Thompson 2004, pp. 111–23). The non-statutory national framework for RE, published in October 2004, recommended that in addition to the study of Christianity, pupils should study Buddhism, Hinduism, Islam, Judaism and Sikhism across Keystages 1–3 and other religious traditions and secular philosophies, where appropriate (QCA 2004, p. 12).

---

1   A humanist may be co-opted on to a SACRE, but not on to an ASC.

A Part of Educational Provision

Perhaps because of the fact that education was originally conceived as a religious imperative, RE and worship have always been seen as part and parcel of school in England and Wales. RE is timetabled through the day, taught by professionally trained teachers who are paid just as any other teacher and who are in all respects equal in status. While not part of the national curriculum introduced in 1988, RE is part of the statutory 'basic curriculum'. RE has an officer and team at the national Qualifications and Curriculum Authority (QCA) dedicated to it and benefits from national initiatives such as reviews of the curriculum, assessment and IT.

Government Reports on Religious Education

I now examine selected government reports on religious education in schools. This will further illustrate the history of the subject and also throw into relief the challenges that face us today. I consider the line taken on the teaching of the subject and the role of the teacher. An advantage of investigating government reports is that such reports tend to be broad and far-reaching and take into account the views of a wide range of people. Their intentions are advertised and comments invited from interested individuals and associations. The Spens Report, for example, received a very great number of submissions. This means that any particular view that may happen to prevail within the profession is balanced by the views of those outside the profession.[2]

The Spens Report

The Spens Report of 1938 was the product of a five-year enquiry into secondary education. Its chapter on 'Scripture' began: 'We believe that there is a wide and genuine recognition of the value and importance of religious instruction and the teaching of Scripture in schools' (Spens 1938, p. 206). Agreed syllabuses had enabled controversy to be overcome and shown that proper religious instruction could take place. No substantial body of opinion in favour of an entirely secular secondary education existed and 'the great majority of parents prefer ... that their children should continue to receive some kind of religious instruction during their post-primary education' (p. 208). The Bible should be included in education because it opened up a 'religious interpretation of life' without which 'no boy or girl can be counted as properly educated'. The report went on: 'The traditional form which that interpretation has taken in this country is Christian . . . the Bible is the classic book of Christianity and forms the basis of the structure of the Christian faith and worship' (p. 208). Scripture should be taught with a view to understanding what the books of the Bible were intended to mean by their authors. The 'objective' approach

---

2   Compare Schools' Council (1971), which confined its discussions entirely to those within the teaching profession.

would increase intellectual respect for and interest in religion. It also (it was thought) sidestepped awkward questions about denominational interpretations.

The Role of the Teacher

Aware that their approach might be misunderstood, the report continued:

> By the word 'objective' we do not mean that teachers of Scripture should confine themselves to literary criticism and the provision of an 'historical' background; nor, certainly, that they should not themselves have a strong sympathy with a religious interpretation of life. It can hardly be disputed that the best teacher is one whose interest in the subject and desire to teach it proceed from religious faith … [to teach 'objectively'] enables teachers to take a position from which they can most easily and effectively reply to questions raised incidentally by their pupils, as well as explain the divergencies in Christian thought, without incurring the suspicion of either insincerity or prejudice – personal or denominational. (p. 209)

It was recognised that some teachers might want to apply Christian principles to modern-day problems, both personal and social. Others might want to lay emphasis on the Bible as a call to the Christian life. Spens did not prohibit this and acknowledged that this aspect of religious education could be very effective. More qualified teachers were needed, a plea that would be repeated often in years to come. Provision for teachers in post was a priority. Leave of absence should be given to teachers to study for a degree in theology and other qualifications. Grants should be given for vacation study plus a portion of the fees. Every elementary school child (although their brief was for secondary education!) should be provided with portions of the Bible in attractive format.

The Crowther Report

The Crowther Report of 1959 was concerned with the 15–18 age group. Crowther wanted guidance to be given to the young, while aware that the young were in no hurry to accept it. Advertisers sought to entice them to buy their products, thus making the young feel important and encouraging their natural tendencies to resist the restraints that family and school imposed on them. The temptation was for adults not to make the effort to encourage high standards and ideals. Yet 'nothing could be more fatal to their influence with the young than the reserve which prudence dictates or legislators decree' (Crowther 1959, p. 175). In relation to the requirements of the 1944 Education Act, it was stated that 'there is no period in life when people more need what the Education Act means when it refers … to "religious instruction", and no period when it is more difficult to give':

> The teenagers with whom we are concerned need, perhaps above all else, to find a faith to live by. They will not find precisely the same faith and some will not find any. Education can and should play some part in the search. It can assure them that there is something to search for and it can show them where to look and what other men have found. (p. 44)

This meant Christianity: 'It is the endeavour to discover and to understand the central affirmations of the Christian faith so that (whether they accept it or not) they at least may know what Christians believe' (p. 275).

The Newsom Report

Newsom, published in 1963 after two years' work, considered the education of pupils aged between 13 and 16 who were of average, or less than average, ability. It is remarkable for its forthright advocacy of Christian teaching, in the year when the RE profession experienced a dramatic loss of nerve for such teaching (Thompson 2004, ch.1). Newsom concentrated heavily on evidence from the schools and its view on RE and worship attended to the views of pupils.

The report spoke of fostering the spiritual and moral development of pupils, of fulfilling personal needs:

> they [the pupils] want to know what kind of animal man is and whether ultimately each one of us matters – and – if so why and to whom ... they need to know what answer the Christian faith gives. This ought to be given in the most direct and plainest way possible ... the schools of the land need immediately Christian teachers who ... speak with informed conviction in a language the pupils can understand and who in terms of scholarship have kept on the Christian frontiers of today. (quoted in Birnie 1964, p. 17)

Newsom, like Spens, recommended that teaching must be more than moral instruction or exhortation. Nonetheless, moral instruction, undergirded by Christian belief must be given. It was no use leaving this to chance. Like Crowther, Newsom argued that it was wrong to leave the young to fend for themselves. The same was true for spiritual development. The committee had been impressed by their experience of worship in schools and noted that pupils sometimes said that what they missed about schools was the saying of prayers. In relation to religious instruction they recommended the SCM materials which started from problems and moved to the Bible, rather than beginning from the Bible.

The Role of the Teacher

Pupils wanted teachers who 'know what they are talking about' (Newsom 1963, p. 56). Teachers needed to be able to show pupils how a Christian would set about solving problems encountered in life. Thus a teacher needed to be up to date in their scholarship. Newsom said: 'The best schools give their pupils something which they do not get elsewhere, something which they know they need when they receive it, though they had not realised the lack before' (pp. 55–6). The view of a pupil was quoted to the effect that unless the teacher was a 'right and religious man' he would be no better able to explain things than the pupils were. Newsom wrote:

> They want to be told the truth. 'It is no use', we were told in discussion, 'putting up a smokescreen and retiring in flight behind it'. The teacher who is not prepared to expose himself in honestly grappling with these ultimate problems had better leave them alone. His lessons must carry conviction. This is not the same as trying to convert his pupils. Above all, they don't want to be 'got at'. (p. 52)

The integrity of the teacher was very important. Pupils would learn the truth of what was taught by how they saw teachers behaving.

The Plowden Report

Plowden published in 1967 after three years' work and was concerned with primary schools. A minority of members of the Commission did not believe that Religious Instruction (RI) should be included at primary level and contributed a note of reservation. Other members believed that RI and worship should set the tone of living and learning for the whole school. Still others found themselves between these two positions. The view taken by the Commission was to continue with the provisions of the 1944 Act since surveys had revealed widespread support for RI and daily worship in the country. RI should 'meet the wishes of those parents who have specifically accepted that their child should have this instruction' (Plowden 1967, p. 207).

Like Newsom, Plowden advocated the imparting of a Christian view of life to the young. Plowden reflected the work of Ronald Goldman whose voice may be discerned in the following statement. Young children, it was argued,

> need a simple and positive introduction to religion. They should be taught to know and love God and to practise in the school community the virtues appropriate to their age and environment … Children should not be unnecessarily involved in religious controversy. They should not be confused by being taught to doubt before faith is established. (p. 207)

The agreed syllabuses should be recast so as to impart concepts as opposed to facts. While accepting Goldman's strictures about the use of the Bible, Plowden nonetheless accepted that stories about the life and teaching of Jesus should be given to even the very young children, while a systematic study of his life was best at the latter stages of primary education: 'They may be led to find in him the expression of that which, in ways appropriate to their development, they have learnt to be good and true' (p. 208). Stories from non-Christian traditions should be included and given sympathetically, the example of Saladin was suggested. Bible stories, hymns and prayers required careful delivery but they were still what RI and worship was about.

Common standards and values were of extreme importance and children who were withdrawn from RI and worship should nonetheless be expected to conform to the general life of the school. The unstated assumption here was that school life was to be modelled on Christian teaching.

The Role of the Teacher

Being a report into primary education, Plowden had to face the issue of how far it was appropriate for the class teacher to teach RI. HMIs had conducted a survey of the attitudes of teachers to taking RI which revealed that 8 per cent of women teachers and 16 per cent of men teachers were either reluctant or not much interested. Plowden concluded that there was no great difficulty in staffing the subject and was keen for the class teacher to give RI where possible. Their advice to those teachers who were 'reluctant' was to concentrate on those aspects of the teaching with which they were comfortable, ethics or history perhaps. In this way they could be honest and avoid introducing children to controversy:

> It is essential that the teacher who is prepared to give religious education should be honest and sincere in his teaching, and should not pretend to beliefs he does not hold. For the non-believing teacher or one of different religion this may mean stressing the ethics and the history of Christianity rather than its theology. (Plowden 1963, p. 207)

Plowden pointed out, in relation to the 1944 Education Act, that 'too little thought was given to the training of teachers' (p. 207).

The Swann Report

The Swann Report of 1985 enquired into the education of children from ethnic minorities. It viewed RE[3] as important and dedicated a lengthy chapter to the subject (33 pages) that also considered separate schooling according to faiths. Swann engaged with the professional RE literature, quoting several authorities. It has the feel of a manifesto for change, although the changes advocated were by then firmly entrenched in the thinking of opinion-formers within the profession, if not in schools at large. The view taken was, in essence, that of the Schools' Council Working Paper 36, *Religious Education in Secondary Schools*, published in 1971 under the directorship of Ninian Smart, then Professor of Religious Studies at Lancaster University:

> We find ourselves firmly in favour of the broader phenomenological approach to religious education as the best and indeed only means of enhancing the understanding of all pupils, from whatever religious background, of the plurality of faiths in contemporary Britain, of bringing them to an understanding of the nature of belief and the religious dimension of human existence, and of helping them to appreciate the diverse and sometimes conflicting life stances which exist and thus enabling them to determine (and justify) their own religious position. (Swann 1985, pp. 474–5)

Swann's view of RE was clearly influenced by sociological concerns, in particular 'cultural pluralism'. Swann had studied several ways of approaching the subject and came out strongly in favour of the phenomenological approach while acknowledging criticisms of it. In arguing that it was the only approach suited to the situation Swann broke new ground. Earlier reports had not claimed a monopoly for their recommendations.

Swann emphasised that Christianity should continue to hold a central place in the teaching of RE. But educational institutions should not 'transmit a sectional view as if it were the only publicly defensible one' (p. 472, quoting John Elliott). To worries

---

3   By 1985 the term 'religious education' had replaced the term 'religious instruction' in common usage. The 1944 Education Act used 'religious education' to refer to religious instruction and collective worship, thus linking the two activities. The 1988 ERA replaced RI with RE.

that this meant downplaying the importance of Christianity the report replied that their aim was to 'to set the consideration of Christianity, in all its spiritual depth and fullness, within a wider context of the true significance of the religious dimension to life, in all its forms' (p. 473).

Swann stated that the majority of teachers in schools with a multi-faith population were in favour of the phenomenological approach. Such teachers told the committee that a substantial number of their colleagues, especially those working in 'all-white' areas, still saw their work in terms of scripture and Bible study. Ethnic communities offered evidence referring to the provision of RE their children had received. Swann felt strongly that the education system should respect and reflect the faiths of its citizens and not compare them negatively to Christianity. An understanding of minority faiths would help to counter negative stereotypes amongst ethnic majority youngsters and thus go some way to combating racism. It was pointed out, however, that some Muslims wanted a confessional teaching of Islam for their children and 'saw no need for a broader approach' (p. 474).

The Role of the Teacher

Great emphasis was put on the need for the teacher to acknowledge and welcome cultural diversity. A teacher must have 'respect and understanding of the cultural heritage which belongs to the children growing up in our society' (Swann 1985, p. 560). When it came to selection for teacher training any teacher showing negative attitudes towards ethnic minorities or the development of a culturally plural society would be unlikely to be able to 'fulfil the professional responsibilities of a teacher in preparing pupils to live harmoniously in today's pluralist society' (p. 569). In relation to RE, a teacher would have to endorse the phenomenological approach as the latter was linked to the promotion of cultural diversity and, implicitly, with the view that religious faiths must be presented as equally worthy forms of life. It was recognised by the committee that adopting this role might be difficult for certain teachers: 'considerable skill and sensitivity were required on the part of a teacher, who might well have a personal commitment to a particular faith, in order to present other faiths as valid in their own right' (p. 489).

It is perhaps this concern that led some RE teachers, when asked how they handled their own beliefs, to say that they preferred to keep them to themselves, lest they had an influence on the way pupils viewed matters: '[they] deliberately avoided expressing their own views in the classroom, in the belief that these would inevitably condition pupils' perception of different religions' (p. 487). Others stated that they would explain and defend their own beliefs if asked. A section on resources highlighted the problem of obtaining textbooks that did not present religions other than Christianity 'in negative or inaccurate terms' (p. 488). Teachers were advised to use such texts as examples of negative stereotyping, the purpose being to instruct pupils to avoid such errors. Speakers could be invited into the classroom to bring to life the faiths concerned and enhance pupils' appreciation of the presence of a range of faiths within the locality and society in general.

Discussion

It is clear that Swann distanced itself from earlier ways of approaching RE. Yet there are important commonalities between Swann and the earlier reports outlined above. In this section I discuss both the commonalities and differences with a view to asking how far Swann represents a continuation of the tradition of RE teaching and how far it should be viewed as a new departure. I treat the earlier reports as a unity, aware that this is to mask some differences.

Commonalities

1. Both recognise a need for pupils to work out a philosophy of life. Crowther writes of the 'need to find a faith to live by', and acknowledges that pupils will not all find the same faith. Swann writes of pupils 'determining their own religious position'.
2. Both accept the right of pupils to be, in the words of Spens, 'made aware of the fact of the existence of a religious interpretation of life'. Or, as Swann puts it, of being brought to 'an understanding of the nature of belief and the religious dimension of human existence'.
3. Both accord a central place to Christianity, and, although Swann argues against any notion of Christianity being presented as the favoured faith, Swann writes of its spiritual depth and fullness.
4. Both endorse RE as an important part of the curriculum of pupils. Neither regards Britain as a secular society having outgrown religion. Swann's brief highlighted the fact that for minorities religion provides an important sense of identity and considered that RE fulfilled an important role in promoting social cohesion.

Differences

1. *What is being taught.* The earlier reports take it for granted that Christianity is the religion to be taught (although the law allowed for flexibility) with, in the case of Plowden, selected stories from other religions. Swann, reflecting the religious needs of ethnic minorities and the need for the host community to recognise and accept such minorities, argues for a more prominent place for the teaching of other religions. The latter could be seen as a development of the tradition. However, Swann goes further. Christianity must not be singled out from other religions since this would be to deny the 'true significance of the religious dimension to life, in all its forms'. For Swann, Christianity is one of a type, the religious type. Religions are expressions of 'religion' and this is thought to lend validity to them all. Behind Swann's view is a particular theological position that is taught to all pupils as true. It is worth pointing out that while it would be possible for a teacher to teach in the way the earlier reports suggest, *and* accept Swann's position, it would be very difficult for a teacher who believed that Christianity was true in a way that other religions were not, to teach in the way Swann advocated. Swann

acknowledged this. A teacher must accept the view, in the classroom at least, that all religions presented to children are valid options. In effect, Swann followed an assimilationist view in relation to the religions. All religions may be subsumed under the same category and should be seen as similar in nature. There is, Swann argues, a 'nature of belief'. This is ironic in view of Swann's policy of resisting assimilation as a way of dealing with ethnic minorities within the host culture.

2. *The role of the teacher.* The earlier reports presume that the young need direction in morality and in religion. The teacher's role is to open up and advocate the Christian faith and it is presumed that this is best done by one who has experience and inner conviction. Swann takes the view that the young should be presented with a wide range of belief systems from which a choice may be made. The teacher must take care not to influence the choice made by the pupil and to this end, some teachers choose not to reveal their own beliefs. In the earlier reports, the problem was always the teacher who did not have faith. Newsom's solution was for only specialists to teach the subject. Plowden advised the doubting teacher to concentrate on those aspects of religion with which he or she felt comfortable and could therefore convey with sincerity. For Swann the problem is reversed. Difficulty lies with the teacher who has faith. Such a teacher would have to use 'considerable skill and sensitivity in presenting other religions as valid options'.

Comment

There are important similarities between Swann and the earlier reports. But the differences have set RE on a very different course[4] such that it is not overstating the case to argue that a rupture in the tradition has taken place. There are obvious advantages to Swann's recommendations. Such a way of teaching avoids imparting any sense of superiority or inferiority. It recognises the contribution of other religions and can open up the riches of cultures and preserve insights that might be lost. It allows religions to interact, clarify and perhaps modify and enhance their sense of who they are and what they believe. It perhaps works best when children have a strong sense of their religion, what they believe and practise. These children already know what it is to be religious. My concern is with those that do not and, it may be granted, this means very many children in our society today.

RE, post-Swann, does not explicitly attempt to guide children into any particular religion or religious understanding. Hence children are always addressed as if on the outside of religious life. No religion is valued for its own sake or offered as the religion to be believed and followed. It is common for children to be presented with an array of different religions in the limited time allowed for RE. A premium is put on individual choice with little or no external guidance given as to how pupils might begin to choose between them. Pupils are likely to conclude that they are being

---

4   This is not to say that Swann, on its own, brought about such changes. Clearly there were many factors at work in the changes that have taken place in RE over this period which are not considered here.

asked to make an arbitrary choice, based on nothing more than some subjective preference. Children learn that all choices are supposedly good choices and that it is a matter of little consequence what they end up believing. The idea that religion spiritually compels one to believe and presents one with the truth is bypassed. Such a form of teaching may also have the unintended effect of undermining the role of the teacher. There is surely something wrong when a teacher has to prevent the young from gaining access to his or her hard-won insights. In the words of David Martin, the 'religious educationist [who] finds himself with nothing to impart other than the ideology of the experiencing self. He can only move amongst his pupils proclaiming that he is as profoundly human as they are' (Martin 1973, p. 18).

Can we find a way of re-ordering RE so that children avoid the sense of being an outsider? Can we avoid giving the impression that religion is somehow inevitably subjective and lacking in rational justification? Can we find a way of allowing teachers to invest themselves in their teaching? Swann is important for reminding us that we live in a world of many religions but children do need to feel what it is to belong somewhere. They need an introduction to religion that gives religion credibility and purchase and to which they feel a sense of debt rather than something over which they have power of attorney. At this point alarm bells ring and concerns about what is appropriate for children who come from a mixed background arise. These are genuine and important concerns. Swann takes the view that there is neutral ground to stand on here – that there is some knowledge which is open to all rational people which may safely be drawn upon, knowledge which is 'safer' than that accorded to those possessed of a religious temperament. Yet it is not difficult to see that far from adopting a neutral view, Swann promotes a particular theological view which, because it is presented as neutral, escapes criticism.

As it happens, we have an example of what constitutes a natural progression. Hansard confirms that Parliament intended the 1988 ERA to give to parents belonging to principal religions other than Christianity in Britain the right for their children to have a RE in which their own religion played a central role (Thompson 2004, ch. 9). At the same time the Act signalled that, in the main, children would learn by means of the Christian traditions. Both the fact that Swann represents a rupture in the tradition and the fact that Parliament has legislated for a continuance of that tradition, albeit with some modification, should give pause for thought in a democratic society. It should certainly make us question the view of Swann that the phenomenological approach, or a modern day variant, is the only acceptable one. Swann reflects important concerns about the desire of minority religions to find respect and recognition within society. The law accords the principal religions, as of right, a place on SACREs and ASCs in areas where their presence is significant. The agreed syllabus may reflect their beliefs and practices so that their children may receive an education in their own religion (as well as an understanding of Christianity). This gives religious minorities equal rights in relation to access to RE. The intention of the law was to provide for a plurality of ways of doing RE. This is untidy and necessitates much work on the ground. However it is the reason why we have SACREs and ASCs. The question is how far concerns about cultural pluralism necessitate a pedagogy in which all religions are presented as 'valid options' and children addressed as if religion makes no claim upon them.

References

Birnie, I. (1964) 'What has RE to offer?' *Learning for Living*, 4 (2), 16–18.

England and Wales. A report of the Consultative Committee of the Board of Education on Secondary Education with special reference to Grammar Schools and Technical High Schools (1938). London, HMSO (The Spens Report).

England and Wales. A report of the Central Advisory Council for Education (1959) *15 to 18*. London, HMSO (The Crowther Report).

—— A report of the Central Advisory Council for Education (1963) *Half our Future*. London, HMSO (The Newsom Report).

—— A report of the Central Advisory Council for Education (1967) *Children and their Primary Schools*. London, HMSO (The Plowden Report).

—— The report of the committee of inquiry into the education of children from ethnic minority groups (1985) *Education for All*. London, HMSO (The Swann Report).

Martin, D. (1973) 'The Naked Person'. *Encounter,* June, 12–20.

Qualifications And Curriculum Authority (2004) *Religious Education – The Non-Statutory National Framework*. London, QCA.

Schools Council (1971) *Religious Education in Secondary Schools*, Schools Council Working Paper 36. London, Evans/Methuen.

Thompson, P. (2004) *Whatever Happened to Religious Education?* Cambridge, Lutterworth Press.

Chapter 7

Religious Education and the Misrepresentation of Religion

Philip Barnes

Abstract

British Religious Education has misrepresented the nature of religion in efforts to commend itself as contributing to the social aims of education, as these are typically framed in liberal democratic societies. Contemporary multi-faith religious education is placed in context and its underlying theological and philosophical commitments identified and criticised.

At a recent Editorial Board meeting of a leading international journal in religious education, at which I was present, one of the members remarked that the journal should contribute more to the 'export' of British RE.[1] The speaker believed that post-confessional developments in British RE, that is, post-1970 developments, provide an example (or paradigm) for educators from other national contexts to follow. Such a viewpoint is widely shared among professional educators in Britain (Hull 2005; O'Grady 2005; Keast 2006). The commonly recited narrative of modern British RE is of confessionalism giving way to neutrality, commitment to professionalism, and indoctrination to education. It is a tale of progress and the triumph of reason over unreason. In truth, as a number of recent writers have pointed out (Copley 2005; Thompson 2004), the story is more controversial, convoluted and ideological, resulting in educational losses as well as educational gains. Apart from pedagogical concerns about the failure of some versions of post-confessional, multi-faith RE to engage pupils' interest and the accusation that thematic teaching has the potential to confuse pupils (see Barnes 2003, pp. 38–9) there is growing disquiet across a range of issues. In September 2005 the Religious Education Council for England and Wales (which for the most part adopts a positive attitude to developments in RE) complained about 'the prevailing liberal/secularist assumptions' that undermine the significance of RE and noted that many faith community members are concerned

---

1   The term 'British RE' is used to draw attention to ideas and influences that are common across RE in the three nations of England, Scotland and Wales; if pressed the ideas considered and criticised are more characteristic of English RE and educators than Scottish or Welsh education.

about how their faith is portrayed and treated in schools – such concern undoubtedly gives encouragement to calls for the creation of new faith schools that reflect Britain's religious diversity (see RE Council 2005). Others allege that neutral presentations of religious phenomena result in religious indifference (Watson 1993, pp. 43–6). One of the most serious criticisms to emerge in the last few years is the allegation that despite claims to 'objectivity', the form of RE that followed the collapse of Christian confessionalism in education in the late 1960s was in some respects just as partisan and uncritical as that which it succeeded: if not Christian confessionalism it was confessionalism of a sort – albeit more moderate, liberal and ecumenical.

The purpose of this article is to articulate a new perspective on modern British RE that both complements and, in part, subsumes existing critiques. My argument, while controversial, is straightforward: it is that British RE has misrepresented the nature of religion in efforts to commend itself as contributing to the social aims of education, as these are typically framed in liberal democratic societies such as Britain in terms of furthering tolerance, respect for difference and social cohesion. The irony is that the misrepresentation of religion by religious educators has in fact contributed to British multi-faith RE's failure to achieve the social aims upon which it sets so much store and in terms of whose achievement it often (rhetorically) commends itself as making a significant contribution to education, even though there is no empirical evidence to support this claim. My contention is that current representations of religion in British RE are limited in their capacity to challenge racism and religious intolerance, chiefly because they are conceptually ill-equipped to develop respect for difference.

The thesis that British multi-faith RE, as it has evolved and developed, is ill-equipped (by virtue of pursuing inaccurate representations of religion) to contribute to the social aim of preparing pupils to live in and to contribute to a multicultural society is controversial and will be resisted by some. Much intellectual effort and energy has been invested in the British paradigm of multi-faith RE. Moreover, as Foucault has shown (1973 and 1977), disciplinary and educational paradigms are intimately connected to structures of power and influence in a society; intellectual elites rarely relinquish influence (allied as it is to professional and institutional status) on the basis of 'rational' arguments alone. The negative conclusion that current models of multi-faith RE in Britain have revealed themselves as not particularly well suited to preparing pupils to participate in a multicultural society, however, does not entail that all such models are defective. There is no insurmountable reason why multi-faith RE cannot combine good pedagogical practice with accurate representations of religion in such a way as to make a real contribution to the development in pupils of religious tolerance and respect for cultural and religious difference.

Liberal Protestantism, Tolerance and Multi-Faith RE

Although the Schools Council Working Paper 36, *Religious Education in Secondary Schools* (1971) enjoined teachers in the early 1970s (under the influence of Ninian Smart, 1968; for discussion see Barnes, 2000) to move to a multi-faith model of RE, it did not use the designation 'multi-faith', which came to be adopted later, instead it recommended a *phenomenological* approach. The use of this approach, it asserted, enables pupils both to gain an authentic understanding of religion and to develop the virtue of tolerance (Schools Council 1971, pp. 21–8).[2]

The intellectual roots of the phenomenology of religion proper can be traced to Liberal Protestant attempts in the late nineteenth century to develop a methodology for the study of religion that was descriptive, broad ranging and objective; less driven by Christian polemics against other religions and more conscious of the divisive legacy of religion in the modern world. Deeply influenced by Friedrich Schleiermacher's appeal to religious experience in the search for a credible foundation for religious knowledge (and no doubt aping Descartes' foundationalist quest for epistemic certainty), the phenomenology of religion located the 'essence' of religion in the 'pre-reflective experiential depths of the self', and regarded the public or outer features of religion as 'evocative objectifications (i.e. nondiscursive symbols) of internal experience' (Lindbeck 1984, p. 21). This interpretation of religion, as developed by Gerardus van der Leeuw, Friedrich Heiler, Mircea Eliade and others in the twentieth century, gave rise to two methodological principles that became central to the phenomenology of religion, that of *epoché*, which denotes the suspension of judgement and the bracketing of one's own beliefs and values, and that of *eidetic* vision, which is the capacity to grasp the essence of religious phenomena by means of empathy and intuition. Phenomenologists of religion believed that through use of these principles, the 'objective' meaning of religion would be laid bare (see Barnes, 2001a).

The reinterpretation of religion in terms of inner subjectivity and commitment brings obvious advantages to the liberal Christian apologist, for if the ground of religion is situated within the self in private experience, free reign can be given to criticism of the public aspects of religion. Effectively religion is removed from the realm of public knowledge and the realm of the sacred privatised. Religion becomes concerned with inner experience and the hidden life of the soul and not with public knowledge. Such a reading of religion supports an easy accommodation with culture, for religion is withdrawn from the public world of economics, morality and politics. The emphasis upon inner experience also creates the possibility of reconciling the religions to each other. If religious experience has priority over its conceptualisation in beliefs and doctrines (following Schleiermacher) then the religions can posit agreement at the foundational level of experience, even though the experience is expressed in different doctrinal ways. The Sacred is manifest through all the great religions of humankind.

The attractiveness of the phenomenological approach to religious educators should be obvious. Phenomenological RE can claim to be multi-faith, neutral and 'objective' – no religion is privileged over another.[3] Formally, the critical evaluation

---

2   For discussion and an assessment of Religious Education in Secondary Schools, see Barnes (2002a).

3   Not that RE in 'common' schools in a pluralist society should favour one religion over others, but it should make pupils aware of the contested nature of religion and introduce them to the skills and considerations that are relevant to the assessment of religion and religious phenomena; this modern British RE has failed to do.

of religious beliefs and practices can be set aside, bracketed out as the phenomenology of religion's methodology demands, yet informally the truth of religion is assumed: the irreducible truth of religious experience that reveals itself in eidetic vision. Religious believers can be persuaded that their ultimate commitments will be unchallenged in the educational domain and liberal religious educators can persist in their assumption that the different religions participate in or point to some deeper spiritual reality. In this way the controversial issues of assessing religious claims to truth and of adjudicating between rival doctrinal claims are simply overlooked. RE is freed from challenge and possible controversy. The phenomenological approach provides the means by which the Liberal Protestant thesis of the unity of religion can be inculcated in the young.

As multi-faith, phenomenological RE rose to prominence in the 1970s, however, certain weaknesses about its capacity to further the social aims of multicultural education soon became apparent to teachers. The notion that acquaintance with the beliefs and values of minority groups *by itself* will considerably reduce religious prejudice enjoyed little support from experience. The second major criticism strikes right to the heart of the phenomenological methodology as it was propounded in Working Paper 36. According to the phenomenology of religion and the phenomenological approach to RE, an appreciation of others and of their beliefs and values is linked to a deepening sense of religious understanding: as religious understanding develops so too does a positive appreciation and estimate of religious diversity. Religious understanding in turn is brought about by abstracting oneself from one's own beliefs and values and then in this state entering imaginatively into the subjective life-world of others (this process of abstraction, as we have noted, also has the potential to provide an existential insight into the truth of religion). Working Paper 36 affirms that by suspending judgement and bracketing out one's own beliefs, one is enabled to enter into the experience of others, and in this way to gain a 'sympathetic understanding of the[ir] inner life': 'A Christian child can become a Jew for a day' (Schools Council 1971, pp. 23, 26). But is this pedagogical technique possible for pupils? A psychological perspective on children's cognitive development suggests that most pupils in primary schools are incapable (conceptually) of adopting a viewpoint contrary to their own (the evidence is summarised and discussed by Kay 1997). At this stage in their cognitive development they are incapable of adopting a third person perspective on situations and experiences; a limitation that in some cases endures until well into secondary level education.

If classroom experience revealed that multi-faith RE in the form of the phenomenological approach was less effective in challenging racism and religious intolerance than its first advocates had anticipated, this does not necessarily undermine its potential in this area. The phenomenological technique for acquiring a positive attitude to religious diversity may be deficient, but ongoing research that identified a link between notions of superiority and prejudice was received (uncritically) by religious educators as confirming their assault on religious superiority, in the conviction that in so doing they were simultaneously challenging racism and religious intolerance. In acknowledgement both of weaknesses in the phenomenology approach and of new developments, the term '*phenomenological* RE' gradually fell into disuse, to be replaced by '*multi-faith* RE'. The theological commitments, however, remained the same: the different religions are regarded as equally valid expressions of the Sacred. The ecumenical thesis that all religions mediate salvation offers the prospect of religious and social harmony. A few prominent examples may be cited to illustrate the continuing and abiding nature of this particular theological commitment in modern British multi-faith RE.

Educational Expressions of the Essential Unity of the Different Religions

In an editorial in the *British Journal of Religious Education* in 1992, John Hull introduced the word 'religionism' to refer both to the view that one religion is true to a degree denied to other religions and to the attitude of superiority that expresses itself as intolerance towards adherents of other religions. Religionism, he affirmed, is rather like racism – there is the racist belief that one's own race is better than others and there are racist attitudes that show themselves in acts of discrimination against individuals from other races (Hull 1992, p. 70). In his opinion, it is the denial of the truth of other religious traditions than one's own that is the cause of religious bigotry and intolerance. Consequently, it is recommended that within the educational context pupils should be taught explicitly that all religions are equal (i.e. epistemically equal as to their truth), in the sense that no one religion should be presented in education as *regarding itself* as true in any way that is denied to other religions (he also believes that this interpretation should also become part of the self-identity and self-understanding of the different religious communities themselves).[4]

This same interpretation of RE's contribution to social and moral education, predicated on the same liberal theological commitments, was also affirmed by signatories of a 'Declaration by Christian and Muslim Religious Educators in the University of Birmingham' in the immediate aftermath of the terrorist attacks of 9/11 (the declaration was widely circulated at the time and was posted on the website <www.studyoverseas.com> on 23 October 2001):

> we call upon our fellow Christians and Muslims *to abandon the competition* which has defiled our mutual relations for centuries. We confess that *this spirit of competition* has contributed to the climate in which extremism and fanaticism appears in both Christianity and Islam. We invite our fellow Christians and Muslims to enter into a new partnership in which we will work together for the good of humanity ... [my emphasis]

> [Religious education, conceived in this way, will] provide an education for understanding in both these two religions [i.e. Christianity and Islam], so that ignorance, prejudice and intolerance may be eliminated.

Finally, we may refer to a recent article by Geoff Teece (2005), in which he proposes that John Hick's theological advocacy of religious pluralism, according to which there are many equally valid and authentic ways of salvation, provides a 'foundation' for RE. (The obvious question to ask is why does RE in a pluralist democracy need a theological foundation?) Teece entreats religious believers to be 'epistemologically humble', by which he means that they should conclude that their own religious

---

4   For an extended critique of Hull's position, see Barnes (2002b).

ꭈns are no better warranted than the religious convictions of others. The ꭎꭎmption that the different religions represent different but complementary revelations of the divine, he believes, supports learning and teaching in RE and its inculcation in the young will contribute to a 'fruitful' and 'appropriate critical education for the twentieth-first century' (Teece 2005, p. 39).

Certainly there is a degree of advocacy in the examples we have cited, for there will be those in the teaching profession who remain unconvinced by the rhetoric of liberal religion. Yet this must not be allowed to obscure the fact that for many religious educators, particularly the intellectual elite and those involved in teacher-education, the essential unity of the different religions currently both underwrites the justification of RE in the school curriculum and guides educational practice in the classroom (cf. Wright 2004, pp. 191–4). There are two critical issues that emerge from recognition of this situation. First, there is the issue of why the theological and religious commitments of one particular form of (what was originally) Liberal Protestantism are privileged in this way. In a pluralist society where the truth of religion is disputed and where no single form of religion commands widespread allegiance it is inappropriate to use publicly funded schools, which are by intention and design open to all, to further one particular religious creed, in this case the Liberal Protestant creed of the unity of religions. The second critical issue is the way in which commitment to the thesis of religious unity has led to the misrepresentation of religion in education, and ironically contributed to the failure of RE to realise the very aims that the misrepresentation of religion was intended to achieve! I have considered the first issue elsewhere (see Barnes and Wright 2006), and it is now appropriate to consider the second issue in more detail by building on the critique of phenomenological RE that has already been developed.

The Misrepresentation of the Religions

Many modern British religious educators have found a use for religion and a justification for its compulsory inclusion in the curriculum of all schools: the aim of RE is to deconstruct exclusive claims to religious truth, and hence implicitly to inculcate in pupils the liberal conviction that the different religions are equal and complementary paths to religious fulfilment. That this representation of religion in education is pursued from the best of motives is undeniable, but that it is a misrepresentation of the nature of religion is equally undeniable, a misrepresentation that ultimately works against the realisation of the legitimate moral and social aims of education, the very aims that religious educators themselves wish most devoutly to achieve.

To inculcate in pupils the idea that the religions are complementary and not in competition with each other, clearly contradicts both the contemporary self-understanding of most religious adherents and the doctrinal logic of the different religions. It also means that representations of religion in education are required to go to considerable lengths to ignore and minimise the doctrinal and propositional aspects of religion that tell against the essential unity of the religions. We shall expand upon each of these points in turn, in order to give substance to the claim that the nature of religion is misrepresented in British education.

Traditionally and historically, adherents of the major religions have regarded themselves as advancing alternative claims to truth and as sustaining rival identities. One normally contrasts Christian religious identity with Muslim religious identity; one does not normally think of an individual as a Muslim and a Christian, or as a Jew and a Buddhist. Religious identities tend to be exclusive in a way cultural and ethnic identities are not.[5] Individuals 'convert' from one to the other; often such conversions are on the basis that the new religion is believed to be true to a degree denied to the old religion, though no doubt there are psychological and social mechanisms at work as well. Religions are typically represented by their followers (Western academic elites aside) as being both particular and exclusive. To present the different religions in the classroom as acknowledging the truth of each other is to falsify the self-understanding of most religious adherents; it also presents to pupils a picture of religion that is often contradicted by their experience elsewhere – in the home, where religious commitment is regarded as exclusive, and in the media, where attention is given to religious conflict and the contrary claims of different religions.

There is a straightforward reason why adherents of the different religions do not regard other religions as complementary and equally authentic: the religions endorse different religious doctrines; they hold to different and well-nigh contradictory systems of belief (see Christian 1972 and 1987; Griffiths 2001). For example, Christians believe that the divine is personal and Trinitarian; Jews and Muslims deny this, although they agree that God is personal, thus creating a contrast with Advaita Hinduism and Theravada Buddhism (the former believes that the divine is an impersonal principle, whereas the latter denies the existence of any substantial reality, divine or otherwise). There is also disagreement on the nature of the religious life, the religious quest and the religious end (*telos*). It is not just that the religions differ, it is that they are different in fundamental ways. Each version of religion, moreover, considers that its beliefs and doctrines faithfully represent and picture the true nature of reality. Simply, the different religions each claim to be true. For the Muslim, there is no God but Allah, and Muhammad is the prophet of God: to enter paradise one must believe the teachings of the prophet and observe the practices that express the teachings. By contrast, the Christian trusts in God's grace in Christ for salvation. By analogy with the canons of ordinary perceptual knowledge, where 'agreement' between experiences is required to justify the claim that they are of the same object, the different descriptions of the divine in the various religions should not be regarded as having a common referent; the descriptions are not only different but in particular instances actually conflict with each other; what is asserted by

---

5   This, of course, does not entail that religious identifies are fixed and unchanging, for what was once regarded as 'alien' can over time be incorporated into a religion's self-understanding and identity; and there can be religions that self-consciously synthesise elements from other traditions, as in some varieties of Buddhism and in Shintoism.

one religion is denied by another.[6] The case for the essential unity of the religions collapses on the irreducible dissimilarity of the different religions.

The standard liberal theological response has been to posit the primacy of experience over beliefs and doctrines. Experience lies at the heart of religion, whereas beliefs and doctrines are secondary and revisable. This is the position of most phenomenologists of religion and many of the advocates of the phenomenological or multi-faith approach to RE. It is on the basis of this interpretation of religion that the role of doctrines and beliefs in religion is minimised in British RE. Modern textbooks give the impression that religion centres on communal experiences facilitated by participation in religious rites and practices. The phenomena of religion are organised under such generic themes as festivals (or celebrations), founders, reformers, pilgrimage, rites of passage (or the life cycle), worship, and so on. Admittedly, there is usually a (short) section devoted to beliefs and doctrines, with a particular focus on the concept of the divine, but the importance attached to the propositional or doctrinal element in religion is minimised; and with good reason, for if beliefs are constitutive of religion, as most religious adherents maintain and the logic of religion and religious practice would seem to require, it is very difficult to maintain (intellectually) the view that the different religions are equally valid and complementary. Their beliefs suggest otherwise. The notion, however, that experience has primacy and immediacy over beliefs and concepts (and accordingly that religious experience has immediacy over religious beliefs), is, for philosophical reasons, developed by Wittgenstein in the *Investigations* (2002), highly problematic and controversial (see Barnes 1994; 2001a and 2001b). Such a position is incapable of supporting the theological axiom that in essence the religions are one.

There is a further level at which misrepresentation of the nature of religion occurs, when, in order to effect a reconciliation between the different religions, it becomes necessary to revise their beliefs. The Qur'an cannot literally contain the very words of God because those words condemn other religions (at best) as less true. Christians cannot believe that Jesus was God incarnate, for this in turn entails that Christianity has a uniqueness denied to other religions. Theologians such as John Hick (1973, pp. 120–47) and Maurice Wiles (1992, p. 77) for example, who press for a more inclusive attitude to other religions, acknowledge that some of the cardinal doctrines of the different religions have to be revised and reinterpreted. In the case of Christianity they acknowledge that a radical revision of Christian belief and doctrine is required to effect a new and more liberal understanding of Christianity's relation to others religions. Yet acknowledgement of the fact that religious beliefs and doctrines have to be revised to fit the ruling liberal paradigm of religion is absent from modern British educational discourse. What is offered to pupils in schools is a particular vision of what religion should be (as reconstructed by liberal theological interpreters), not what it is: this move towards the idealisation of representations of religion is further encouraged by the refusal, inherited from phenomenology, to subject religion to close analysis and criticism – we noted how one's critical faculties

---

6   I have developed a number of philosophical objections to the thesis of religious unity in Barnes (1990), and I have questioned the use of John Hick's pluralist theology by religious educators in Barnes and Wright (2006).

have to be set aside in order to intuit the presence of the Sacred in and through religious phenomena. What presents itself as a neutral programme in RE for the advancement of mutual respect and toleration in society, on closer inspection reveals itself as having radical implications for the interpretation of religion and for the presentation of the 'truth' of religion in schools. Religious believers will feel that their religion and the nature of their religious commitment are being falsified in the name of good community relations; they will feel patronised by educators who maintain that they know the 'true' meaning of religion and that this true meaning conflicts with what religious believers traditionally claim.

The Undermining of Respect for Difference by British Multi-Faith RE

It might be contended that the misrepresentation of religion in education is a necessary evil, and that it is better to challenge and to attempt to change the self-understanding of religious people, if their religious beliefs encourage prejudice and intolerance, than to ignore the problem. Perhaps the misrepresentation of religion is in fact the lesser of two evils: it may be unethical to misrepresent the self-understanding of religious people in education, but this is eminently preferable to the baleful consequences for society that result from representing religions faithfully and ignoring the bigotry and intolerance they encourage. Although some will baulk at the suggestion that religions should be knowingly misrepresented in education (and it runs counter to much of my argument and our natural educational intuitions), we need to pause and consider its attraction. To fail to see its attraction is to fail to recognise the ambiguous character of religion. The notion that the different religions are in harmony with each other and that recognition of this by religious adherents yields positive fruit for society implicitly presupposes that the religions, when stripped of their inessentials features, are good. There are reasons for believing that this is a questionable assumption (see Barnes 2005). For example, no religion can purge religious intolerance from its history; and more seriously, not all religions can purge from their sacred writings all encouragements and inducements to violence against 'non-believers'. Even the assumption that the different religions are both good and evil in equal proportions (in either their essential or inessential features) is also questionable, though this is an assumption that many religious liberals may feel bound to endorse because it also affirms the principle of equality between religions (and for some liberals this is an overriding principle). The strategy that religion should be misrepresented in schools in the service of social harmony does have something to commend it; one can imagine the opposition from some religious adherents if a suggestion is made that their particular sacred writings openly condone acts of violence against others (even if it is the case scripturally), whereas the sacred writings of other groups do not. It might be better for public institutions to inculcate the belief that all religions can have a negative effect on society in equal measure, rather than state any evidence that might suggest otherwise (in keeping with this it could also be taught that the different religions have equally good effects on society).

The deliberate misrepresentation of religions in public education is not without its attractions, but it remains highly questionable whether the misrepresentation that the religions are equally valid and complementary paths to salvation is one that should be pursued as an educational aim in schools. This is because the inculcation of this particular misrepresentation is more likely than not to undermine respect for difference, while simultaneously failing to challenge religious intolerance and bigotry.

Religious believers who recognise that their cherished religious values and convictions are being misrepresented in education (in order to square them with the equal truth of other religions) will conclude that their views and beliefs are not respected. They will sense that there is no real respect for difference. If there were true respect for difference then the differences between the religions would be faithfully acknowledged and not ignored or explained away as secondary. The educational strategy of convincing pupils that the religions are in essential agreement actually undermines respect for difference in a further sense. Consider the logic of the strategy. One is encouraged to accept adherents of other religions and to relinquish intolerance of them on the ground that their ultimate convictions are in agreement with your own. You adopt a positive attitude to 'the other' because the other shares a similar and complementary commitment to the divine. Acceptance of the religious other is predicated on religious agreement (in essential experience). But this carries the implication that no such respect for difference may be forthcoming in those cases where there is genuine disagreement, and for those who resist the liberal temptation to view all religions as true. If there were true respect for religious difference there would be no need to attempt to convince pupils of the essential agreement between the religions. In a sense the liberal strategy has the capacity to 'demonise' the other just as effectively as those who believe in the exclusive nature of the truth of their particular religious commitment. The line between insiders and outsiders is drawn in a different place, this time between inclusivists and exclusivists rather than say between Muslims and Jews, or Hindus and Muslims, but the same binary distinction is employed. Respect for religious difference is compromised when those who are to be accepted and affirmed must first relinquish any claim to uniqueness or religious distinctiveness.

By attempting to press on pupils the liberal theological principle that all religions are equal, British multi-faith RE has failed to inculcate true respect for difference. Equally by devoting its educational energies to the pursuit of this principle it has failed to engage fully with the complex web of interrelationships between beliefs, attitudes and feelings that combine on occasions to encourage religious intolerance and discrimination. There is no direct connection between belief in the exclusive truth of one's own commitments and intolerance of those who hold contrary commitments. Belief in the superiority of humanism over Christianity, for example, does not (logically) sanction humanists to be intolerant of Christians. Superiority of belief need not issue in an attitude of superiority! The two are quite distinct. We would not think of counselling liberal politicians to acknowledge that conservative policies are as convincing as liberal social policies on the grounds that the difference between them is used by some conservatives to encourage intolerance and disdain of liberals. In any case it may be that freedom of expression and freedom of conviction should be paramount, even if individuals espouse viewpoints that encourage some to be intolerant and bigoted.

Conclusion

To conclude that modern British RE has misrepresented the nature of religion (or more accurately the nature and self-understanding of the different religions) and that this misrepresentation has actually worked to thwart efforts to realise the legitimate moral and social aims of education does not mean that it has not made some contribution to challenging religious intolerance and racism. Multi-faith RE should be regarded as giving 'recognition' (see Taylor 1994, pp. 25–73) to the diversity of religions that are practised in contemporary Britain, and in this way minority religions feel that their distinctive contribution to society is publicly affirmed, though obviously not every religious group can be affirmed in this way. Equally, multi-faith RE, at one level, provides reliable descriptions of different aspects of the main 'world' religions, faithful accounts of religious rites and pilgrimage, and so on. Such teaching no doubt challenges crude caricatures and distorted accounts of non-Christian religious phenomena. But such positive features are limited. The achievements of modern British, multi-faith religion education need to be enlarged and integrated into a new and more ideologically critical form of RE that facilitates both dialogue and respect between people from different communities with different commitments.[7] True dialogue respects difference and true respect facilitates dialogue.

References

Barnes, L.P. (1990) 'Relativism, Ineffability and the Appeal to Experience: A Reply to the Myth Makers'. *Modern Theology*, 7 (1), 101–114.

—— (1994) 'Rudolf Otto and the Limits of Religious Description'. *Religious Studies*, 30 (2), 219–30.

—— (2000) 'Ninian Smart and the Phenomenological Approach to Religious Education'. *Religion*, 30 (4), 315–32.

—— (2001a) 'What is Wrong with the Phenomenological Approach to Religious Education?'. *Religious Education*, 36 (4), 445–61.

—— (2001b) 'Ideology, the Phenomenological Approach, and Hermeneutics: A Response to Professor Lovat'. *Religious Education*, 36 (4), 572–81.

—— (2002a) '*Working Paper 36*, Christian Confessionalism and Phenomenological Religious Education'. *Journal of Education & Christian Belief*, 6 (1), 3–23.

—— (2002b) 'The Representation of Religion in Education: A Critique of John Hull's Interpretation of Religionism and Religious Intolerance'. *International Journal for Education and Religion*, 3 (1), 97–116.

—— (2003) 'World Religions in British Religious Education; Critical Reflections and Positive Conclusions'. *Journal of Religious Education*, 51 (2), 34–41.

—— (2005) 'Was the Northern Ireland Conflict Religious?' *Journal of Contemporary Religion*, 20 (1), 53–67.

—— (2007) 'Developing a New Post-Liberal Paradigm for British Religious Education'. *Journal of Beliefs and Values*, 28 (1), 17–32.

---

7   I have provided a preliminary sketch of such a form of RE in Barnes 2007.

—— and Wright, A. (2006) 'Romanticism, Representations of Religion and Critical Religious Education'. *British Journal of Religious Education*, 28 (1), 65–77.

Christian, W. (1972) *Oppositions of Religious Doctrines*. London, Macmillan.

—— (1987) *Doctrines of Religious Communities: A Philosophical Study*. New Haven, Yale University Press.

Copley, T. (2005) *Indoctrination, Education and God*. London, SPCK.

Foucault, M. (1973) *The Order of Things: An Archaeology of the Human Sciences*. New York, Vintage Books.

—— (1977) *The Archaeology of Knowledge*. London, Tavistock.

Griffiths, P.J. (2001) *Problems of Religious Diversity*. Blackwell, Oxford.

Hick, J. (1973) *God and the Universe of Faiths*. London, Collins.

Hull, J. (1992) 'The Transmission of Religious Prejudice'. *British Journal of Religious Education*, 14 (2), 69–72.

—— (2005) 'Religious Education in Germany and England: The recent work of Hans- Georg Ziebertz'. *British Journal of Religious Education*, 27 (3), pp. 5–17.

Kay, W.K. (1997) 'Phenomenology, Religious Education, and Piaget'. *Religion*, 27 (3), 275–83.

Keast, J. (2006) 'An RE for Europe?' *Recourse*, 28 (3), 13–15.

Lindbeck, G. (1984) *The Nature of Doctrine: Religion and Theology in a Postliberal Age*. London, SPCK.

O'Grady, K. (2005) 'Professor Ninian Smart, Phenomenology and Religious Education'. *British Journal of Religious Education*, 27 (3), 227–37.

RE Council (2005) *Towards a National Strategy for Religious Education*. London, RE Council.

Schools Council (1971) *Religious Education in Secondary Schools*, Working Paper 36. London: Evans/Methuen.

Smart, N. (1968) *Secular Education and the Logic of Religion*. London, Faber and Faber.

Taylor, C. (1994) 'The Politics of Recognition'. In Amy Gutmann (ed.) *Multiculturalism*. Princeton, Princeton University Press.

Teece, G. (2005) 'Traversing the Gap: Andrew Wright, John Hick and Critical Religious Education'. *British Journal of Religious Education*, 27 (1), 29–40.

Thompson, P. (2004) *Whatever Happened to Religious Education?* London, Lutterworth Press.

Watson, B. (1993) *The Effective Teaching of Religious Education*. London, Longman.

Wiles, M. (1992) *Christian Theology and Inter-Religious Dialogue*, London, SCM Press.

Wittgenstein, L. (2002) *Philosophical Investigations*. Oxford, Blackwell.

Wright, A. (2004) *Religion, Education and Post-Modernity*. London, RoutledgeFalmer.

Chapter 8

Religious Education, Atheism and Deception

Marius Felderhof

Abstract

Being honest with oneself is one of the most testing demands in life. It is not something the religious educator should evade. The prescriptions by theorists for Religious Education are shown to possess inherent ambiguities that contain the potential of deception. The call to include atheism in the curriculum is a particular case in point. Through an examination of five different forms of atheism clear educational conclusions are drawn. Either atheism cannot be taught for good reasons or many professional RE teachers are led, perhaps unwittingly, into committing a deception.

Deception and Ambiguity

In 1848 S. Kierkegaard wrote a book, *The Point of View* (published posthumously), in which he confessed that 'from the point of view of my whole activity as an author, integrally conceived, the aesthetic work is a deception' (Kierkegaard ET 1939, p. 39). He continued: 'A deception, however, is a rather ugly thing. To this I would make answer: One must not let oneself be deceived by the word "deception". One can deceive a person for truth's sake, and … one can deceive a person into the truth.' In other words, yes, he had deceived, but this was mitigated morally because his deception was done for the sake of truth and the person.

Now Kierkegaard was above all a religious educator and it was precisely in his role as an educator that he deceived. In his aesthetic works he was not presenting life as a *religious* author but as a spectator, as an outsider to Christianity, showing its character entirely from a non-religious point of view. How a non-believer would come to understand Christianity. The question to be asked is whether it is in the nature of being a religious educator that one must deceive the pupil/reader in this particular way or is the connection between being a religious educator and this kind of deception just an accidental relationship? Could the religious educator be honest? Or, if some form of deception is necessary, then in what sense are his successors as religious educators also engaged in the same deceit today? Can they exonerate themselves from moral blame by using Kierkegaard's excuse of 'deceiving into the truth'? Or are his modern counterparts genuine deceivers, perhaps with the excuse of being unwitting deceivers? In such a case there is a double deception – deceiving and self-deceiving!

I raise the possibility of deception because in the attempt to understand the pedagogical approaches of the religious educator one notices purposes, strategies and methodologies that are often less than straightforward, and perhaps less than honest. Evident ambiguities could be attributed to a simple lack of clarity; on the other hand, they could be symptoms of deception. If the latter, what is the nature of the deception?

A recent appeal to include atheism in the RE curriculum in Britain (IPPR 2004) is a case in point. To teach atheism under the guise of RE would appear to constitute an obvious candidate of deception. Innocently and naively, one might expect RE to communicate religious life, not the a-religious or irreligious life.

So why is this demand to teach atheism raised at all, and why now? Some RE teachers may even think that the issue was conceded long ago, for example, with the publication of the 1975 Birmingham Agreed Syllabus. In this particular syllabus pupils were invited to take a minor course 'in a stance for living which shares many of the dimensions of religion whilst not admitting realities transcending the natural order' (City of Birmingham 1975, p. 10). At that time the wording was a barely disguised code for admitting Marxism and Secular Humanism into the RE curriculum. Many other syllabi followed suit (e.g. Redbridge 1987, p. 14).[1] Atheism is already required to be taught. With this history the purpose of the call by the Institute for Public Policy Research (IPPR) to include atheism could be to make this requirement absolutely explicit and independent of its religious import. Atheism would then be included in its own right, without the caveat in the Birmingham Syllabus that made the teaching of atheism legally acceptable; namely, that by introducing atheism the 'course [on atheism] will highlight the distinctive features of religious faith'. (The caveat had been legally necessary because legal opinion, less tolerant of deception, could not ignore the question of intent.) Alternatively, the renewed demand to include the teaching of atheism in RE was raised solely in the cause of some blatant politicking, namely, to influence those who were about to draft the national framework for RE into a direction[2] that serves the purposes of a secularising lobby. If successful, this could end in deceiving pupils about the true nature of religious life and the religious educationist about the nature of the education provided.

By not stating openly what is at stake, an atmosphere of smoke and mirrors is created in RE with the new appeal to teach atheism. At one level the appeal is trite. Not many would have thought it possible to teach anything religious without (a) examining the challenges to the sense of religious life[3] or without (b) building hermeneutical bridges between the religious life and the overwhelmingly secularised world in which we live. If teaching atheism is not done for these obvious reasons, one

---

1 The Redbridge Syllabus (1987) was designed to 'help young people to come to an understanding of the nature of religion (including ethical, non-theistic traditions)', p. 14. Thanks to Penny Thompson for this reference.

2 Note the subtitle of the IPPR report, *Getting the National Framework Right*.

3 Logically, $p = \sim \sim p$, which suggests that any examination of p can lead to a discussion of $\sim p$.

must conclude there are additional and more serious demands at stake. If the IPPR wanted more than an examination of religious sense or the building of hermeneutical bridges to religion in teaching atheism, what is it? Unless these expectations are spelled out, it is difficult to evaluate the substance of what is being demanded.

Educational Values and Ambiguity

Similar smokescreens hinting at deception are rife elsewhere within RE; for example, when theorists make appeals on behalf of certain values. They regularly advocate critical openness, rationality, freedom, tolerance of the beliefs of others, coming to one's own beliefs, the relevance of one's experience, so that one wonders what occasions their exhortations. The list enumerates intellectual virtues that most take for granted in a liberal society; in many respects they are platitudes (Mitchell 1967, pp. 107–108; 1980, pp. 59–60). Perhaps reference to such platitudes are occasionally necessary in order to upbraid a teacher who is overly zealous in inculcating the answers her pupils need to pass examinations or to chastise a teacher who teaches a particular curriculum and in a style, of which one does not approve, having judged it to be too narrow or too overbearing. Nevertheless, it is inconceivable that anyone should challenge what was being advocated and deliberately set out to make a case for being uncritical, close-minded, irrational, slavish, intolerant. Though in individual cases a person might be judged to be such, no religious believer defends himself with some perverse, postmodern claim that these particular counter virtues and values happen to be the ones he owns. So what is the real purpose in the constant repetition of the exhortations to critical openness, rationality, freedom, tolerance and the like?

The belabouring of platitudes hides ambiguity. Advocating the cultivation of these capacities and dispositions in children within RE is one thing, to imply covertly that religions might be inherently antagonistic to such values and virtues and consequently also to teach children to adopt a willingness to doubt the whole value and status of religious life as such is quite another. In this state, one could conclude that religious life would first have to be justified in secular terms. Akin to the appeal to teach atheism, this demand could rule out a religious understanding before the educational process even begins. It is prima facie the case that one is not conveying a *religious* understanding when one is providing secular justifications. It may be the case that some expressions of religious life manifest deficiencies and failures here or there, according to its own norms, but to suggest that religious life in its entirety is questionable and requires an a-religious justification is quite another.[4] No RE, it is hinted darkly, must be allowed into state schools until this challenge to religious life as such has been answered. If one cannot do this (and it is assumed that one cannot), one must proceed on the basis that it has not been answered and adopt a policy of agnosticism.

Should the religious person be required to answer the challenge? And should the religious educator always proceed on the presumption of an agnostic, a-religious or

---

4 The logic is similar to that explored by J.L. Austin in *Sense and Sensibilia* (Austin 1962) with respect to sense experience.

even an atheistic basis? Perhaps the answer to these questions will become clearer when one examines some of the different guises that atheism can take. There is no attempt here to be comprehensive in the treatment of atheism, only to highlight certain features that make significant differences to how anyone with a religious interest can respond educationally.

Atheisms and RE

First, the most familiar and the least problematic form of 'atheism' is the Biblical fool who said in his heart there is no God.[5] Despite the atheistic avowal St. Anselm tried to show how the fool was implicitly committed to God (Hopkins and Richardson 1974).[6] The fool's atheism, if this is indeed what it is, was more of a practical kind. It is the atheism of one who does not act or live from what 'he knows' or tacitly assumes; essentially he does not feel and act 'appropriately'. For if one assumes that God is the God who issues moral commands, to act immorally without fear, remorse or guilt is a form of 'atheism' or godlessness.

Implicit in this godlessness is a lack of seriousness, a presumption that within any person one can separate the affective and conative faculties from his cognitive faculty.[7] To suppose such a separation a genuine possibility is, for example, to think that it is either intelligible or reasonable for a person to know another is in pain *and* yet to feel no pity or to have no impulse to act and to console. But this is either absurd or it is inhuman.[8] From this it is clear the fool's atheism cannot be taught and one is bound to reject any claim that one should attempt to do so. Teaching this form of atheism is impossible because it is either unintelligible[9] or it amounts to a demand to communicate a lack of seriousness,[10] which would effectively undermine any educational process that is about the formation of persons.

The case of the fool's atheism is nevertheless instructive because it is not unusual for religious educators and academics to assume just such a separation of the cognitive from the affective and conative faculties. Conceptually it is already

---

5   Ps. 14:1; 53:1.

6   St. Anselm's *Proslogion*.

7   As Wittgenstein observes, the obstacle to understanding may lie in the will (Wittgenstein ET 1980, p. 17e).

8   J. Astley discusses the issue of the separation of the cognitive and affective in his chapter in this volume (p. 000). He notes the difficulty in the position of D.Z. Phillips (Phillips 2001) when he speaks of the 'hermeneutics of contemplation', but what Phillips 'contemplates' is the logic and grammar of 'God' not what the term denotes. Were he to do that, he would only have the choice facing the devils in James 2:19 to tremble or to worship.

9   It depends on the meaning of 'know'. If to 'know' entails appropriate affections then it would be unintelligible to deny them.

10   I mean by a lack of seriousness as that which happens in the failure to acknowledge the interconnection of the three traditional faculties of human beings. How can one be said to feel something deeply if there is neither thoughtfulness nor impulse to act? Or what is the impulse to act without thoughtfulness or emotion? Or can one really say that one has thought deeply about anything when this is done without passion or without any intention or impulse to act? Seriousness is evident when one faculty entails the others.

done through the distinction in the widely used attainment targets, 'Learning about' and 'Learning from' religion. It is then assumed that one might freely enquire into religious matters 'cognitively speaking' without making any impact on their pupils' affections and dispositions to act.[11] The refrain that pupils must be allowed to decide for themselves is evidence of this. This is an illusion. Any communication of the 'truths' of religious life will make a claim on the pupils' affections and commitments and reveal when and how these are reasonably made and rightly felt. On the other hand, given the connection between the three faculties, any cognitive presumption of agnosticism or atheism will have a corresponding impact on the pupils' feelings and decisions.

Second, religiously, the more familiar form of 'atheism' occurs at those times in life when one is beset by doubts and uncertainties, perhaps one has lost the sense of the love of God in the midst of suffering or death; Christ's cry from the cross, 'My God, my God, why hast Thou forsaken me'[12] might be paradigmatic. The mystics have spoken of the dark night of the soul, a deep religious depression that can set in, moments when God can only be described as the void. Or alternatively the religious protests against wickedness and evil that one encounters in the Psalms or Job might qualify as forms of religious atheisms. Theology implies yet another, reflective form of it in its apophatism[13] or in its *via negativa*. The *Eclipse of God* (Buber 1953), *When the Gods are Silent* (Miskotte 1967) or the years wandering in the wilderness are recognised as part of the rhythm of religious life.[14] They are all indicative of times when words fail, when easy orthodoxies and traditional conceptions no longer do justice to the complexities of the experience of life. This kind of atheism is deeply tied to the religious sense of life, the one feeds off the other. It would be inconceivable to provide RE where this form of atheism did not arise because it is an intrinsic element of religious life as such.[15] This is not to say that it must appear at every phase of the curriculum, that is, it must be communicated to 5-year-olds as well as to 18-year-olds.[16]

Third, another form of atheism might resemble Wittgenstein's reaction to the picture of the last judgement (Wittgenstein 1966, pp. 53ff.). A person may understand

---

11 Sometimes the reverse is the case. They are not expected to come to any cognitive conclusions but are nevertheless expected to draw moral guidance from them. Michael Hand in the IPPR report (p. 6) comments on this: 'Pupils are not expected to adopt religious beliefs, but they are expected to draw guidance from moral teaching based on those beliefs. This expectation is incoherent.'

12 Mark 15:34.

13 See e.g. Pseudo-Dionysius the Areopagite, *Mystical Theology*.

14 Mark 9:24, 'Lord, I believe, help thou mine unbelief.'

15 This is why a theologian can presume to teach atheists about atheism (Turner 2002, pp. 3–22).

16 I was always struck, at a time when topics were popular in primary schools, that teachers might choose to talk about 'hands' in 'RE'. The theme would discuss the caring hands of doctors and nurses, the protective hands of the crossing lady etc but they never discussed the pointing finger or accusing hand, or the clenched fist or threatening hand. No doubt the nurturing of hope and confidence in young children is more important than the realism of life.

it, but it may still mean nothing to him. Perhaps this is the situation of those within our secular society who have some familiarity with the vestiges of religious life. There is some understanding but it means nothing to them. They are not inclined to use religious pictures and concepts or to practise the religious life in any recognisable way. In so far as they do use religious language, for example, in forms of abuse or 'swearing', it has been emptied of any real religious content. Perhaps this is the state of many in our present society as some have declared (Brown 2001). If this is the case, it is difficult to see how this form of atheism could constitute a serious element in a RE curriculum. Indifference to religion can hardly be the substance of RE other than as a description and brief report on the state of contemporary society. On the contrary, the urgency of RE emerges from the perception that unless efforts are made to give the next generation some access to the meaning of religious life, an understanding of it will also be lost and culturally much of the past will become virtually unrecognisable. This conclusion may render RE into something that is by nature backward looking. However, open enquiry and an investigative spirit will examine the possibilities of the past for their present and future viability. This is the stuff of education: to give the latest generation access to the cultural resources of the past with the potential for renewal in the present and future.

Some sociologists, who have detected this indifference to religion in contemporary society and stridently announced the death of Christianity in Britain, have simultaneously tried to issue the reassurance that people nevertheless do have a sense of transcendence (Brown 2001, p. 197).[17] In doing so the social commentators are not being consistent. By introducing the concept of transcendence into people's lives in their analysis of society they are introducing a key religious concept. The consequence of this acknowledgement is that what they effectively report is *not* an indifference to religious life. More likely, they are reporting a certain animus towards traditional religious life[18] that they (and the people they study) already know or presume to know. What they actually desire is the renewal of religious discourse, which would once again articulate the depth of life for which they long. In the context of RE, however, their complaints about the inadequacy of traditional concepts and institutions do not in themselves amount to a renewal and as such can hardly occupy a significant place in the RE curriculum except as a footnote in the *via negativa*. If there are some in Britain who can claim a more developed and coherent form of religious life than the mere expression of the inadequacy of Christianity supposes, then this new religious movement would have to be judged on its merits. Whether it deserves any attention within the framework of RE would depend on its depth,

---

17 Prof. Callum Brown affirmed this in conversation. And he wrote 'British culture is pioneering new discursive territory' (Brown 2001, p.1 97). Note how many people will say, 'I am not religious but ...'. This may be indicative of a certain alienation from organised religious life and a lack of ease for whatever reason with traditional religious and theological discourse but it is not a-religiousness.

18 (Brown 2001, p. 2) 'One could say, not altogether flippantly, that the decline of Christian certainty in British society since the 1950s has meant that respectability has been supplanted by respect – in which moral criticism of difference has been replaced by toleration and greater freedom to live our lives in the way we choose.' This comment hides a deep resentment.

insight, coherence, consistency, impressiveness and other logical and relevant criteria internal to religious life. The stumbling block for the questing social commentators is that most in this culture will still find that Christianity best meets these criteria and thus warrant the bulk of attention in the curriculum (Felderhof 2005).

Fourth, there is a methodology of study, which systematically excludes religious concepts and categories. Some refer to this as *methodological atheism*. In examining the causal nexus of the world any appeal to purpose (*telos*) or to God is specifically excluded. To introduce God would simply bring the 'scientific' study of the causal operation of the universe to an end. Reference to God as the 'first cause' or the 'uncaused cause' is often a source of confusion as it introduces an equivocation into the concept of 'cause' and a change in the category of one's understanding or shift in one's method. Essentially to speak of God is no longer to do physics or chemistry.

Methodological atheism is not confined to the physical or natural sciences. It might equally well be deployed within the social and human sciences. The connectedness between events, or the developments in human social life, is discussed entirely within the framework of either causal or human determination. The affirmation of this framework is essentially axiomatic in that the introduction of a reference to 'transcendence' or 'the eternal' as a significant 'causal' factor would again simply show that one was no longer studying or operating within the terms of reference of the social and human sciences.

In principle, the religious person need not, and normally does not, object to the disciplines marked by such forms of methodological atheism. It has proved productive and has greatly developed human understanding of the self and of the physical universe. Indeed, this is no less true of religious phenomena per se. Religious Studies, *on principle*, develops the understanding of religious phenomena entirely within the framework of causal and human determination. The understanding that such study provides of religious life is valuable in its own right. Religiously, it is also valuable precisely because it reminds the student of the human-centric (or egocentric) nature of so much of our understanding and activity.

What is also clear is that there is a degree of discomfort with this phenomenological study of religious life since it almost entirely avoids a direct engagement with characteristically *religious* categories, such as 'the eternal/the Divine', and characteristically *religious* concepts, such as forgiveness of sin. The methodological atheism that is employed ensures the exclusion of all the religious (and theological) reflection that uses such categories and concepts. The shift in the character of enquiry is marked through a shift from religious discourse into some meta-discourse that is often evident in the use of indirect or circumlocutory language. Thus to admit that 'one exists before God', which entails fear and trembling, becomes a claim about 'human beliefs concerning God', which entails no such thing; or, where 'believing in God', which entails trust and obedience, becomes a claim concerning 'human beliefs that God exists' which entails neither. It should be observed that the elements in these pairs of phrases obviously do not denote the same thing, though people often slide from one to the other. Or, compare 'rite of passage' with 'confirmation', which again evokes a distinct shift in understanding. The fact is that RE has relied a great deal on religious studies as supposedly the best and only way of conveying the 'religious world' to the young in a largely secular and otherwise religiously plural world. However, the critical point is that the *exclusive* reliance on the methodological atheism of religious studies (logically) can do nothing other than convey an atheistic understanding within RE. It is not surprising that secular humanists find such study of religions entirely acceptable since it indirectly endorses their understanding of the world. Within this context the demand for the teaching of atheism is again puzzling since RE is currently almost exclusively devoted to its perspective.

To demand, in reaction, that RE should focus its attention on Christianity is of no avail. Christianity can equally be studied in this methodologically atheistic way and perhaps this is precisely what is intended when RE theorists advocate the study of Christianity as a 'world religion'. It is not the *object* of study but the *methodology* of study that is the issue here. What does help is to recognise that the adoption of the methodology is axiomatic. One could critically choose to act differently and adopt a methodology in RE that is more sympathetic to the sense of religious life, notably to enter the religious world to which most are likely to relate and test the sense of the religious form of life, examining the account believers give of it. Traditionally this was what was always done and, as Thompson notes in her chapter, was the methodology the various government reports assumed RE teachers used.

Fifthly and finally, there is the atheism that treats all religions as failed explanations – for in a genuinely scientific hypothesis, according to LaPlace, God is redundant (Koyre 1957) – or, they are treated as hypotheses that fall by the wayside either due to counter evidence or to lack of evidence. This form of atheism is bolstered by the fourth way because in the pursuit of potential explanations one might rely on disciplines that by their nature employ a form of methodological atheism. Not surprisingly the explanations that are consequently presented appear to be devoid of any religious force (Phillips 1976).

From those, for example natural and social scientists, whose lives are utterly committed to developing *explanations* (a) of events in the world and (b) of developments in life, one might expect a religious indifference. This is because religious categories and concepts do not appear to have a bearing on such explanations (Phillips 1976).[19] But it seldom works out like this in practice. Some scientists and non-scientists alike insist on seeing religious life and understanding as if it were some rival 'scientific' hypothesis or as a theory that they must see off the field with an appeal to the 'evidence' (Wittgenstein 1966). Reflection on the existence of God is for them a discussion akin to establishing the existence of the Himalayan Yeti or the tenth planet. Their anger or dismay is aroused by the supposed failure of their religious antagonists to acknowledge the relative weight of evidence for each hypothesis.

That the existence of God is not a hypothesis is evident from the fact that religiously nothing could conceivably count against God's existence. As in the case of Job, the worship of God is deemed proper whatever happens to oneself or whatever happens in the world. Faith in God is not conditional on this or that event or consideration. We are just not in the position to scrutinise God's credentials. The

---

19 See especially chapter 3, 'Are Religious Beliefs Mistaken Hypotheses?' Phillips writes later (1976, p. 188), 'It is also confused to think that the issues between religious belief and atheism can be settled by some kind of philosophical demonstration.'

denial that religious belief is a hypothesis is not to deny that faith in God cannot die or lose its sense – or for that matter to observe that one can come to faith through deep reflection. That would patently be a mistake as people can and do lose faith and take offence (or convert); religious people do struggle with senselessness. It is only to deny that this or that piece of 'evidence' would *ever* make the difference and religious belief could therefore never constitute a proper hypothesis.

The denial that religious belief is a kind of hypothesis is not to remove religious life from the sphere of reason and reflection. There is more to understanding than the construction and testing of hypotheses. What reason can do is to show the kind of sense that a religious life can have. Aesthetic interests and moral life are similarly not hypotheses; one deploys one's reason and shows what these interests amount to. One cannot 'prove' the glory of music to the tone deaf nor 'prove' the importance of moral considerations to those who are amoral. They are not hypotheses for the tone deaf and the amoralist to consider in the light of this or that piece of evidence. They may, however, be interests to develop through attention to how people live.

Nor does the denial that religious belief is a hypothesis mean that it is all a subjective matter, a human fancy and projection. Aesthetic interests or moral interests cannot be dismissed as merely subjective; those interests are developed precisely because of how the world is for us, namely, one in which it makes sense to make aesthetic and moral judgements and distinctions. Similarly the religious interest is developed because of the situation in which human beings find themselves, namely, where they are confronted by disclosures that evoke awe and demand worship with the consequent linguistic use of religious categories and concepts.

If a religious believer sometimes treats their faith as if it were a hypothesis it may be due to a misunderstanding or to certain obtuseness of intellect. In any case it is unreasonable to expect that they will always give a good account of their life. It may well be that because of their presumption that religious belief is a hypothesis the religious believer argues a hopeless case, defends a certain ambiguity in the evidence, or appeals illicitly to some privileged, non-public evidence (like the witness of the Holy Spirit) that trumps all other evidence that is adduced. The failure to convince in this way may spur some other religious believers to try harder but it has encouraged yet others to question whether the task should have been accepted at all. They will question whether each religious tradition is in reality an attempt at providing a comprehensive explanation that must be compared to rival explanations.

A closer examination of religious life would show that the religious person who lives before God would not as a religious person treat their life as the expression of an explanation. They might try to understand it, might test its meaning and might try to live more faithfully, might examine how they make judgements. What they cannot do is to step outside it and to treat it as if it were a hypothesis. For on what basis would they judge it? One might as readily step outside the moral life and judge it on its material contribution.

One suspects that the appeal to include atheism in the RE curriculum does not have much to do with any of the first four forms of atheism. It cannot be a demand to introduce less seriousness and more hypocrisy into education by believing one thing and doing another. And religious people have long since ceded that one may understand many aspects of the religious life more deeply through the prism of atheism, and have acknowledged that modern society is increasingly a-religious and accepted that it is valuable to consider the world causally or humanistically. But what the religious person cannot do is to treat a religious tradition as if it were just one hypothesis amongst others. Were they to do so they would destroy its religious character. The appeal to include atheism in RE on a par with religion, as one hypothesis amongst others, amounts to the request to treat religions irreligiously (Phillips 1967).[20] If RE theorists do accept the invitation to treat religious faith in this way they will deceive their pupils into believing they can acquire a religious understanding by this means.

Deception Re-Considered

Kierkegaard took seriously the a-religious life, and as an aesthetic author examined the religious life a-religiously even though he did not share that point of view. The deception was that he did not warn his reader of this tension between the position he presented and the position he owned except indirectly through his employment of pseudonyms as the author. His strategy was to help his reader to come to their senses like the prodigal son in the biblical parable and to discover for themself the inherent despair that Kierkegaard discerned in the exclusively aesthetic life. In this respect the deception deepened because the exposure of the character of the aesthetic life did have a religious purpose for him, though never openly stated in the aesthetic works, by preparing his reader to consider alternatives. The reader was deceived into recognising the truth of their life; it was done for truth's sake, but it was also a deception into the truth in that Kierkegaard hoped his reader would be tempted to embrace an alternative, which he took to be the truth of the religious life.

In the twenty-first century from a very different standpoint but on a par with Kierkegaard, the secular teacher might equally engage in a deception and show pupils what it is to embrace religious life in religious terms, and in which they discover this for themselves. If this deceives the pupils into the truth, whether that be the truth of the void or a genuine depth of understanding that transforms lives, the deception will be morally excusable.

What Kierkegaard did not do was to interpose himself between the reader and the reader's will to live well; the Socratic teacher ironically retreats from the process of coming to understanding whilst fully aware of how they are helping the pupil to come to their own understanding. How does this compare to the habits and position of contemporary teachers of RE? If only under the guise of RE the professional teacher could present the religious form of life from a religious point of view! Instead, contemporary teachers have been led to treat religion as a potential hypothesis and to induct their pupils into an enquiry with a methodology that can only communicate an a-religious understanding. If as a consequence an a-religious view is presented as the mode of *religious* understanding, is this not deception? If such secular teachers

---

20 D.Z. Phillips concludes his article, 'Faith Scepticism and Religious Understanding' (Phillips 1967, pp. 63–79) as follows: 'The man who construes religious belief as a theoretical affair distorts it. Kierkegaard emphasises that there is no understanding of religion without passion. That is why understanding religion is incompatible with scepticism.'

themselves come to think this is *religious* education, are they not doubly deceived? First, by presenting one thing as its opposite, second, in that they themselves cannot recognise this a-religious view for what it is. Of course, the self-consciously agnostic and atheist could offer the moral excuse for this deception, namely, that they were deceiving their pupils into what they believe to be the agnostic or atheistic 'truth'! But what of the others?

References

Austin, J.L. (1962) *Sense and Sensibilia.* Oxford, Oxford University Press.

Brown, Callum (2001) *The Death of Christian Britain: Understanding Secularisation 1800–2000.* London, Routledge.

Buber, M. (1953) *Eclipse of God.* London, Victor Gollancz.

City of Birmingham Education Committee (1975) *Agreed Syllabus of Religious Instruction.* Birmingham.

Dionysius, the Areopagite (1st C/1949) *The Mystical Theology.* Brook, Surrey, The Shrine of Wisdom.

Felderhof, M.C. (2005) 'RE: Religions, Equality and Curriculum Time'. *Journal of Beliefs and Values*, 26 (2), 201–214.

Hopkins, J. and Richardson, H.W. (eds) (1974) *Anselm of Canterbury*, Vol. 1. London, SCM Press.

Institute for Public Policy Research (IPPR) (2004) *Event Report*, Tuesday, 20 January, London.

Kierkegaard, S. (1939) *The Point of View.* Trans. Geoffrey Cumberlege. ET London, Oxford University Press.

Koyre, A. (1957) *From the Closed World to the Infinite Universe.* Baltimore, Johns Hopkins University Press.

Miskotte, K.H. (1967) *When the Gods are Silent.* London, Collins.

Mitchell, B. (1967) *Law, Morality and Religion in a Secular Society.* London, Oxford University Press.

—— (1980) *Morality, Religious and Secular.* Oxford, Clarendon Press.

Phillips, D. Z. (ed.) (1967) *Religion and Understanding.* Oxford, Blackwell.

—— (1976) *Religion Without Explanation.* Oxford, Blackwell.

—— (2001) *Religion and the Hermeneutics of Contemplation.* Cambridge, Cambridge University Press.

Redbridge LEA (1987) *Agreed Syllabus for Religious Education.* Redbridge.

Turner, D. (2002) *Faith Seeking.* London, SCM Press.

Wittgenstein, L. (1966) *Lectures and Conversations on Aesthetics, Psychology and Religious Belief.* Ed. C. Bennett. Oxford, Basil Blackwell.

—— (1980) *Culture and Value.* Ed. G.H. von Wright. ET Oxford, Blackwell.

Chapter 9

Can 'Skills' Help Religious Education?

William K. Kay

Abstract

Skills are a major component in educational discourse on the British scene and an account of how this situation has arisen is given. Skills are examined from a psychological perspective and criticized from both a philosophical and a psychological perspective. Skills discourse is often intellectually incoherent or inapplicable to Religious Education.

Introduction

It is not clear when skills became an accepted and defining part of British education. The Education Reform Act 1988 (part 1, 2 (2) (a)) refers to 'the knowledge, skills and understanding which pupils of different abilities and maturities are expected to have by the end of each key stage' and in (b) to 'the matters, skills and processes which are required to be taught'. So it appears that skills were recognised as being fundamental to educational purposes by 1988. However within the same Act in (part 1, 7 (5) (b)) considerations relating to collective worship refer to 'ages and aptitudes' of pupils rather than to their skills. The term 'aptitude' is more general and stands in an uncertain relationship to the term 'skill'. It is not clear why collective worship should be concerned with the aptitudes of pupils while other aspects of school life should be concerned with skills. One explanation is that the 1988 legislators simply took over parts of the phraseology used in the 1944 Education Act (Butler 1971, p. 119).

The Emergence of Skills

Although, as we shall see, psychologists dealing with the workplace had explored skills, the real driving force behind the emergence of skills within the maintained sector of education in England and Wales appears to have been the Confederation of British Industry (CBI). In the 1980s Mrs Thatcher's Conservative government listened to the CBI and accepted their view that the education system needed to prepare young people for commerce and industry. Someone had to prepare young people in this way and employers balked at the need to 'do the work of the schools for them'. So the government began to modify the curriculum in schools to make it more amenable to the requirements of employers.

According to Wolf (2002, p. 118) core skills were launched on the world in a speech by Kenneth Baker, then Secretary of State for Education, in 1989. He identified these skills as involving communication, numeracy, personal relations, and familiarity with technology, with systems, with changing and social contexts, with language. Very quickly after this the CBI produced a booklet that reflected the examples given by Baker. The next Secretary of State, John MacGregor, asked the National Curriculum Council and the NCVQ (which dealt with vocational qualifications) to incorporate core skills into post-16 course provision. The National Curriculum Council dragged its feet, but the NCVQ moved forward enthusiastically. NCVQ officials argued that by using performance criteria it would be possible to define exactly what was meant by a variety of different levels in the six core skills. Such an argument, in the hard light of subsequent analysis, looks fanciful in the extreme. Wolf suggests that all this happened because educational bureaucracy was keen to justify its existence and simply ignored any criticisms, valid or not, of the agenda of the skills lobby.

In 1992 the new Secretary of State was arguing that it was reasonable to expect people to leave education *at all levels* with core skills. Presumably, therefore, the skills were now to be introduced below the age of 16. And by 1995 the CBI urged that government that 'all learning should develop core skills ... a Core Skills Task force [no less!] should be set up to agree and implement a strategy for core skills in all learning' (Wolf 2002, p. 122). The CBI's confidence in core skills was predicated on the view that, once such skills were firmly planted within the curriculum, business would then save money it had invested in training schemes. At the same time, the government assumed that a business-friendly workforce would benefit the national economy and Britain's international competitiveness.

In 1996 core skills received help from an unexpected quarter. Lord Dearing, writing one of his several reports for the government, accepted that such skills were important to the structure of post-16 education. Once he had rebaptised them as 'key skills' they were ready to be brought out of their 'vocational ghetto' and could be backed by a support programme of £17 million. Once financial incentives were offered, colleges and schools entered pupils for the new qualifications despite scepticism from pupils about whether employers thought the awards worth having (Wolf 2002, p. 125).[1] A cynical explanation for the mushrooming of these unpopular and under-used qualifications lies in the simplicity of the process by which information on pupils can be collected. Boxes can be ticked. Discussions in class can be held. Teachers can note whether pupils contribute or not. Naturally the 'skills' so recorded varied widely and naturally, too, according to Tariq and Cochrane (2003) 'several have questioned the concept of key skills and more specifically their place in higher education' (Hyland 1999, Holmes 2000).

At some point in this history, 'basic skills' were identified as 'the ability to read, write and speak English/ Welsh and use mathematics at a level necessary to function and progress at work and in society in general' (Basic Skills Agency website, March

---

1 According to Hodgson and Spour (2002), 'The Key Skills Qualification is overwhelmingly viewed by students and by practitioners as a "hassle" and without much "currency" with little "use" or "exchange" value.'

2004). The Agency is funded by the DfES and the Welsh Assembly Government but stands independently of them. Its terminology is also applied in the Probation Service (Hudson 2003), though Hudson herself has reservations about the uncritical adoption by the Service of a strategy to promote 'adult basic skills'. In the contexts of the Probation Service and the Basic Skills Agency, the thrust of public spending is remedial and intended to lift the life chances of those who have failed to benefit from compulsory schooling. Hodgson and Spours (2002) speak about 'the origins of remedialism' as dating back to the Further Education Unit report, *A Basis for Choice* that was published in 1979. More recently a broader philosophy is espoused by the Learning and Skills Council (LSC) which, also with public funding, operates at the interface between education and business, or education and employment, but acknowledges that adult learning is desirable for those outside the campuses of institutions of higher education. Meanwhile, for those inside higher education, 'study skills' may be taught as a way of enabling young people to organise their time efficiently though unfortunately, according to Adey *et al.* (1999, p. 3), 'there is no systematic evidence for the effect of study skill programmes'.

Skills in RE

The *Non-Statutory Guidance on RE* (QCA, nd, but probably 1999)[2] aligns the teaching of religion with skills of different kinds. This may seem to be an opportunistic attempt to justify RE by showing that it is able to make a contribution to the curriculum conceptualised in terms of skills. Nevertheless it is a sustained attempt. The key skills identified by Dearing are all present. RE helps children in their encounter with different forms of written and spoken communication, with different uses of language and all this helps children to talk with knowledge and understanding about their own beliefs and those of others. Similarly information technology and social skills are enhanced by RE. Even problem-solving and information technology benefit from RE. Thinking skills, we are optimistically told (p. 19), and financial capability – even enterprise education as well as creative thinking skills – are all within the purview of RE.

Oddly enough, though, none of the skills appear to be present on pages six and seven of the *Non-Statutory Guidance* where national expectations on the two attainment targets are given. Neither is there any reference to skills in the more compressed and concise account of attainment targets on pages eight and nine. Yet, by page 16 skills have found their way back into the discourse. We are informed that 'learning from religion is concerned with developing in pupils the capacity and skill to respond thoughtfully and to evaluate what they learn about religions'. By p. 18 we are told that good practice in RE is 'about developing skills, e.g. the skill of living in a plural society, and attitudes, e.g. empathy'. We may well wonder how 'living in a plural society' can be reduced to a set of skills or whether, if this is really what RE is intended to promote, the curriculum has been properly devised to this end.

---

2   Downloadable from <http://www.qca.org.uk/6163.html> (accessed 16 June 2006).

Within RE, skills certainly surface in the major examination syllabuses. For example, the AQA GCSE religious studies syllabuses of 2005 all include reference to key skills and show how there are opportunities to develop these skills within religious studies. So communication at level one is indicated by the ability to take part in discussions, to read and obtain information, and then to write different types of documents. Level two asks for ability to contribute to discussions, to give short talks, to read and summarise information and to write different types of document. Similar reference to key skills is to be found in the Edexcel specifications. There is, also, the general assertion that the Edexcel specification builds upon the 'knowledge, understanding and skills established by the statutory requirements', though without indicating which statute is in mind.

The upshot of this is that there is a contrast between four things:

- the skills of responding thoughtfully to religion and evaluating what is learnt (which QCA promotes);[3]
- the skills of living in a pluralistic society (which stems from good RE practice according to QCA);
- the skills needed to study religion as an academic subject (which Edexcel promotes);[4]
- and the key skills that come via the CBI, the conservative government and Lord Dearing from the vocational world beyond the school gates.

And all these are *different* from the skills identified by heavyweight examiners. Giles (2002, p. 156), writing as an A-level examiner of long standing and the Chief Examiner for Edexcel, speaks of the need for the development of 'analytical skills' during the post-16 process and of the development of 'evaluative skills' within successful RE.

By the time *Religious Education: The Non-Statutory National Framework* was published in 2004, there was no stopping the language of skills. The document normally uses skills within the formula 'knowledge, skills and understanding' so that it is not always easy to see whether what is being referred to is to do with knowledge, or to do with skills or to do with understanding. From time to time the document does refer to specific skills and its most usual line is to argue that RE contributes to the aims of the national curriculum as a whole. Thus (on p. 8) we are told that RE contributes to 'skills in literacy and information and communication technology (ICT)'. Later we are told that RE helps to develop 'skills of listening' (p. 13) as well as 'key skills' and 'thinking skills' (p. 14). The key skills are to do with communication (p. 15) and the thinking skills are concerned with interpreting and analysing information from religious traditions (p. 16). The main thrust of this argument is to underline the usefulness of RE and its compatibility with the rest of

---

3   It is not clear whether this skill is the same as making 'informed responses' (AT 2, level 5), even though at the next level (AT2, level 6) pupils only have to 'respond'.

4   So Edexcel (GCSE for 2004) aims to develop in pupils the ability to examine and academically study religion and wants students to do this by learning to recall, select, organise and deploy knowledge as well as describing and analysing religion, giving personal responses to it and evaluating different responses and communicating effectively.

the skills teaching going on in the classroom. In this way skills discourse, implicitly, makes a case for the inclusion of RE within or alongside the national curriculum, and it is arguable that this is the prime political purpose for such discourse in the document.

Skills in Psychology

The original work done on skills in psychology tended to focus entirely upon physical action (Hockey 1996; Holding 1981). Indeed a *Dictionary of Psychology* defined skill as 'rapidity and precision (usually) of muscular action' (Drever 1964). This is why Michael Argyle (1972, p. 59) says 'by motor skills are meant such things as cycling, skating, driving a car, playing the piano, typing, sending and receiving morse …'. They require physical practice and may be learned – which differentiates them from reflexes – but are subsequently performed, or may be performed, without conscious thought. This means that skills exclude reflexes and, in most cases, the higher mental functions like the interpretation of texts.

Originally psychology began its exploration of the workplace in the days when manual work was far more common than it now is and the concern of psychologists was to find ways to improve production or to compare the efficiency of people of different ages or genders. Nowadays the workplace has become less obviously manual in its main emphasis, the term 'skill' often refers to an organised action sequence rather than to one action on its own. In addition psychologists usually make a distinct between the level of skill that has been acquired (or competence) and the proficiency with which that skill is exercised (performance). So performance may fall below competence because of tiredness or other disabilities.

Analysis of the concept of skill has resulted in a 'skill–rule–knowledge' framework (Rasmussen 1986). Knowledge of a situation evokes a rule and the rule evokes a skill. Mistakes may then be classified as either those that are knowledge-based because of a failure to understand the situation, rule-based because of a failure to apply the correct rule, or lapses and slips where the skill itself is performed ineffectively or not performed at all.

Although skills have been studied within applied psychology in relation to the workplace, there is little or no reference to skills in connection with child psychology and its application to education. Admittedly, simple motor skills relating to walking, jumping or holding a pencil have been described but the basic tradition of developmental psychology has been concerned with the growth of the intellect and the stages through which this goes. There is a strong Piagetian emphasis within child psychology and this has been concerned with the ability of pupils to perform mental operations and the relationship between these operations and physical activities (Plowden 1967; Piaget 1977; Donaldson 1978). None of this literature is concerned with the growth of skills.

One searches in vain within the mainstream of psychological literature on child development to discover any major discussion of the progress of children's learning in terms of the acquisition of more and better skills. The main tradition of child psychology has always seen education as being concerned with other mental attributes like the increasing power of the mind to manipulate symbols to represent abstractions or the growth of understanding through the acquisition of concepts (Lovell 1968; Brunner 1974; Bryant 1974; Gross 1992; Lee and Gupta 1995; Malim and Birch 1998). Thus, as we shall see, one of the main critiques that may be levelled against the representation of educational development in terms of skills is that the skills are not located within any larger developmental picture. They simply exist as freestanding units of behaviour outside a theoretical account of the mind or of social intercourse. Nor are they related to each other in any meaningful way although, for instance, skills involved fingering musical instruments may well be linked by neural pathways with skills involved in typing, and one would expect similar synergies between other sets of skills.

Application and Critique of Skills

Within the classroom and within RE the skill–rule–knowledge model is more promising than the model of skill as a simple repeated activity or an organised action sequence. Yet, even if we consider that the skills exercised by pupils learning about or learning from religion make use of the skill–rule–knowledge framework, there are numerous processes and concepts that need unpacking if this framework is to be properly understood and applied. We need to understand exactly how these rules are formed that link skills and knowledge, how complex these rules might be and exactly what the relationship between different and competing domains of knowledge might be in the enactment of particular skills.

For instance we can imagine the quite simple skill based upon the spelling rule that the letter 'i' comes before 'e' except after letter 'c' where there is a long 'ee' sound. We might then imagine that the skill of writing correctly follows the application of this rule in the context of knowledge about writing sentences. Yet we can also imagine a much more complicated skill evoked by the rule that 'you should never lose hope' in the context of personal disasters. There is an enormous gap between writing sentences and personal disasters in terms of the complicated connections each has with the mental, social and emotional aspects of an individual's life. So, because the contexts differ, everything else changes; the skills are incommensurable.

The thing to notice is that the skills stand in quite different relationships both to religion itself and to classroom practice. Some skills are as a *consequence of* engagement with religion rather than a *precondition for* engagement with religion. The skills needed to study religion either arise out of classroom practice or are acquired elsewhere. But the point is the skills are then applied to the subject matter of religion. On the other hand, the key skills within the different GCSE syllabuses are intended to be strengthened by, or to arise from, a study of religion. Here religion facilitates pre-existing skills. Similarly, the skills of living in a pluralistic society are intended to arise out of classroom practice where religion is well taught.

Moreover, it can easily be seen that the skills might be applied in very different ways and areas. The skills needed to study religion are, presumably, specifically academic skills and similar to the other skills that might be required for studying any other subject (say, history) although they may be adapted to cope with the uniqueness of religion as a field of discourse and as a way of life. They would comprise the skills needed to 'recall, select, organise and deploy knowledge of the specified content' (Edexcel, GCSE, 2004, p. 6). The key skills, however, are intended to be a general product of education. They stand ready for use outside classroom in the workplace or in society at large. Yet these skills are different from 'the skills of living in a pluralistic society'. Such skills are likely to be related to social behaviour and tact, to an understanding of religious taboos and customs, and, one would have thought, be best manifested when informed by attitudes of respect and consideration for other people. In other words, living peacefully in a pluralistic society surely depends more upon attitudes than the technicalities of particular skills.

Then again, consider the rules that governed the utilisation of particular skills. It is hard to imagine simple rules that might inform the general skill of responding thoughtfully to religion and evaluating what is learnt from it. Which aspects of religion? How thoughtfully? What type of learning? Even the rules relating to the study of religion must vary depending upon which aspects of religion are under consideration or whether several religions at once are being contrasted. Are the rules governing the skills needed to study religious ethics identical with the rules governing the skills needed to study religious worship? Probably not, since worship is an activity much less subject to rational investigation than ethics. Ethics concerns the deduction of correct courses of action from general principles (in deontology) or with consequences (in utilitarianism). Worship reflects an emotional understanding of the deity who transcends reason.

Of greater concern than all this is the imprecision of the vocabulary applied to skills. Almost any activity from thinking to mountain climbing could be put into the discourse of skills. We might talk about thinking skills, mountain-climbing skills, swimming skills, novel-writing skills, theatre-directing skills, marriage skills, child-rearing skills and so on. Almost any human endeavour can be fastened onto the word 'skills' as if this explains what is needed. Do marriages fail? Then more marriage skills are needed. Is your novel badly received? Then you need more novel-writing skills. The process of adding the word 'skills' to any activity is such as to remove thought and analysis from it (cf. Barrow 1999).[5] A simple idea is behind this: skills are like a magic substance that we have to add to human activities of any kind, and the more of this magic substance the better. All we have to do is to look at 'good practice' (whatever that is – and that is another question), and then acquire the skills to emulate the good practice. Apart from in some specific areas (like the reading abilities; Nation, Clark and Snowling 2002) there is little or no analysis of why it is that some people are more skilful others. I have heard teachers talk as if, with practice, everybody can acquire all the skills they need to achieve all the purposes they desire.

---

5 To quote Barrow (1999, p. 133): 'The serious consequence of everybody calling everything indiscriminately a "skill" is that they are losing the ability to note the differences. Whether their casual use of language led them to fail to discriminate, or a failure to discriminate led them to abandon specific terminology, is a question I will not pursue. What seems plain is that there is a widespread tendency both to call everything a "skill" *and*, an appalling error, to see everything on the model of a specific, discrete, physical, trainable behaviour.'

In addition there is no obvious sequence by which the skills may be acquired in this simplistic model. Each skill can be acquired in any order, at any time and by anybody. There seems to be little recognition that one set of skills, for example, knowing how to hold a pencil must precede another set of skills, for example, writing sentences. Nor is there any obvious theory that links together motor skills and what might be called thinking skills. We do not know whether thinking skills are intended to direct motor skills or whether thinking skills are simply in a domain of their own. Nor do we know, in the skill–rule–knowledge framework, whether we need thinking skills to acquire knowledge or whether we need thinking skills to acquire the rules that might then help us to apply the other skills called for by particular situations. And, if we do not need thinking skills to help us gain knowledge and apply rules correctly, what do we need – knowledge, other rules, other kinds of skill?

If we try to construct an answer to these questions, we shall have to put skills into a developmental sequence that rests on theoretical assumptions. In effect, we return to the mainstream of educational psychology, and this will immediately challenge the slipshod use of language the skills lobby has fostered.

Conclusion

From this discussion of the emergence of skills and application within RE, I wish to draw these conclusions.

First, the emergence of skills into educational discourse probably comes from the language of motor skills and occupational skills as it was mediated through the concerns of the business community. This is to be contrasted with a philosophical understanding of the curriculum based upon knowledge. Skills are knowledge-free.[6] In this respect they are particularly well adapted to the postmodern climate that denies any overarching narrative or absolute knowledge.

Second, skills are egalitarian because they are predicated on the assumption that everybody can acquire them with sufficient effort. Skills are fundamentally seen as being generated by practice and, since they are largely assumed to be disconnected from each other and from any theory of cognitive development, they do not carry the unwelcome weight that a knowledge-based curriculum bears. If you lack knowledge, you are stupid or lazy but if you lack skills, a little training will put this right.

Third, discourse about skills is incoherent. There is no agreed definition of skills, of their breadth, of their relationship to one another, of whether they may be arranged in a hierarchy or are acquired in a set sequence. We do not know whether some skills contain other skills or whether all skills are of the same basic type, that is, there is something they have in common which is why they are called 'skills' in the first place.

Fourth, the assessment of skills is no easier than the assessment of knowledge. Indeed, it may be more difficult to assess skills since it is not clear how they are linked with intellectual output. It is because people possess certain skills they may perform certain actions. But which skills lead to which actions? Hodgson and Spour

---

6   Even if they may be applied in a skill–rule–knowledge framework.

(2002) make the point this way, 'early concerns about the practicalities of introducing and assessing core/key skills within all post-16 programmes were borne out by the experience of GNVQ programmes, as several school and college inspection reports testify (e.g. FEFC 1994, HMI 1996)'. In the case of intellectual skills it is not clear which set of skills leads to which sort of intellectual output. There is no direct and observable line joining the invisible skill and the presumed product of that skill in the form of a tangible piece of work.

So, six conclusions relevant to RE can be drawn:

1. It is necessary to distinguish (a) the skills needed to study religion and (b) skills arising from a study of religion. Moreover, if religion is a unique field of discourse, then the study skills required to address it will be, at least partially, different from the skills needed to address other fields of study. So, just as we would expect subject-specific skills to be used for the study of mathematics or French, we would expect subject-specific skills to be used for the study of religion. No one seems to know what these subject-specific skills might be (Schools' Council 1977, p. 17), and this is partly because of disagreement about the nature of religion (cf. Fitzgerald 2000; Milbank 1990).

2. The inclusion of key skills within syllabuses appears to be adding confusion about how teaching should occur and how religion should be studied. If Wolfe's historical analysis is correct, key skills were probably included as part of a drive to ensure that all education provides a useful spin-off for business or the vocations. In this sense, key skills are included within a RE syllabus as a means of further justifying the presence of RE within the curriculum and as a way of attempting to provide unifying threads across a wide variety of disciplines.

3. There appears to be confusion between attitudes (or moral qualities like empathy or tolerance) and skills. To apply the term 'skill' to what is entirely an emotional quality (empathy) appears to be entirely misplaced, a category mistake. Emotion does not belong either to the field of cognition or to the field of motor activity. This, of course, does not mean that there may not be appropriate expression and management of emotion, 'emotional intelligence' (Goleman 1996), but this is a quite different matter. Moreover there is also confusion between the skills and knowledge/concepts so that a failure to distinguish between each leads to curricular incoherence.

4. The realistic assessment of skills appears to be as complicated as the assessment of knowledge. Indeed whereas a traditional understanding of examinations has recognised that knowledge can be directly tapped, skills are much more difficult to unearth since different mental processes may result in similar intellectual outcomes. This is a logical point: unobservable mental processes can only be detected by their consequences. Since the relationship between putative skills and their consequences is uncertain, we do not know if several consequences are the result of one skill or whether one consequence is the result of several skills.

5. The skills identified as relating to RE do not map on to religion as a multidimensional topic of study. The famous six dimensions of religion

identified by Ninian Smart (1968) do not have any obvious relationship with the skills base that has been identified as being relevant religion. So the skills that are said to be necessary for the study of religion or to be a consequence of studying religion appear to be disconnected from the concept of religion in all its multidimensional glory. And, if religion is viewed in a different way from that advanced by Smart, then how should skills be related to this undefined other model?

6. Such work as has been carried out on the religious element of young people has been in terms of concept and attitudes and not in terms of skills. The work of Goldman (1964) on concepts or Francis on attitudes (Kay and Francis 1996) has ignored a conceptualisation of religion in terms of skills. There is no long-standing literature on the development of religion conceived in terms of skills. We do not know, for instance, whether some religions promote some skills and others promote others. We do not know at which ages certain skills might appear — if indeed age is relevant. The entire study of religion and childhood has been carried out on a different basis from that presumed by skills. Naturally, the study of religion could be restarted but, at the moment, the use of skills within syllabuses or within classrooms and the connection between those skills and religious development is a black hole of ignorance.

References

Adey, P., Fairbrother, R., Wiliam, D., Johnson and Jones, C. (1999) *Learning Styles and Strategies: A Review of Research.* London, King's College.

Argyle, M. (1972) *The Psychology of Interpersonal Behaviour.* Harmondsworth, Penguin.

Barrow, R. (1999) 'The Higher Nonsense: Some Persistent Errors in Educational Thinking'. *Journal of Curriculum Studies*, 31 (2) 131–42.

The Basic Skills Agency (2004). Available from <http://www.basic-skills.co.uk/site/page.php?cms=2> (accessed 22 June 2006).

Brunner, J. (1974) *The Relevance of Education.* Harmondsworth, Penguin.

Bryant, P. (1974) *Perception and Understanding in Young Children.* London, Methuen.

Butler, R.A. (1971) *The Art of the Possible: The Memoirs of Lord Butler.* Harmondsworth, Penguin.

Donaldson, M. (1978) *Children's Minds.* Glasgow, Fontana.

Drever, J. (1964) *A Dictionary of Psychology.* Harmondsworth, Penguin.

Edexcel, GCSE, 2004.

Fitzgerald, T. (2000) *The Ideology of Religious Studies.* Oxford, Oxford University Press.

Kay, W.K. and Francis, L.J. (1996) *Drift from the Churches: Attitudes toward Christianity during Childhood and Adolescence.* Cardiff, University of Wales Press.

Further Education Funding Council (FEFC) (1994) *General National Vocational Qualifications in the Further Education Sector in England.* Coventry, FEFC.

Further Education Unit (FEU) (1979) *A Basis for Choice.* London, FEU.

Giles, A. (2002) 'The Birth of a New Religious Studies at Post-16'. In Lynne Broadbent and Alan Brown (eds) *Issues in Religious Education.* London, RoutledgeFalmer.

Goldman, R.J. (1964) *Religious Thinking from Childhood to Adolescence.* London, Routledge and Kegan Paul.

Goleman, D. (1996) *Emotional Intelligence.* London, Bloomsbury.

Gross, R.D. (1992) *Psychology: The Science of Mind and Behaviour.* 2nd edn. London, Hodder and Stoughton.

Her Majesty's Inspectorate (HMI) (1996). *Assessment of General Vocational Qualifications in Schools 1995–96.* London, HMSO.

Hockey, R. (1996) 'Skilled Performance and Mental Workload'. In P. Warr (ed.) *Psychology at Work.* 4th edn. Harmondsworth, Penguin.

Hodgson, A. and Spour, K. (2002) 'Key Skills for All? The Key Skills Qualification and Curriculum 2000'. *Journal of Education Policy*, 17 (1), 29–47.

Holding, D.H. (ed.) (1981) *Human Skills.* New York, John Wiley.

Holmes, L. (2001) 'Reconsidering Graduate Employability: the "Graduate Identity" Approach'. *Quality in Higher Education*, 7 (2), 111–19.

Hudson, C. (2003) 'Basic Skills Provision for Young Offenders on Probation Supervision: Beyond a Rhetoric of Evidence-Based Policy?' *British Journal of Educational Studies*, 51 (1), 64–81.

Hyland, T. (1999) *Vocational Studies, Lifelong Learning and Social Values: Investigating Education, Training and NVQS under the New Deal.* Aldershot, Gower.

Lee, V. and Gupta, P.D. (1995) *Children's Cognitive Development.* Oxford: Blackwell in association with the Open University Press.

Lovell, K. (1958) *Educational Psychology and Children.* London, University of London Press.

Malim, T. and Birch, A. (1998) *Introductory Psychology.* Basingstoke, Macmillan.

Milbank, J. (1990) *Theology and Social Theory: Beyond Secular Reason.* Oxford, Blackwell.

Nation, K., Clark, P. and Snowling, M.J. (2002) 'General Cognitive Ability in Children with Reading Comprehension Difficulties'. *British Journal of Educational Psychology*, 75, 549–60.

Piaget, J (1977), *The Origin of Intelligence in the Child*, Harmondsworth, Penguin. First published in French in 1936.

Plowden Report (1967) *Children and their Primary Schools.* London, HMSO.

Qualifications and Curriculum Authority (QCA) (nd) *Non-Statutory Guidance on RE.* London, QCA.

—— (2004) *Religious Education: The Non-Statutory National Framework.* London, QCA. Available from <http://www.qca.org.uk/7250.html>.

Rasmussen, J. (1986) *Human Information Processing and Human Machine Interaction.* Amsterdam, North Holland.

Schools' Council Religious Education Committee (1977) *A Groundplan for the Study of Religion.* London, Schools' Council.

Smart, N. (1968) *Secular Education and the Logic of Religion.* London, Faber and
    Faber.
Tariq, V.N. and Cochrane, C.A. (2003) 'Reflections on Key Skills: Implementing
    Change in a Traditional University'. *Journal of Education Policy*, 18 (5), 481–98.
Wolf, A. (2002) *Does Education Matter?* London, Penguin.

Chapter 10

Is there Anything Religious about Religious Education Any More?

Joe Fleming

Abstract

Religious Education is concerned with explicit or implicit attempts to explore and encounter God, to experience the sacred, to search for faith, to call people to live spiritually. Such attempts may be made not just in RE classes, but in poetry, arts, history, philosophy, literature. The context within which RE takes place at the present time presents considerable challenges to the religious educator. The culture in which schools function is often hostile to religious life. This is compounded by certain difficulties within the field of the theory and practice of RE.

The Context of RE in Australia

I commence with a brief outline of the Australian context in order that the particular points being made can be interpreted and adapted by the readers in their own settings. Context and history are very important components to our making sense of things. For what I argue as an interpretation of RE in an Australian setting may not be a valid interpretation in other cultural and educational contexts. Furthermore my experience has been within Catholic education in Australia (Catholic schools, Catholic university and Catholic administration) and I am writing out of that experience and background.

Organizational Context

At an organizational level there are three separate systems of education provision in Australia. In Australia responsibility for education is the responsibility of the individual states and not the Federal Government, although the Federal Government provides extensive funding.

State (or public) schools comprise about 65 per cent of the school population. Since colonial times (1870s) educational policy has insisted that state education is secular and no RE is taught as part of the formal compulsory curriculum. What this means in current practice is that over time various state governments have given permission for religious groups to offer some optional RE, and in some states there is an agreed syllabus of Christian RE. For example, in Victoria, one of the largest states, the Council for Christian Education in Schools teaches RE to those children who opt for it in about 50 per cent of state primary schools but nothing in the secondary sector. On the other hand, in New South Wales, the other large state, there is a different model (see Maple, above, in Chapter 5).

Catholic schools comprise approximately 20 per cent. The responsibility for RE rests with the local bishop and the local Catholic Education Office. Across Australian Catholic schools RE is a compulsory element of the curriculum in all years of schooling with approximately two–three hours of classroom instruction per week. There is no national curriculum; however, there is a large degree of commonality among the dioceses in terms of content and methodology.

Approximately 15 per cent of schools are in the independent system. These schools include a range of religious traditions, predominantly Christian but also Jewish and Islamic schools. The extent and nature of RE in these schools is largely determined by the Principal and School Board and the nature of the connection with a religious tradition. The Australian Association of Religious Education and the Dialogue Australia Network bring together staff from the independent and Catholic sector to develop curriculum and theoretical approaches to RE. Also various religious denominations have well developed RE programmes for their schools.

Some Cultural Features of RE in Australia

For religious educators in Australia, and given my reading of the literature, elsewhere in the English-speaking world, there are a number of powerful realities that impact, and indeed may limit, the extent to which the religious dimensions of RE can be achieved in contrast to the ways that were once clear and possible. While I speak out of a Catholic Christian context in Australia, I would propose that the substance of the realities is experienced in a more global way. Reflecting on the educational landscape in Australian Catholic schools I detect three critical realities. Two of them will be addressed here and the third will occupy the discussions in the section of this chapter on theoretical approaches to RE.

Three realities in the Australian landscape
They are:

1. Christianity as a point of reference for meaning making is no longer dominant in the lives of teachers and students.
2. There is a greater awareness that students are citizens of the world and that they are living in a religiously diverse world.
3. There is an ongoing struggle to refine a theory of RE that meets the needs of teachers and students within present cultural realities.

My sense is that while these realities certainly challenge what we have traditionally understood to be the place of RE in schools, they also present possible positive readjustments to the needs and contexts of young people in schools. It has always been the case that RE changes; there are new and reshaped models, new starting points, new students, new cultural realities to be addressed.

Any difficult realities present in the world of schools and the issues that flow from them, must be confronted with courage, confidence and wisdom. I am constantly aware of the strength that we gain from hope in God, in the Spirit who is ever with us in our endeavours. We are toilers for the reign of God. A theology of despair is a contradiction. Wanting God to be present in a different way is fickle. What is required is resolve, not retreat. If 'the world is charged with the grandeur of God' then where is God in our current world? In a very real and tangible sense RE is the servant of students, not the servant of ecclesial or political authorities, and certainly not the servant of academics. A prerequisite for the success of RE is a profound engagement with the lives of those people to whom it is given. As Boeve has argued: 'Teaching religion … firmly starts from the places where pupils stand. Its goal is to challenge them to reflect upon their own identity and the formation of that identity' (Boeve 2004, p. 239).

Perhaps the most dramatic and troubling change for Catholic and Christian schools has been that the Christian religion is no longer the starting point, the foundation on which to understand the world and the role of the individual in the world.

Reality 1: The place of Christianity in the landscape

Christianity is just one among many possible options that are part of the cultural context of the young, regardless of the religious tradition into which they were born. Religious affiliation now, more than ever before, is about choice and not so dependent upon, or an outcome of, the religious identity into which one was born. The place and position of a Christian view of life, its control and influence have diminished significantly in the last 50 years. The essential task of the religious educator in the school classroom is, in the words of Scott:

> Ultimately, the teacher of religion is not a catechist or evangeliser for the Church. He or she is an advocate for intelligent understanding of one's own religious tradition in relation to other people. What's at stake is understanding ourselves better through appreciating other religious ways as best we can. The choice is between ignorance and empathy. The school teacher of religion chooses life, chooses enlightenment, chooses revelatory understanding. This is our sacred vocation. (Scott 2005, p. 77)

The strength of concern about the decline of the Christian basis for meaning is a key element of the 1998 statement by the Catholic Congregation for Education, *The Catholic School on the Threshold of the Third Millennium.* The document states that among the many problems facing Catholic schools is that in countries of long standing Christianity there is 'a growing marginalization of the Christian faith as a reference point and a source of light for an effective and convincing interpretation of existence' (Congregation for Catholic Education 1998, par. 1).

More recently, in the United Kingdom, a study commissioned by the Catholic Education Service called *On the Way to Life* (2005), states in its introduction that there are four main challenges that need to be faced by Catholic schools. The first of these challenges is:

Although religion has not been erased from the cultural consciousness, it remains deeply problematic for a secular society. The Church needs to find ways of resisting the secularisation thesis, or it will become a guest at its own wake. At the same time it must engage contemporary culture by finding new ways of entering the discourse. (Catholic Education Service 2005, p. 7)

Finally, a recent volume from the University of Leuven states: 'In many traditional Christian societies Christian faith no longer enjoys the monopoly it once had in giving meaning to human existence. The process of secularisation has seriously restricted the all inclusive importance of the Christian horizon of meaning' (Boeve 2004, p. 233).

In Australia the natural consequences of this cultural tendency was highlighted in a 2005 study by Dr Saker from the Edith Cowan University in Perth, Western Australia. Saker conducted a survey of 133 students, all of whom were graduates of Catholic secondary schools in Western Australia. Critical in this survey is the fact that those surveyed were young women and men who attended Catholic schools, and who presumably came from Catholic families. Moreover, these young people had undertaken a degree in education, which included Catholic studies in order to teach in Catholic schools, and which would involve most of them in the teaching of RE.

The extent of the concern from the researcher and for the authorities in the Catholic Archdiocese, which published the findings in their magazine (*The Record* 2005), can be gleaned from the title, 'Catholic any longer?' in reference to Catholic schools. The fact that the young people who were planning to teach religion in Catholic schools were more representative of the culture than they were of the Church caused alarm bells to ring with the Catholic authorities.

The survey results (*The Record* 2005) were published under the following three headings. They are a clear example of one aspect of current culture in relation to institutional religious beliefs and practices and the effectiveness of RE in schools.

1. Responses to questions on involvement in worshipping communities:

    *   12.8 per cent of those surveyed attend Sunday Mass regularly.
    *   82 per cent rarely, or simply never, participate in the Sacrament of Reconciliation.

2. Responses to questions on the moral teachings of the Church:

    *   *Marriage and divorce*: 47.2 per cent believed that the Catholic Church's teaching on marriage and divorce was not 'relevant to today's world'.
    *   *Contraception*: 77.4 per cent disagreed that the use of contraception was sinful and that every sexual act must be open to procreation.
    *   *Sunday Mass obligation*: 62.4 per cent did not agree that missing Mass on Sunday was sinful, nor did they agree with the Church's teaching on Sunday Mass.
    *   *Beginning of life*: 69.9 per cent agreed with the Church's teaching on when life begins and that the abortion of an unborn child is murder, but believed

that a woman should be able to kill her child if the child is conceived by rape.

- *Sex outside marriage/same sex*: 59.4 per cent did not accept that sexual intercourse outside marriage was sinful or 66.2 per cent that homosexual acts were sinful.
- *Papal authority*: 67.7 per cent agreed that the Pope has the power to make statements on behalf of the Church, but disagreed that when the Pope makes ex cathedra statements he speaks infallibly.

3. Responses to questions about RE:

- Nearly 52 per cent of students surveyed strongly agreed or agreed that their RE classes aroused interest among senior students.
- 58.6 per cent did not see their RE classes as a waste of time.
- Just under 35 per cent of students strongly agreed they would attend if their RE classes were voluntary.
- 52.7 per cent of students strongly agreed or agreed that they gained a lot from their classes.
- 12.1 per cent strongly agreed or agreed that the classes were taken seriously by senior students.
- 55.6 per cent strongly agreed or agreed that their overall RE programme influenced their religious development.

Three main conclusions were reached by Dr Saker:

- The Christian message had been an important one in their lives but family is more important;
- RE is achieving the aim of having children understand the message of Jesus;
- The link between understanding the message of Jesus and actually belonging to, or agreeing with, the doctrine of the religion is another matter.

Reality 2: A religiously and culturally diverse landscape

The second reality, which I will mention briefly, deserves a bigger canvas than I can provide in this chapter. Nevertheless it is critical that religious educators recognise that students in Australian schools are living in a religiously and culturally diverse world. The religious and cultural mix in Australian society has changed. Whatever may be said about the shortcomings or blessings of this reality and whatever we have concluded about pluralism and globalisation, it is a fact that this is the world in which we now live. In Australia the extent of the change can be seen in simple immigration figures. According to the Christian Research Association (2002) in 1971 the following percentages of immigrants according to religious affiliation were: Catholic 34.9 per cent; other Christian 42.8 per cent; No religious affiliation 10 per cent. In 1996 the figures were: Catholic 20.6 per cent; other Christian 27.4 per cent; No religious affiliation 24.5 per cent.

Now under half of those coming to Australia state they have an affiliation with the Catholic/Christian religion. This of itself demands that RE must change. It must adapt its content, its methodologies, its sensitivities, its outcomes, and its theoretical base. Lane (2004) calls upon those involved in RE to embrace a new understanding of RE:

> To be religious in the present and the future will require that we be inter-religious. Inter-religious dialogue is no longer an optional extra, but rather an imperative arising out of the very nature of Christian faith itself. Further, the way of inter-religious dialogue implies a new way of being Christian in the world and a new way of doing theology. From now on there is, as it were, a new way of describing Christian faith and a new source for the performance of Christian theology, namely the encounter with other religions ...
>
> Finally, if we are to deepen our grasp of Christian faith and Christian identity then we must be prepared to pass over to the religious point of view of others and return from that experience to a deepened appreciation of our own Christian faith. In brief, Christian faith in the context of a multicultural world has much to give as well as to gain through the encounter with other living faiths. (Lane 2004, p. 80)

What conclusions may be drawn from the material in this section?

1. That there is an even greater need now than in our immediate past to have a strong emphasis on the religious component of RE. In the past the culture was in many ways supportive of a religious worldview as a basis of making meaning. This is no longer the case. Consequently schools will need to place more emphasis on this dimension in the attempt to offer a viable religious basis for life.
2. That the needs of the youth must be central to the task of the religious educator. We must enter their world and within that world be a voice for a religious view of life. We must start with them.
3. That there must be an on-going professional religious development of teachers who enter our schools. Experiences such as retreats, reflection days, moments devoted to spirituality are just some of the ways in which staff can be called to examine the religious dimension of their own lives.
4. That the religious component of school life must be open to other religious points of view. While a confessional approach, that is, one in which a particular religious tradition of the school has pride of place, is appropriate it must nevertheless be open to other traditions. Indeed if one is going to understand what is it to be Christian in our current world it can only be done by understanding Christian identity in relation to Islamic identity, Jewish identity, Buddhist identity etc.

Theoretical Approaches to RE

The somewhat suggestive title of this chapter is not to be alarmist or to invent issues for the sake of discussion. Moreover it is certainly not intended to be a criticism of those who are engaged in the many fields of RE. However, in Australia, as well as elsewhere, the issue of religious identity is very much on the agenda. It is a question that crosses parish, synagogue, mosque and temple spaces etc. as well as religiously affiliated schools. A central element in these discussions is what is happening (or not happening) in the RE that takes place within schools, as RE has always been seen as .

a linchpin in the development of religious identity and inducting new members into the community (Scott 2005).

In many ways this section of the chapter is a return to an old and recurring debate about what is meant by RE. It is not my purpose to detail this debate, or to try and solve it. What is attempted is to ask a range of questions that may contribute to answering the question: Is there anything religious in RE any more?

Question 1: Can we move RE out of the school classroom?

Some limitations on the discussions about RE follow from where we place it! All too often RE is restricted to formal classes that occur in schools with a religious affiliation. There are a number of problems with this restriction.

Firstly, it is the family that is, and should be supported in their role as the primary and most significant religious educators. The values, beliefs and practices of the family, how they embrace the religious dimensions of life, are vitally important in the everyday but, nevertheless, extraordinary education of the entire family.

Within the Catholic tradition there has always been a strong emphasis on the family as the place for a broad education into a religious way of living. The *General Directory for Catechesis* (1997) devotes a section to parents, as the primary educators of their children, stating 'the childhood religious awakening which takes place in the family is irreplaceable' (Congregation for the Clergy 1997, par. 226). This is a critical point that schools, teachers, and perhaps even parishes can forget. Schools, teachers and parishes are there to support families in this endeavour and not to be a substitute for them.

Moreover, school notions and constructions of education should not undermine the educational dimension of the family life:

> The family, as religious educator, engages in many forms of learning. Education within the family takes place in a unique manner and in a way that differs from other educational forms. Current educational language, however, has been constructed in such a way as to eliminate the enormous educational influence of the family. (Cunnane 2004, p. 99)

Secondly, the local religious community should be a significant place of initiation and nurture of its members. Whether this is parish, mosque, temple or synagogue, the religious community is the second natural home of RE. It is here that beliefs, rituals, ethical responses, questions, answers and challenges are all encountered. It is here that the religious community draws on its traditions of sacred word, of past holy women and men, of moral and ethical beliefs etc. In these settings there is a natural coming together of religion and education.

In the United States, Groome (1980) also stressed the role of the worshipping community in RE:

> The nature, purpose, and context of Christian religious education calls for a way of knowing that can hold the past, present and future in fruitful tension, that fosters free and freeing lived Christian faith, that promotes a creative relationship with a Christian community and of that community with the world. (Groome 1980, p. 149)

In the United Kingdom, Kevin Nichols stated that: 'We realize nowadays that even the best schools have, by their very nature, limitations. In this day and age, however much better our schools become, the catechetical responsibility of the parish must increase, not diminish' (Nichols 1981, p. 29).

The third home for RE is the school. Yet, even within school there is a need to disentangle RE from the confines of the formal RE classroom. I have argued (Fleming, 2002) that within the total life of the school there are three interlocking and overlapping domains of RE. There is the formal RE classroom, where there is teaching and learning about the elements of the religious tradition, and whose merits should be tested against standard pedagogical and educational principles. But there is much more to RE in schools than these few minutes per week! There are at least two other domains. The first of these is the domain of religious, moral and ethical activities offered within school but, nevertheless, outside the formal curriculum. Typically, for example, in Catholic schools these activities would include sacramental programmes, retreats, social justice involvement (e.g. St Vincent de Paul groups) and the like. In addition, other subject areas in the school can also have a strong impact on the RE of students, such as art, literature, history and science, just to name a few. Secondly, there is the domain of the broad religious dimension that is present in school and educates pupils about the dignity of the human person, the rights of people, respect for other religious traditions and so on, which is embedded in the ethos of the school rather than in its formal classroom teaching. This ethos should be conveyed in the school vision and mission statement and brought to life in pastoral care programmes, assessment and reporting policies, classroom management, and all the interpersonal and relational activities that occur in the normal life of the school.

Question 2: Does RE know where it is going?

A reading of any introductory work on the theory of RE may leave the beginner somewhat puzzled. There appears to be a conglomeration of conflicting and ever changing theoretical approaches to RE to which the newly qualified teacher is introduced. How are they to choose which theoretical approach is suitable for their school? Are the theories of equal worth? Is this a sign of a lack of coherence or is it a sign that RE is an active, ongoing and adaptive process, which has at its centre the necessity to respond to the needs and challenges of religious and cultural contexts?

Some guidance may be gained from those who have attempted to map of theories of RE. An Australian academic, educator and researcher Maurice Ryan, surveyed the literature of RE and argued that three rival conceptions of curriculum were being translated into the RE classroom. He calls these conceptions of the RE curriculum 'catechetical, educational and phenomenological' (Ryan 1999, p. 19). The 'catechetical' refers to the conception of the RE curriculum as leading people to faith, or that RE is primarily catechesis. 'Educational' conceptions of RE emphasise the grounding of RE in educational theory. Finally, the 'phenomenological' conception of RE treats the study of religions as a phenomenon of society and culture.

Ryan's work links with that of Lovat, who also divided the landscape of RE into three models: the specific or faith-forming model where 'the overall goal is to convince, convert or strengthen commitment' (Lovat 1989, p. 1); the inter-faith model, which aims at greater understanding of the world without any interest in evangelising; and the integrated model, which (as its title suggests) brings together a critical dialectic of the faith components of religion and the role that religion plays in the world. Yet another attempt at mapping the field was made by Rossiter (1981).

Whilst the efforts of mapping RE theory focused on the aims of RE, four major pedagogical approaches have been used in Catholic schools over the last 60 years.

Approach 1: Doctrinal
Until the 1960s, RE in Australian schools was structured around the Catechism. Catechisms contained questions and answers on important items of Catholic knowledge, belief and practice. Students learnt the answers by rote (Australian Hierarchy 1963). The aim of the doctrinal approach to RE was to ensure that students memorised the body of doctrine that was central to the Catholic tradition. It assumed that rote learning of the doctrinal content would lead students to understanding, belief and practice of the Catholic tradition.

Approach 2: Kerygmatic
A change in approach occurred in the mid-1960s. The kerygmatic approach to RE, based on the proclamation of the message of salvation as found in Scripture, became popular. This approach grew out of the work of Jungmann (1962) and Hofinger (1962) who had been influenced by the upsurge in scriptural scholarship in Europe. The kerygmatic approach used the key stories in scripture as the focus of RE.

Approach 3: Life-Centred
Following Vatican II, the doctrinal and kerygmatic approaches were replaced by life-centred, experiential catechesis. The starting point of this approach to RE was neither the authoritarian reproduction of doctrine of the Catechism, nor the humanly conceptual approach of the kerygma, but the lived experiences of those being educated (Welbourne 1995). This reform in RE was a response 'to the Second Vatican Council's ideas about divine revelation' where it was argued 'that God was present and working in the lives of people now' (Ryan and Malone 1996, p. 41).

Approach 4: Educational
The next phase of RE was in the 1980s. This period can be characterised as the development of RE curriculum on educational grounds. The educational dimensions were stressed equally much, if not more often, than the catechetical dimensions of RE. The work of international researchers (Moran 1970, 1983, 1989; Groome 1980; Boys 1982, Goldman 1965; Grimmitt 1973; Smart 1973, 1975), and Australian scholars (Rummery 1975, 2001; Rossiter 1982, 1987, Lovat 1989, 1991), has drawn attention to the necessity to bring developments in education and the related social science disciplines of psychology and sociology into RE. One of the major results of their work has been the transformation of the language of RE and a new balance between 'religious' and 'educational' considerations. Various theories of RE have sometimes favoured one or other aspect at the expense of the other. Most of these researchers have argued that the RE in the classroom must be subject to overriding educational considerations.

The question remains, what is an appropriate approach for the present time? A brief response is that any approach must be properly educational. The approach must also respond to the issues raised earlier: the diminishing influence of the Christian worldview as a system of meaning making for the young; the need to be inter-religious. There must also be a clear distinction between catechesis and RE and it is this point that I now turn.

Question 3: Can an appropriate distinction be made between RE and Catechesis?

Catholic schools are an essential and major part of the missionary activity of the Church. So are parishes and families. When the Church articulates the understanding of such things as evangelisation, catechesis, religious instruction and RE it often uses a broad brush stroke to cover all aspects of its mission. All too often the Church documents were not clear on whether the RE spoken about was applicable to parish, family or school. The type, purpose and processes of RE in these three contexts is not the same. RE that takes place in the classroom looks and feels nothing like the RE that takes place in the family. To understand the necessity for the distinctions we need to turn to Catholic teaching on RE.

The following group of documents issued by the Conregation for Catholic Education represents the key documents of the Catholic Church in relation to RE as it is in schools and it is from these that an appropriate theory of RE for schools needs to be drawn:

> *The Catholic School* (1977)
> *Lay Catholics in Schools: Witnesses to Faith* (1982)
> *The Religious Dimension of Education in a Catholic School* (1988)
> *The Catholic School on the Threshold of the Third Millennium* (1998)

In the Australian academic scene this attempt at delineating the various contexts of RE was first of all undertaken by Rossiter (1982, 1987). Some of the major points raised by Rossiter were:

- RE in Catholic schools has long been regarded primarily as education in faith or more intensively as catechesis.
- Most teachers take the view that catechetical purposes can be achieved in RE in schools.
- Catholic Church documents use 'catechesis' and 'RE' interchangeably.
- There has been a failure to adequately transpose catechetical aims and ideals into the educational settings of schools.
- RE in a broad sense refers to all the activities that go on in school.
- Faith education has a special place in school but the form and shape of it is different depending on what is being undertaken, e.g. prayer, liturgy, voluntary groups, teaching and learning about the tradition etc.

His examination of Church documents led him to this conclusion:

The Church documents use the term catechesis in two senses – a broad sense, to cover all of the efforts to promote a life of faith in Christians; and a strict sense, to describe the voluntary, faith-sharing dialogue of believers who meet precisely for the purpose of encouragement and expression of personal faith. (Rossiter 1987, p. 11)

It needs to be made clear what is being stated here: in the Catholic school, faith is central and also that catechesis in the technical sense occurs and is encouraged. That is, there can be, and is, a sharing of faith within a faith community in a school setting. But RE, while assisting in this catechetical endeavour is much broader. What is being argued here is not a replacement of one for the other, or even an argument that one is more important than the other. What is required is a careful delineation of the terms so that the various tasks that are undertaken within the life of the school community can be better aimed at catechesis or RE. The *General Directory for Catechesis* describes it this way:

The relationship between religious instruction in schools and catechesis is one of distinction and complementarity: there is an absolute necessity to distinguish clearly between religious instruction and catechesis. What confers on religious instruction in schools its proper evangelizing character is the fact that it is called to penetrate a particular area of culture and to relate with other areas of knowledge. As an original form of the ministry of the word, it makes present the Gospel in a personal process of cultural, systematic and critical assimilation. (Congregation for the Clergy 1997, par. 73)

In the same paragraph it adds that RE in schools should:

- appear as a scholastic discipline
- present the Christian message and the Christian event with the same seriousness and the same depth as other disciplines
- engage in a necessary inter-disciplinary dialogue.

The Congregation for Catholic Education (1988) also proposed a delineation of the terms. It stated that:

There is a close connection, and at the same time a clear distinction, between religious instruction and catechesis, or the handing on of the Gospel message. The close connection makes it possible for a school to remain a school and still integrate culture with the message of Christianity. The distinction comes from the fact that, unlike religious instruction, catechesis presupposes that the hearer is receiving the Christian message as a salvific reality. Moreover, catechesis takes place within a community living out its faith at a level of space and time not available to a school: a whole lifetime. (Congregation for Catholic Education 1988, par. 68)

And later it is striking in its statement of aims:

The aim of catechesis, or handing on the Gospel message, is maturity: spiritual, liturgical, sacramental and apostolic; this happens most especially in a local Church community. The aim of the school however, is knowledge. (Congregation for Catholic Education 1988, par. 69)

Given this analysis of the theoretical landscape of RE and how it has sometimes been used in schools, what conclusions can be drawn in relation to the overall question of this chapter? I offer the following concluding points:

1. RE occurs in the home, school and religious community. A full assessment of the religious component needs to include all these contexts and not just the school.
2. RE theory has been through a number of adjustments, necessarily changing in response to a changing culture.
3. In the most recent RE theory, the educational dimension has been a powerful transformer of RE curriculum. However, to the extent that the educational concerns overshadow the religious component it fails to be a wholesome theory. What is required in schools is a healthy and lively interplay between the religious and the educational dimensions.

References

Australian Hierarchy (1963) *Catholic Catechism, Book Two*. Sydney, E.J. Dwyer.

Boeve, L. (2004) 'Beyond Correlation Strategies: Teaching Religion in a Detraditionalised and Pluralised Context'. In H. Lombaerts and D. Pollefeyt (eds) *Hermeneutics and Religious Education*. Leuven, Leuven University Press, pp. 233–54.

Boys, M.C. (1982) 'The Standpoint of Religious Education'. *Religious Education*, 76 (2), 128–41.

Brennan, O. (ed.) (2005) *Critical Issues in Religious Education*. Dublin, Veritas.

Catholic Archdiocese of Perth (2005) *'Catholic any longer?'* Perth, Catholic Archdiocese of Perth.

Catholic Education Service (2005) *On the Way to Life: Contemporary Culture and Theological Development as a Framework for Catholic Education, Catechesis and Formation*. London: The Heythrop Institute for Religion, Ethics and Public Life.

Christian Research Association (2002) 'Australia's Religious Communities'. A multimedia exploration CD-Rrom, 2nd edn 2004. Christian Research Association: Australia.

Congregation for Catholic Education (1977) *The Catholic School*. Strathfield, NSW: St Paul's Publications.

—— (1982) *Lay Catholics in Schools: Witnesses to Faith*. Strathfield, NSW: St Paul's Publications.

—— (1988) *The Religious Dimension of Education in a Catholic School*. Strathfield, NSW: St Paul's Publications.

—— (1998) *The Catholic School on the Threshold of the Third Millennium*.

Congregation for the Clergy (1997) *General Directory for Catechesis*. Strathfield, NSW: St Paul's Publications.

Cunnane, F. (2004) *New Directions in Religious Education*. Dublin, Veritas.

Fleming, G. (2002) 'An Analysis of Religious Education Coordinators' Perceptions of their Role in Catholic Secondary Schools in the Archdiocese of Melbourne'. Unpublished PhD thesis: ACU National.

Goldman, R. (1965) *Readiness for Religion: A Basis for Developmental Religious Education*. London, Routledge and Kegan Paul.

Grimmitt, M. (1973) *What Can I Do in RE?* Great Wakering, Mayhew-McCrimmon.

Hofinger, J. and Reedy, W. (1962) *The ABCs of Modern Catechetics*. New York, W.H. Sadlier.

Groome, T. H. (1980*) Christian Religious Education: Sharing our Story and Vision*. Blackburn, Victoria: Dove Communications.

Jungmann, J.A. (1962) *The Good News and its Proclamation*. New York, W.H. Sadlier.

Lane, D.A. (2004) 'Faith in the Context of a Multicultural World'. *The Living Light*, Summer, 68–80.

Lombaerts, H. and Pollefeyt, D. (2004) *Hermeneutics and Religious Education*. Leuven, Leuven University Press.

Lovat, T. (1989) *What Is This Thing Called Religious Education?* Wentworth Falls, Social Science Press.

—— (1991) 'The Critical Model of Religious Education: Justification and Some Evaluation'. *Word in Life*, 39 (2), 18–20.

Moran, G. (1970) *Design for Religion: Toward Ecumenical Education*. London, Search Press.

—— (1989) *Religious Education as a Second Language*. Birmingham, AL, Religious Education Press.

—— (1983) *Religious Education Development. Images for the Future*. Minnesota: Winston Press.

Nichols, K. (1981) *Cornerstone*. Slough, St Paul Publications.

Rossiter, G. (1981) *Religious Education in Australian Schools*. Canberra, Curriculum Development Centre.

—— (1982) 'The Need for a "Creative Divorce" between Catechesis and Religious Education in Catholic Schools'. *Religious Education*, 77 (1), 21–40.

—— (1987) 'The Place for Faith in Religious Education in Catholic Schools'. *The Living Light*, 24 (1), 7–16.

Rummery, R.M. (1975) *Catechesis and Religious Education in a Pluralist Society*. Sydney, E.J. Dwyer.

Rummery, G. (2001) 'Catechesis and Religious Education in a Pluralist Society Revisited'. *Journal of Religious Education*, 49 (2), 4–15.

Ryan, M. (1999) 'The Classroom Religion Program in Catholic Schools: Three Rival Conceptions of Curriculum'. *Journal of Religious Education*, 47 (3), 19–26.

—— and Malone, P. (1996) *Exploring the Religion Classroom*. Wentworth Falls: Social Science Press.

Scott, K. (2005) 'Continuity and Change in Religious Education: Building on the Past, Re-Imagining the Future'. In O. Brennan (ed.) *Critical Issues in Religious Education*. Dublin, Veritas, pp. 79–88.

Smart, N. (1973) *The Phenomenon of Religion*. London, Macmillan.

Smart, N. and Horder, D. (1975) *New Movements in Religious Education*. London, Temple Smith.

Welbourne, A.E. (1995) 'Critical Religious Educators: The Role of Graduate Studies in their Professional Development'. Unpublished PhD thesis, University of New England.

PART 3

Introduction

Perhaps now more than ever before it is necessary to face up to the reality of religions and their challenge to human life. The chapters in this final section focus on how Religious Education (RE) can respond to this new situation. Chapter 11 asks us to pay attention to the prophetic call of the religions and take seriously their probing questions about society and individuals within it. And what of the teacher of RE? What analogy is appropriate to describe the teacher's task? Is it going too far to expect (or allow for) the teacher to model religious life? And if not, what sort of life is the teacher to model? This raises the question of how far education is to be understood as nurture (see chapter 14). Perhaps we cannot escape responsibility for nurturing the young. Indeed, picking up a theme found in the first section, it is only through nurture that personality can be formed and sense made of life. So what is the responsibility of the RE teacher? Is it to endorse the secular view of religion that has come to be the norm in schools while at the same time modelling religious life or is this to engage in a dismembering of RE as chapter 11 suggests? The Christian has an opportunity within community schools to model religious life as a counterweight to the largely secular nurture that children will receive in some (or many?) community schools. Perhaps what is needed is for the teacher of RE (see chapters 12 and 13) to explore spiritual, moral and metaphysical realities in ways similar to those employed in the teaching of art and literature where meaning is expressed through metaphor, narrative, poetry and figurative language. Such an approach has the advantage that it is faithful to the subject matter of religion. And is it the case (see chapter 15) that the distinction between so-called confessional and non-confessional forms of teaching is largely a myth? Religion is inescapably transformative. This being so, RE should not be afraid of engendering a religious response in pupils.

Chapter 11

Dismembering and Remembering Religious Education

John Sullivan

Abstract

Recent cultural shifts affect the context in which Religious Education is conducted, not the least of which is a renewed sensitivity to the conflictual and challenging nature of religion. There is now both an opportunity and a duty to bring out for pupils in RE key features of the demands that a religion makes on its adherents and the way it poses probing questions about our individual and communal life. There are three closely linked weaknesses in some contemporary understandings of RE. Cumulatively these three defects bring about a dismembering of religions. A better understanding of the relationship between teacher, pupil and subject matter in RE can help us to avoid such dismembering.

Cultural Context

The revolution in RE that took place from the 1970s was the result of multiple factors. A rounded account would review the role of pressure groups within the teaching profession, secularisation in society, the decline of the churches, intellectual developments in universities that led to new approaches to the study of religion and the increased presence in British society of people of faiths other than Christianity. Major changes in the material conditions of people in our culture also played a part, for example, changes in habits of food consumption, communication, travel, entertainment, household equipment and of transport. Choices, expectations, attitudes, habits, priorities and mindsets all were modified in significant ways that influenced the reception of teaching about religion.

In addition to, and, indeed, closely implicated in all these factors, the RE revolution was, in part, a response to a cultural assimilation of existentialism, a form of philosophy that is suspicious of history, concerned for authenticity, wary of orthodoxy (seen as imprisoning), in favour of freedom, unimpressed by loyalty (seen as a remnant of tribalism) and such existentialism saw much danger in claims to truth, especially Truth with a capital T, since the concern for establishing and promulgating truth was tantamount to totalitarianism, being judgemental, and led to indoctrination, one of the bogey-words of the period (on existentialism, see Warnock 1970; Livingston 1971, pp. 345–84; Macquarrie 1973). The post 1939–45 War world had seen what could go wrong with collectivism, of either the communist or the fascist kind. Now it was time for authentic self-expression.

Of course, the emphasis on autonomy and authenticity that is central to existentialism continues to offer a valuable corrective to government pressures towards collectivism and social pressures towards conformity. Autonomy and authenticity are important and integral conditions of any true religious commitment, although perhaps it is time to acknowledge that in many religions the passage to freedom requires first living in the truth, rather than the passage to truth first requiring that we be fully free. To give authenticity top priority privileges the seeker over what is sought. In contrast, to put truth in the foreground displaces seekers to some extent, at least by expecting from them attentiveness, a kind of surrender, a change of mind, a conversion.

I believe we are now in a new cultural situation. It is one in which there is a different kind of space for considering the value of religious ways of knowing, the role of religious communities in a pluralist society, and a new opportunity to wrestle with questions of truth. However, it must be recognised that religion is inherently conflictual; indeed, this is partly why it is often shied away from, in personal conversation, in education, in social affairs, in political debate and in public policy. It can appear to be in the interests of social harmony to side step the conflicts that arise over religion by removing religion from the public domain and relegating it to the realm of the private option. Three types of conflict can be identified here. First, all religions, in one way or another, set themselves against the way the world is: they are counter-cultural; they offer a radical alternative to the status quo. Generally we recognise that when they do align themselves with the status quo, they have blurred necessary boundaries, sold the past, distorted something essential in their nature and strayed from their mission. We can expect some degree of mutual tension, at the very least, between the way of the world and the way of a religion. Second, they are also conflictual internally: clashes of interpretations about their essence, about their doctrines, ethics and forms of worship, about relative priorities, abound and endure over time, even if they shift their particular areas of focus. Third, religions are also conflictual with regard to the inner life of persons, as well as of communities, since they seek to detect and to defeat sinful resistance to the demands of faith. Various kinds of surrender, conversion and transformation are expected to come about through engagement with the disciplines promoted by religions as gateways to the more abundant life, a life with God.

This conflictual nature of religion must not be underestimated, even though it must be acknowledged that religions also contain resources for reconciliation and harmony – with the world, with alternative interpretations of the tradition and within the self. One kind of offence associated with religion is the enduring authority of the past, of tradition, of memory. This can appear to rob us of freedom, the chance to move in new directions. Religions that carry long memories and the apparatus of substantial traditions might seem to impose on us a script for life that is too limiting, one that prescribes our options both prematurely and too tightly. Fear of offence caused by the conflictual nature of religion has led to various developments in religious education. In my view, some of these developments, while having positive features, can inhibit, distort or undermine an adequate understanding of the nature and functioning of religion.

Defective Approaches to RE

In reaction against the offence caused by the authority of tradition, some religious educators shy away from presenting any religious tradition as a whole, as a totality; instead it is ransacked, or, to use less loaded language, aspects of it are interrogated or explored for their potential use as resources to be deployed by pupils as they think fit. While this approach to a tradition, selecting what suits our purposes, might well appear to preserve the independence of the learner, it does so at the expense of denaturing the tradition. Ultimately this renders inaccessible to us those aspects of the tradition we are least likely to search for but of which we are most in need. This kind of response to, and treatment of, the authority of religion contributes, I believe, to three defective approaches to RE, cumulatively amounting to a process I label dismembering.

First, in the process of RE, religion is often dismembered. That is, it is cut off from its object, God. In the neutral space of a public school classroom God cannot be assumed to exist, cannot be addressed and pupils cannot be spoken to as if God is present and addressing them. Yet surely, for many religious traditions, as theologian Robert Martin reminds us, 'the ultimate telos of religious educational praxis is the deepening encounter of persons with God' (Martin 1998, p. 336). In this dismembering religion is also examined from outside of the operation of notions of tradition, authority, commitment and a truth that stands over us. It is separated from an integral way of life and the set of practices that sustain this way of life. Religion is looked *at*, but not *through*. Yet it disfigures a religion to separate too sharply the contexts in which it developed, the teaching it articulates and the set of practices it enjoins on its adherents. As Debray suggests: 'to talk of the historical context [of a religion] without the spirituality that animates it is to run the risk of devitalising it. To speak, on the contrary, of wisdom without the social context that produced it is to run the risk of mystifying it' (Debray 2002, p. 30).

There is both a pedagogical and a hermeneutical problem here; and these two are integrally linked. Unless one narrows down the topic being studied and focuses on some specific aspect, then the 'what', the object of study, lacks concreteness and cannot be grasped by learners. A teacher has to use the part as a way into the whole. Yet by what principle of interpretation do we select the part as representing the whole? Furthermore, as soon as a part is isolated from the whole to which it belongs, it loses important features of its resonance, meaning and significance. If a religion must be dwelt in, at least temporarily, to afford a view as to the difference it makes to see the world through its lens, then merely looking at it from a distance will always suffer major limitations. Yet at the same time, there will also be limits as to how far one can legitimately expect or require pupils to participate in a religion in order to access the worldview it offers.

Second, in dismembered forms of RE, construction is emphasised at the expense of discovery and, as a corollary of this, the authenticity of learners is privileged over the authority of the object of study. One writer puts this point in the following way: 'A great deal of our modern study of religion attempts to give an account of a response without any reference to the stimulus' (Joachim Wach, quoted by Hay 1982, p. 70). Religious statements and claims can easily slip into resembling observations about one's inner state rather than about ultimate reality. This distorts the nature of at least some religions – for example, Judaism, Christianity and Islam – as obedient responses to the prevenient address to us by God and as whole-hearted participation in a faith community.

Earlier philosophical traditions gave priority to the force exercised on our minds by the object of our study, so that, through contact with what is known, knowledge fashions the knower. Since the Enlightenment the emphasis has been on the way that our minds construct knowledge from inbuilt categories we employ in any act of understanding. This shift in emphasis moves learners away from a docile (that is, teachable) attending and submitting to and imitation of what they study and stresses instead the importance of being aware of the way that their methods of investigation will interrogate or question what they are studying. Put more crudely, one might say that 'it' will be examined on 'their' terms, rather than the other way round, which is the usual religious way of working, for 'to know an object truly is to submit our subjectivity, our preconceptions and preunderstandings, to the object's self-disclosure' (Martin 1998, pp. 8, 230, 315). Construction by the learner does have a part to play, during the evaluation of what is learnt and also, potentially, as a necessary accompaniment of the process of ownership of religious truth. However, in religious education, construction is only part of the process and, I would submit, of secondary importance, both in the sense that it occurs chronologically only after and in the light of the primary communication of religious truth from the religious tradition, and also in the sense that constructed truth remains, from a religious perspective, subordinate in importance to truth that is discovered and revealed.

Third, RE too often pays insufficient attention to important features of belief within the life of members of a faith tradition. One aspect of this is the shared character of belief. Believers inevitably display, when pressed about their religious beliefs, an individual tone or colouring with regard to these beliefs, perhaps an idiosyncratic interpretation, a peculiar set of links with the rest of their experience, a special sense of what it means to them. Despite these differences, and despite lapses, in intention they seek to participate in the same form of life, to benefit from the same 'goods' that it offers, to inhabit the same tradition, to share the same overarching narrative and abide sufficiently closely by the same rules and values. Some forms of RE, while positively hospitable to learners in terms of maximising individual psychological space to express who they are and what they feel, can at the same time minimise the nature and demands of group affiliation as integral features of religious belonging and life and as necessary elements in the path to religious knowledge. Allegiance to traditions and to communities that are already in place, in this sense, not chosen by the individual, can come across as arbitrary, partisan, parochial and dangerously divisive (Cahoy 2002, p. 78). The exercise of authentic freedom can seem to require keeping one's options open. If this is the case, then it might appear to many pupils that commitment threatens freedom, for to commit oneself is to accept an option and thereby to refuse or to close down other options. Then the misguided equation of 'the more commitment the less freedom; the more freedom, the less commitment' gets readily embraced, leading to a position which holds commitment as epistemologically suspect because it is thought to lead to close-mindedness (Cahoy 2002, p. 80).

Another neglected feature is the stratification of belief – the way that some beliefs have a control function over others (Sloane 2003, pp. 132, 137, 226, 227, 236). The notion of 'control beliefs' originated with the philosopher Nicholas Wolterstorff. It has usefully been deployed by both Thiessen and Shortt to show the bearing of fundamental religious presuppositions on the way our other concepts are regulated and exercised (Shortt and Cooling 1997, pp. 170, 284–6). There is a hierarchy of beliefs, not a level playing field in which they are all set on the same level. Some beliefs can only be understood in the light of others that are more primary or 'bedrock' in the structure or 'economy' of a faith tradition. Some are more central to the heart of a faith and exercise some kind of influence on how other less central beliefs are interpreted, as well as greater control over behaviour by providing norms for evaluation for our conduct.

Connected to the failure to acknowledge how beliefs are stratified within religious traditions one often detects a forgetfulness about, or an insensitivity to, our duties with regard to our believing (Sloane 2003, p. 95). The neutral, uninitiated, unformed or unspiritual person is not equipped to recognise religious truth in any way that is considered adequate. Their understanding can at best be partial and shallow. We can downplay the role of character and commitments in the acquisition of knowledge.

Robert Martin has addressed several of these themes in a compatible but different way. In some approaches to religious education he suggests, 'methods of spiritual discernment and indwelling – worship, contemplation, and prayer – are attributed only a secondary epistemological status' (Martin 1998, p. 93). Religious education must give young people opportunities to engage with and to deploy religious ways of knowing. Martin poses the challenge: 'If we attempt to know God through some point outside of or apart from God's own self-communication, we will inevitably use ourselves as a measure for who God is' (p. 117). At some point in RE, at least the possibility of divine revelation and its implications for our thinking and behaving must be considered as a counter to relying solely on human modes of perception, reasoning and valuing. He then reminds us that, 'in the process of inquiry, tools function for us not as external objects, but form part of ourselves' (p. 224). Our ways of (and tools for) reading, perceiving, categorising, interpreting and evaluating are not without effect on us as persons. What we are like modifies our use of these ways and tools.

The Role of the RE Teacher

At this point I schematically outline four types of RE that I think contend for dominance in the field. Each has some merit though each has either clear defects or presents complex challenges to RE teachers. In practice, a teacher might well display features of more than one type of approach within the same lesson, either deliberately or unwittingly.

The first of these four types of religious education is where the teacher seeks to convey authoritatively only one particular religious tradition. One might call this 'one-way' teaching. Its plus point is that, at its best, it is strong on conviction. Its shadow side is that it can easily, though not necessarily, slip into indoctrination. Through lack of encounter with 'the other', the boundaries of what is known are less than clear; because of the mono-religious focus, the teacher cannot help allowing assumptions about others to creep into the vacuum caused by omission of consideration of these others. By so concentrating on the authoritative transmission of one tradition, a teacher might well fail to listen properly. If this is the case, they fail to learn from others and from pupils and thus fails the very tradition they represent. Here dismembering occurs because of premature closure and domestication. This kind of teacher stresses distinctiveness while failing to be appropriately inclusive. Those pupils whose voices (and experience) are not heard cannot practise appropriation and ownership. Judgements made in the process of this kind of religious education can be premature. This kind of teaching strives to do justice to the 'seed' at its disposal, but fails to attend to the 'soil' in which it is to be planted. Because of premature closure, such one-way teaching might fail to bring out the incompleteness and unfinished nature of a religion, its shadow side, its ambiguities, and the radical internal differences that struggle for mastery, its ongoing need for critique, reform and purification.

The second kind of RE might give a high priority to the practice of neutrality by the teacher. Here the teacher presides over the airing of multiple viewpoints, none of which are privileged. On the positive side, such an approach might appear to be non-judgemental and facilitate a greater degree of freedom of expression than the first type of RE I have described, with no particular viewpoint being imposed. However, the shadow side of this approach is that no viewpoint or tradition is adequately represented or engaged with, thus leading to all being distorted and downgraded. This kind of teaching can slip into one-way listening (by the teacher) to all without discrimination, thus failing to teach skills of discernment, which in turn undermines the educational efficacy of the teaching. Here dismembering occurs by RE lacking depth, where pupils stand back from the material under study. A supposedly benign space is created by the teacher in the name of tolerance. This way of teaching can fail to bring out the motivational power (for good and for bad) and the comprehensive claims that flow from religious commitments. Teachers and pupils abstain from judgements. The teacher represents no particular 'seed' and thus plants none (knowingly). They do not cultivate the 'soil' so that it is ready to receive any 'seed', leaving this process of cultivation to agencies beyond school.

In the third type of RE, pluralism is the guiding theme. The teacher stresses the importance of recognising and respecting different traditions in a broader view of their nature, history, development, self-definitions and self-expressions. This has the merit of encouraging multiple and mutual listening; it also maintains the integrity of each religion. However, it can tend to accept too readily the self-picture presented by pupils and by religious traditions. It can imply also a fragmentation of truth, import relativism and fail to equip pupils with the capacity for critique of religious claims and lifestyles. Truth and its contested nature receive insufficient attention and examination. The pluralistic approach to RE aims for harmony between people of

different religions but, through a fearful or politically correc‍t
a critical evaluation either of individuals or of traditions, th‍e
level' or 'side by side'. This approach recognises and appr‍o
implies a general blessing on others who seek to engage w‍
engages with this 'sowing' directly nor critiques those wh‍o

Fourth, some RE teachers seek to display and enc‍o
openness and distinctiveness with inclusivity. Such an ap‍
and conversation as a goal, but starts from a position, one that is well gr‍ound‍
that each has something to offer to the discussion. In this type of RE, teachers make at
least provisional assumptions about starting points to get the study under way. They
assume that well-rooted religious faith has more chance of coping creatively and
constructively with difference than a superficial and relatively ignorant tolerance.
They offer an integrated, substantive and comprehensive 'model' or schema of how
a religion works; they mediate as much of an insider's position as is compatible
with respect for individual freedom and the position of other traditions. Formation,
with its four dimensions – ways of thinking, ways of behaving, ways of belonging
and ways of worshipping (Sullivan 2003) – is allowed. This is something much
more substantial than the RE teacher simply conveying information or facilitating a
search, because multiple dimensions of a religion are introduced and the authority
of religion to address us is heeded. This fourth type of RE differs from the first, in
that it is more inclusive of people and positions. It differs from the second, in that
the teacher models the standpoint of religious commitment and makes explicit its
constituent elements and its implications. It differs from the third in that it risks
promoting evaluation and judgement, though buttressed, one hopes, by modesty,
humility, caution, respect and sensitivity.

Brian Hill (2003, p. 36) examines approaches to teaching RE in a way that is
very similar to the analysis I have offered. He describes the major stances in the field
as being exclusive partiality, exclusive neutrality, neutral impartiality and committed
impartiality. In exclusive partiality, only the teacher's value system is presented.
This mirrors what I have called 'one-way' teaching. With exclusive neutrality there
is an avoidance of any teaching of worldviews; this parallels my second category.
In Hill's third type, neutral impartiality, students are helped to examine a range of
values but the teacher remains neutral, though this in fact models a fence-sitting
non-commitment. This reflects what I have called the pluralistic approach. By
committed impartiality Hill means that teachers reveal their own position but treat
all pupils impartially. This ensures that, though pupils do encounter an example of
commitment, they are not forced to agree or to comply with it. This again echoes
my fourth category, which involved combining commitment with openness and
distinctiveness with inclusivity.

Central to Hill's argument in favour of the fourth position is his distinction
between capacities and commitments. He says: 'The classroom, with its ambience
of compulsory curriculum, is not the appropriate ethical context in which to press
for professions of allegiance to certain values for living … The classroom is,
however, an effective and appropriate setting in which to develop human capacities'
(2003, p. 39). Among these capacities he includes remembering, feeling, thinking,
exercising skills, making decisions and taking responsibility. I find his distinction

n clarifying what is legitimate and what is not legitimate for us to attempt classroom. As he says, 'we may test whether students have grasped the ef-structure of a particular religion, ... [but] we may not test whether they have ndividually embraced a religious view' (p. 39). I think Hill's favouring of committed impartiality does more justice to the nature of religion than some of the other types of RE that he and I have outlined, while also preserving the rights of pupils better than some forms of RE manage to achieve.

In contrast, John Hull (2003) celebrates the secularity of the RE teacher as one of the professional strengths of teaching in the UK context: 'The secularity of the profession is the cornerstone of the rationale for the existence of religious education as a required subject in the state schools of a multicultural democracy' (p. 52). This is certainly a view that has much currency among many professional RE teachers in the UK and might almost be described as the orthodox or default position. Hull sees this stance as one that guarantees the degree of independence from religious interference or influence that is necessary for teachers if they are to pursue an educational agenda.

Although I accept Hull's emphasis on the priority to be given to educational criteria when deciding what is to be done in the classroom – for it is not the task of schools to be the primary agency for communicating salvific knowledge – I believe his emphasis serves in important ways to contribute to what I have called the dismembering of religion in RE. He compares the role and task of professional RE teachers with that of the ministry:

> It is the different relationship between the professional and the content matter with which he or she deals, which constitute the difference between the two professions. A minister who did not believe in what he or she was preaching would be considered a hypocrite but a theology graduate who is a religious education specialist teacher is not expected to believe in the truth of the religions covered in the curriculum which he or she teaches. ... the teacher is there to help [pupils] to think clearly about religions and about their own values and should not advocate his or her own personal commitment. (p. 52)

Assuredly, an overbearing teacher can so privilege their own position that they suppress the emerging capacities for reflection and so forth, as described by Hill, a point I have acknowledged in my comments on the defects of 'one-way' teaching. However, this is neither an automatic nor a necessary accompaniment of the communication of conviction and commitment by the teacher, if they exercise pedagogical sensitivity and prudence, qualities that are likely to be enhanced by the practice of the spiritual and moral virtues enjoined by religious traditions, including such qualities as attentiveness, self-control, patience, humility and love for students.

I think that when Hull says 'broadly speaking, religions deal in salvation but the school is concerned with education' (p. 52), he separates out too sharply the drive for sanctity and salvation from the pursuit of understanding and wisdom, as if the former belongs only in the church and the latter only in the school (or university). The well-being and human flourishing to be promoted by education is more closely intimated in the purposes and practices of religions than he allows. It is true that, as Hull says, '[RE] is not for the devotional benefit of religious children, but for the educational benefit of all children' (p. 54), but this does not entail such a sidelining of religious perspectives, practices and concerns in the classroom that religion is thereby rendered something 'foreign' or forbidden, or as something that cannot be integrated into an educational context.

Hull's defence of professional secularity in RE teachers could easily encourage a distancing from both the object of study and the self who studies in teachers and pupils. In response to the increased professionalisation of teaching, too little has been made of the character of teachers as the primary source of their teaching. In parallel with the important resource of the teacher's personhood, Gloria Durka reminds us that 'to teach morally is to help make students keenly aware that their *own character* is at stake' (Durka 2002, pp. 32, 55). She also makes the striking assertion that 'it is only on the basis of a religious account of teaching that its true character can be fully grasped ... The connection between moral and spiritual virtues to excellence in teaching is one of interdependence' (p. 76). If she is right, then to the degree that Hull's prescriptions for RE separate out too sharply the personal stance and commitments of the teacher from the dance between teacher, pupil and subject matter, the effective teaching of religion is diminished.

The publication of George Steiner's *Lessons of the Masters* (Steiner 2003) brought home to me starkly one particular feature of the debate about RE: the cultural retreat from accepting a strong view of the role of the teacher. It seems to me that the teaching profession as a whole, including RE teachers, have bought into this retreat, to the ultimate detriment of effective learning. This retreat seems due to many factors and influences: it is connected partly to the legacy of existentialism, partly to increased secularisation, partly to the earlier shift in the Enlightenment, from the object of knowledge to the subject who knows, and partly to other factors, such as loss of deference in social attitudes, an emphasis on equality and erosion of trust in established authorities. It is reflected in Hull's treatment of the relation between teacher, pupil and subject matter in RE as well as in misunderstandings of the first three types of religious education I have analysed above.

Steiner does not talk about the concern by teachers to avoid indoctrination, the desire to display inclusiveness in the classroom, or the widespread heightened awareness of the power-laden associations of all forms of discourse. All these play a part in the retreat from a strong view of teaching. Yet the case he makes is, I believe, entirely compatible with the worthy aspirations of promoting freedom of thought, of taking careful note of pupils' experience and voices and of seeking to avoid unduly privileging any particular standpoint. These goals are mistakenly confused by many teachers – at all levels – as being opposed to any notion of teaching as a strongly directive activity, one that might revolve around the dialectic between mastery and discipleship.

Steiner makes a powerful case for such a view of teaching, one built up by reference to many different teachers across many centuries, and in relation to many different disciplines. Let me pick out the relevant aspects of what he has to say. He refers to three principal structures of relation between teachers and their students: destruction, subversion and exchange:

> Masters have destroyed their disciples ... They have broken their spirits, consumed their hopes, and exploited their dependence and individuality ... In counterpoint, disciples, pupils, apprentices have subverted, betrayed, and ruined their Masters ... The third category is that of exchange, of an eros of reciprocal trust and, indeed, love. By a process of interaction, of osmosis, the Master learns from his disciple as he teaches him. (p. 2)

In one way or another, teaching is an exercise of power. Teachers have to be politicians as well as being artists and students. That is, they have to show a facility in the exercise of influence if they are to get the vote of attention from their pupils, if they are to protect their classes at least temporarily from competing attractions and distractions, if they are to co-ordinate the energies of disparate people for engagement in a particular task, if they are to maintain the trust of those who employ them and if they are to retain the confidence of communities to which they are accountable. As Steiner puts it, 'the pulse of teaching is persuasion. The teacher solicits attention, agreement, and, optimally, collaborative dissent. Persuasion is both positive – "share this skill with me, follow me into this art, read this text" – and negative – "do not believe this, do not expend effort and time on that"' (p. 26).

The very word, 'disciple', used in an educational context, can seem to imply, on the part of teachers, pretensions that wildly exceed their mandate. It might seem to suggest that teachers have too low a regard for their pupils, expect unquestioning and unthinking obedience, mere imitation instead of authentic and independent action. Steiner does not envisage strong teaching, as from a master to a disciple, as necessarily having these negative connotations. 'The Master learns from the disciple and is modified by this interrelation in what becomes, ideally, a process of exchange. Donation becomes reciprocal' (p. 6). Only when teachers offer something deep from within themselves are they likely to activate, stimulate and arouse something similarly deep from within their pupils.

Steiner is well aware of the heights to which his strong notion of teaching can reach, as well as of the depths to which it can sink if abused; for the underlying eros that pervades all kinds of teaching can be corrupted as well as ordered for good. The calling of the teacher is 'to awaken in another human being powers, dreams beyond one's own; to induce a love for that which one loves; to make of one's inward present their future' (pp. 183–4). This can be a

> terribly dangerous enterprise. The living Master takes into his hands that inmost of his students, the fragile and incendiary matter of their possibilities ... To teach without grave apprehension, without troubled reverence for the risks involved, is a frivolity. To teach greatly is to awaken doubts in the pupil, to train for dissent. It is to school the disciple for departure. (p. 102)

This is not a case of someone trying to impose his own way as the only or the last word on a subject, but as a starting point, a foundation, a vantage point from which to stand.

I have suggested that there is a danger that some approaches to RE tend towards dismembering religion. Have teachers allowed themselves and their pupils to be adequately addressed by the religious tradition or traditions? I have also suggested that retreating from an appropriately strong form of teaching does not necessarily serve pupils well, enhance their freedom or promote an adequate growth of understanding. Religious education can focus on truth as well as on toleration, on judgement as well as on empathy; it can promote commitment, as well as search, and facilitate indwelling and practising a religion, as well as observing it. Implicitly I have indicated ways in which the teaching of religion can be a process, not of dismembering, but of remembering.

References

Cahoy, W. (2002) 'A Sense of Place and the Place of Sense'. In Stephen Haynes (ed.) *Professing in the Postmodern Academy*. Waco, TX, Baylor University Press, pp. 73–111.

Debray, R. (2002) *L'Enseignement du fait religieux dans l'école laique*. Paris, Odile Jacob.

Durka, G. (2002) *The Teacher's Calling*. New York, Paulist Press.

Hay, D. (1982) *Exploring Inner Space*. Harmondsworth, Penguin.

Hill, B. (2003) 'Bridging the Divides: A Christian Brief for Values Education in Schools'. *Journal of Religious Education*, 51 (3), 34–43.

Hull, J. (2003) 'The Blessings of Secularity: Religious Education in England and Wales'. *Journal of Religious Education*, 51 (3), 51–8.

Livingston, J. (1971) *Modern Christian Thought*. New York, Macmillan.

Macquarrie, J. (1973) *Existentialism*. Harmondsworth, Penguin.

Martin, Robert. (1998) *The Incarnate Ground of Christian Faith*. Lanham, New York, University Press of America.

Shortt, J. and Cooling, T. (1997) *Agenda for Educational Change*. Leicester, Apollos.

Sloane, A. (2003) *On Being a Christian in the Academy*. Carlisle, Paternoster Press.

Steiner, G. (2003) *Lessons of the Masters*. Cambridge, MA, Harvard University Press.

Sullivan, J. (2003) 'From Formation to the Frontiers: the Dialectic of Christian Education'. *Journal of Education and Christian Belief*, 7 (1), 7–21.

Warnock, Mary (1970) *Existentialism*. Oxford, Oxford University Press.

Chapter 12

On the Grammar of Religious Discourse and Education

David Carr

Abstract

Some dubious philosophical assumptions underly modern conceptions of religious discourse and education – as apparent, for example, in tensions between literalist and expressivist readings of religious discourse and confessional and non-confessional approaches to Religious Education. However, whilst literalist interpretations of religious discourse are rejected (and any consequent religious fundamentalism) in favour of a non-literalist conception of religious narratives as epistemically continuous with forms of imaginative human art and literature, rejected too are idealist, social constructivist and relativist interpretations of story in favour of a realist account of religious and other serious cultural literature as truth-focused forms of objective human enquiry, knowledge and understanding. On this view, although the language of religious narrative is no less metaphorical, analogical and/or figurative than that of great poetry, it is – no less than great poetry – concerned with the objective exploration of spiritual, moral and metaphysical reality.

> It's said that to reverse its doom
> And save the entangled Soul, to earth
> God came and entered in the womb
> And passed through the gate of birth;
> ... Then braced by iron and by wood,
> Engrafted on a tree he died,
> And little dogs lapped up the blood
> That spurted from his broken side

Edwin Muir: 'Thought and image' (Muir 1960, p. 133)

RE, Knowledge and Truth

I shall argue here for two main claims: (i) that any satisfactory account of RE requires to be grounded in a conception of religious texts, narratives or discourses as actual or potential sources of human knowledge and understanding; (ii) that such texts and narratives are apt for appreciation – primarily though not exclusively – as non-literal modes of representation or expression that are significantly continuous with such (other) forms of creative literature as poetry, novel and drama. On the face of it, these two claims may seem incompatible – precisely to the extent that if religious narratives are stories they cannot be true, and if they are true they cannot be stories. Still, I shall try to show that failure to appreciate the significance and/or non-literal truth of stories is ultimately debilitating to the teaching of both creative literature and RE.

I shall begin, however, by attending to the evident problems of two familiar – and frequently contrasted – accounts of religion and RE. First, on what might be called a 'traditional' view of religion, religious claims and texts may be taken as literally descriptive of natural historical or 'supernatural' events. On an extreme Christian version of this view, the Genesis account of God's seven-day creation of the world and humanity, the Exodus story of God speaking to Moses from a burning bush, and the Gospel narrative of Satan's appearance to Christ in the wilderness are taken to describe actual historical events that Christians might deny only on pain of heresy or blasphemy. Likewise, the faithful might be required to hold that heaven, hell and purgatory describe actual places of after death reward, punishment and purgation, and that bread and wine are actually transformed in the Eucharist into the body and blood of Christ. Religious believers of all faiths who take the narratives, parables and theological doctrines of religious texts to be literally descriptive of natural or supernatural events are often referred to as 'fundamentalists', and educational approaches that encourage others to accept the literal truth of such texts are sometimes referred to as 'confessional'. That said, the distinction between literal and non-literal approaches to religious discourse is not exactly coextensive with that between confessional and non-confessional approaches to religious initiation, and confessional approaches may allow scope for less literal interpretation of sacred texts. Thus, for example, one may doubt whether all contemporary Christian advocates of confessional approaches would insist that Jonah was literally swallowed by a whale, or that the infant Jesus was actually visited by three kings, and I suspect that few would take the parables of Christ to be anything other than morally instructive fiction.

Needless to say, any thoroughgoing literalist interpretation of religious texts or narratives is hard to sustain. First, one need not doubt that such great religions as Judaism, Christianity and Islam have historical bases in the lives of their founding figures and key prophets, in order to appreciate that they also exhibit mythopoeic adornments that also occur in folk tales around the world, and that are not to be taken as historically descriptive. Secondly, it is not just that it may be overly credulous to take some of the more 'supernatural' elements of religious narratives literally, but that such literalism also runs the risk of missing the religious point. Interestingly, the conservative Roman Catholic philosopher Elizabeth Anscombe once argued in an article on transubstantiation (Anscombe 1981) that the main religious question is hardly settled by insisting that any talk of real presence is merely symbolic, since the real issue is really that of precisely what it could or should be said to symbolise. At the risk of drawing a rather different conclusion from any that Anscombe might have accepted, it is arguable that even if miracles – understood as anomalous discontinuities in the causal order – do occur, they would not be in themselves indicative of anything other than such discontinuity, and would still require appropriate interpretation to warrant religious significance. On this view, the key question about (say) Christ's transfiguration or his walking on the water – even on a literal interpretation of such stories – would be that of their precise *religious* import. On the face of it, however, there would seem no better case for literally interpreting the creation myths of Genesis, than there is for so doing in the cases of Bunyan's *Pilgrim's Progress* or Milton's *Paradise Lost*.

Beyond Literalism and Confession

Still, it may be that related interpretative problems have also informed the various approaches to RE recently developed as alternatives to confession. On the face of it, many of such approaches seem to have been prompted by both epistemic and political considerations and concerns. On the one hand, the political issue – at any rate, as this has related to the religious dimension of the traditional British state school curriculum – is essentially that of the justice of any confessional teaching of Christianity in the increasingly pluralist climate of contemporary British society. On the other hand, the epistemic issue has assumed more urgency in face of the apparent drift of a formerly (at least nominally) Christian population towards a more secular-liberal climate – as measured, perhaps most notably, by a decline in church attendance and growing scepticism about the very rationality of religious belief. That said, although such trends have certainly led some post-war educational theorists and policy makers to doubt whether RE has any legitimate place in contemporary schooling, it would appear that these concerns pull in rather different directions: whereas the epistemic consideration may point in the direction of entirely eliminating RE from the school curriculum, the political consideration might point more in the direction of providing wider curricular access or exposure to religions other than Christianity.

In the wake of the so-called 'phenomenological' turn, RE in the British common school seems to have gone in the directions of both more and less. In view of a new multicultural focus on religions besides Christianity, the religious curriculum has certainly broadened in scope, but it would also appear to have lost some of its former character and substance by abandoning any and all 'confessional' attempt to initiate children into the creeds and doctrines, devotional and moral practices, of Christian faith. To be sure, phenomenological or non-confessional approaches vary somewhat. Whereas in some contexts they seem confined to largely 'value-neutral' description of the ceremonies and rituals of major faiths, in others they have been combined with more open approaches to moral education. On such approaches, the Old Testament story of Joseph and his brothers or the New Testament parable of the Good Samaritan may be taken as pretexts for more general moral discussion of the evils of envy and bullying, or the importance of care and concern for others. On the positive side, indeed, neither of these aims of contemporary RE, nor the demise of traditional or at any rate sectarian confessional approaches, needs to be regarded as pure loss. There is clearly much to be said for acquainting those of one culture with the customs and practices of another, or with urgent issues of moral life and association, and it is of course far from clear what legitimate business common schooling might be said to have with the initiation of young people into any given religion – even that of their own parents and community.

However, it may be thought a less positive side of non-confessional approaches that such albeit valuable teaching of comparative cultural studies and/or moral education still falls rather short of RE: indeed, one may have some concern for the success of any such cultural lessons and/or moral education where such instruction proceeds in the absence of much sense of the real religious significance of cultural customs and moral values. As a regular observer of primary RE teaching, I have often been struck by the evident difficulties faced by trainee teachers – particularly those of little or no personal religious faith or background – in making sense of aspects of Christian as well as non-Christian culture and moral belief. How, for example, might one make cultural sense of the widespread artistic representation of the divine in Christian art and its absence from Islamic art, unless one appreciates how these faiths differ on the nature of God and/or the theology of divine–human relations? Or how might the parable of the slaying of the landlord's son by the wicked husbandmen be appreciated in terms other than moral banalities about fairness and the evils of violence failing some appreciation of the theology of incarnation? Indeed, how might the parable of the workers in the vineyard be understood at all, without reference to the very peculiar Christian vision of divine justice? From this viewpoint, contemporary non-confessional approaches may have more in common with literalism than might at first appear. For whereas fundamentalists hold that religious texts and narratives cannot be meaningful unless they are literally true, non-confessional approaches seem often to assume that since such texts cannot be literally true, they could have meaning only as local cultural warrants for this or that social custom, or – more idealistically – as aspirations to universal moral ideals. But, in so far as that is so, non-confessional approaches may well throw out the baby of religious knowledge and understanding with the bath water of confession.

Religion and Cultural Narrative

However, a way out of the tangle of confusion that bedevils any contrast between confessional and non-confessional approaches to religious discourse and education is suggested by recent moral and social theoretical focus on the idea of narrative. In this connection, the influential British philosopher Alasdair MacIntyre (1981) has argued that since human action is essentially rational and purposive – so that one is hard put to understand human moral and other conduct in terms other than the adoption of appropriate means to the achievement of rational ends or goals – it is also not possible to explain human identity and agency in the reductive causal categories of natural, social or behavioural science. Thus, for MacIntyre, understanding human identity is not a matter of identifying (logically or empirically) necessary conditions of physical or psychological continuity, but of understanding the roles played by individuals in narratives that others relate concerning them or which they tell about themselves: the unity of a person, he maintains, is the unity of a character in a story, and any agency associated with personhood so conceived has to be grasped in the context of such narrative. Apart from such narratives, indeed, human actions defy rational individuation or interpretation. The idea that humans understand themselves, not least as moral agents, through narratives or stories seems a promising one for making sense of religion and RE – not least since religious texts are clearly rich in stories and narratives – and MacIntyre himself precisely takes such accounts to play a key role in human self-understanding.

That said, the communitarian idea of religious texts as narratives is also not unproblematic. Certainly on some radical interpretations, the term 'narrative' seems to have acquired an unhelpfully wide sense as any sort of scientific, religious, moral, political or historical theory or explanation through which human agents might seek to account for their circumstances: it would seem to be in this rather indiscriminate sense of narrative that some post-structuralist or postmodern thinkers (see Lyotard 1984) have sought to question the epistemic status and force of all human (especially scientific) explanations, presumably on the genealogical grounds that no one local cultural construct could lay claim to greater objective status than any other. But however tempted philosophers of religion and RE might be to embrace the view that science is no more objective than religion, this is clearly an epistemically hazardous and self-defeating sense of narrative. The trouble here is that the sense of narrative from which such sceptical philosophical conclusions are derived clearly presupposes a contrast between creative invention and what is clearly not so: from this viewpoint, if all human explanations are narratives, then we might as well say that none are. On the other hand, however, if stories of human invention are distinguished from objective scientific accounts, the problem for any narratival conceptions of moral identity and agency is precisely that of avoiding collapse into some kind of moral or religious relativism. Indeed, those concerned to pursue culturally grounded and sometimes rearguard political agendas of national or tribal recognition, and who regard religious and national beliefs and customs as ways of sustaining communal solidarity via a sense of difference from others, have sometimes taken comfort from MacIntyrean and/or related communitarian views. Still, the dangers of such thinking in a world of deep racial and cultural divisions and tensions needs little emphasis, and it is surely by that same token disastrous to try to construe religious or moral meaning and significance in terms of such partisan concerns.

Despite MacIntyre's valiant efforts to develop an objective but culturally 'internalist' account of practical rationality (MacIntyre 1992), the problem clearly persists that any such practical reason is either capable of reliably arbitrating between the claims of rival traditions, in which case it has a culture transcendent objective basis, or it is not – in which case relativism rules after all. But there is another possibility: that narratives are really rival, but some are right and others wrong – or, at least, that some narratives contain more truth or objective insight than others in terms that precisely resist MacIntyrean practical resolution. On this view, MacIntyre is right to make the connection between great religious and other cultural stories and moral and/or spiritual self-understanding, but wrong to regard any genuine self-understanding as a function of local participation in social traditions. On the face of it, any human interest in such questions as whether there is a God, or whether humans as biologically or evolutionarily continuous with other animal species are rational by virtue of possessing immortal souls, is not in the sustaining of this or that local practice, but in achieving a universally transcendent perspective on the nature, flourishing and destiny of humankind – and it is to just such concerns that the great human narratives have precisely been addressed. From this viewpoint, any currently fashionable inclination to construe religious affiliation as little more than club membership supplies a shallow appreciation of religion. Still, this is to revive – in a particularly acute form – the question of how narratives or stories of the normative character that MacIntyre clearly (and surely rightly) distinguishes from empirical scientific theory can yet claim an objective rational status that goes beyond mere aesthetic preference for exotic rites and rituals.

It is worth some present re-statement that to claim that a story is a narrative in MacIntyre's sense is not to deny that it has a literal or factual basis – as of course many Christians and Moslems would want to insist that Gospel and Qur'an narratives have – but it is to say that we do not seek such significance and/or truth in the same way we seek it in empirical theories or hypotheses. From this viewpoint, to look for the religious significance of Buddha in the historical facts of Buddha's life is no less mistaken than trying to find the meaning of Malory's *Morte d'Arthur* in the life of some historical King Arthur. Some such mistake may indeed run through the arguments and counter-arguments of both creationists and evolutionists who appear to regard Genesis and Darwin as offering rival explanations of the origins of species. Creationists mistakenly assume that because Genesis is in some sense significant or true, then Darwinian evolution must be false (which of course it may be); but evolutionists may equally mistakenly assume that because Darwinian theory is significant or true (which it may be), Genesis cannot be. But, in any case, one may also regard as religious narratives stories that no serious person of faith would or should need to consider literally true, such as the *Epic of Gilgamesh*, the *Bhagavad Gita*, the book of Job, Dante's *Divine Comedy*, Milton's *Paradise Lost* or the parables of Christ himself – to which list most Christian believers would also probably add the key themes of Genesis.

Towards an Objective Account of Religious Narrative

For many religious believers, however, such mere assertion may only serve to draw the lines of engagement more clearly. If religious narratives have the same grammar and/or epistemic form as other human stories or fictions – or are otherwise continuous with such stories – they can be only human creations or constructions which must call into question: (1) the divine origins of religion; and (2) the objective truth of religious narratives. Conversely, if there is to be any divinely inspired truth to religious narratives, religious stories *cannot* be continuous with other forms of human creative storytelling. Of these objections, the first – regarding the divine source of religious narratives – is surely a red herring, and basically rests on confusion of epistemic and other (perhaps causal or genetic) considerations. For, in general, it does not follow from any claim that religious narratives are stories that they are not also divinely inspired, or even perhaps directly communicated to men by God or his prophets. In the event, not all religions seem to have claimed such direct divine transmission of religious truths, but the main point for emphasis in any narratival account of religious meaning is only that it is characteristic of religious texts to assume the form of stories, or of normative prescriptions (regarding values to be promoted or virtues to be cultivated) that have ultimate grounding in stories.

The second objection – concerning the truth of such stories – is clearly much more problematic and therefore calls for more comment.

For is it not the case that any assimilation of religious narrative to creative literature must sound the death knell of religious objectivity or truth? Arguably, however, our earlier objection to thinking of religious narratives as socially constructed vehicles of cultural cohesion – that religions seem concerned with the search for universal truths rather than local conditions of group solidarity – is even more directly applicable to the creative efforts of great poets, dramatists and other artists. Indeed, this point might well be pressed on behalf of literary and artistic truth against religious hegemony, sectarianism and hypocrisy. For have not such major writers and artists as Blake, Goya, Dostoevsky, Joyce and Bunuel been precisely concerned to expose the injustice and repression of many organised religions? That said, such examples may also serve to press the case for both perspectives: for have not the great religions often sought to expose local prejudice and temporal powers in the name of universal truth in a not dissimilar way to art? Indeed, it has evidently been the concern of some (though not all) of the lately mentioned artists to defend religious truth against such institutional corruption of religion: Dostoevsky rejects not Christianity but the Grand Inquisitor, and Blake's little vagabond prefers the alehouse to the church precisely because God is more likely to be found there. At all events, despite the mounting tide of post-war and postmodern suspicion of that traditional Western literary canon formerly regarded as the very cornerstone of educated sensibility in Britain and elsewhere (Matthew Arnold's 'best that has been thought and said' (Gribble 1967, p.150)), it remains arguable that the great literary heritage of our own and other cultures is a prime source of objective normative enquiry – and as such to be neglected by or denied future generations only at the very gravest moral peril.

But one may still have questions about the precise epistemic role of great cultural – religious and other – narratives. What, for example, can great religious and other stories teach us that science cannot? Here, one may be tempted to suppose that such stories and narratives are mainly concerned with the 'inner' world of human experience, and religion has sometimes been held to deal with the personal and/or private dimensions of the human mind or soul. But in the wake of modern philosophers like Dewey and Wittgenstein, such a view is less easy to sustain, precisely in so far as it encourages the idea that the realms of human soul and value are those of purely subjective experience and feeling. What art and literature already existed to teach us in advance of modern philosophical writings, however, was much about the objective reality and value of personal human feeling. Wittgenstein criticises the post-Cartesian account of allegedly 'inner' personal experience when he insists in *Zettel* (1967, 89e) that love is not a feeling, since love is put to the test: but, despite the pronounced cognitivism of Wittgenstein's account of emotional life, it may be more accurate to hold that while emotions do have a significant affective dimension, such affectivity is far from subjective or disconnected from the discernment of objective value and truth. On the contrary, if we want to understand more about love – or, at any rate, about a significant variety of human love – we could hardly do better than turn to the literature of romantic poetry, such as the powerfully moving 'Lucy' poems of Wordsworth. Indeed, what Wordsworth appreciated more than perhaps any poet before him (and perhaps more than any philosopher since Aristotle) is the role of appropriate feelings in the cultivation of personally transformative virtue, and the vital role of arts such as poetry in giving such feelings objective expression. In this light, although poetry is a key source of objective knowledge and understanding, it is a source not of the theoretical knowledge of science, but more of what Bertrand Russell (1968) called 'acquaintance knowledge' or of what has been more recently called 'illustrative representation' (Young 2001). Whatever science may have to tell us about the causal conditions of human attachment, or about any neurological impediments to such attachment, it seems ill equipped to afford much if any insight into the emotional meaning or value of love as a profound moral and spiritual reality.

As well as seeking to illumine the experiential or 'aesthetic' aspects of value and virtue, however, literature and the arts are even more evidently concerned with the task of exploring the normative consequences for human flourishing of those practical contexts and dispositions in which such sentiments as love, hate, anger, fear, lust, jealousy, pride, envy, ambition, guilt, remorse and resentment are implicated. It is of some present interest that while the tragedies of Shakespeare, Hardy and Ibsen have been much concerned with the secular moral consequences of human folly, error and vice, other past literary works – from Aeschylus, Sophocles and Euripides to Marlowe and Milton and beyond – have been no less concerned to explore larger metaphysical and religious questions concerning the origins of vice and sin, the relationship of freedom to divine law and responsibility and the proper scope and/or limits of human knowledge, aspiration and ambition, of precisely the kind that seem also to be raised by the creation stories of Genesis. Indeed, although the religious context in which they were originally composed could hardly be more remote from modern Christian or Islamic standpoints, it is clear enough that Aeschylus's *Prometheus Bound*, Sophocles' *Oedipus* trilogy and Euripides' *The Bacchae* are all addressed to issues about the relationship of divine law and order to human freedom that are of equal concern to other religious traditions. Moreover, it is not just that such questions are not obviously resolvable by the methods of empirical natural or social science, but that some of them – from remote antiquity onwards – have themselves been precisely concerned to question the wisdom of any such unfettered scientific *hubris*.

The Continuity of Religious and Other Narrative

By way of example, I shall devote brief attention to a literary theme (more fully explored in Carr 2004a; see also 2004b) that effectively illustrates: (1) the continuity of religious narrative with the wider moral and aesthetic concerns of creative (even secular) literature; and (2) the concern of religious narrative with metaphysical and normative issues that resist complete reduction to the more secular moral and aesthetic concerns of creative art and literature. For although the legend of Faust or Dr Faustus has been subject to secular, post-romantic interpretations concerned with tensions between artistic freedom and conventional morality, it clearly has very much older associations. In his compelling work, *The Myth of the Magus*, E.M.

Butler comments interestingly that 'The Faust of poetry has a hold over men's minds which only the great myths of the world possess, and yet no-one believes in his reality' (Butler 1948, p. 268), and traces the legendary doctor's identity to several shadowy medieval figures. I have elsewhere (Carr 2004) suggested a more direct mythical link to the first-century magician Simon Magus and to the Manichean Bishop Faustus mentioned by Augustine in his *Confessions* (Augustine 1961, p. 92). In order to understand the orthodox Christian demonisation of Faust and/or Magus, the story of his pact with the devil needs to be appreciated as an updated gnostic replay of the Genesis story of the Fall. Unlike Adam, Faust does not just desire knowledge that will make him equal to God, he desires knowledge in the belief that by its attainment he may become God: his is the sin of spiritual pride that Christ resists in the wilderness when Satan tempts him to throw himself from the pinnacle of the Temple.

Briefly, the figure of Faust or Faustus needs to be understood as the embodiment of an ancient dualistic – Manichean or gnostic – theology that conceives human salvation to be the ultimate triumph of a spiritual agency over its gross physical nature. It is just this conception that is challenged by the Christian narrative of the incarnation and resurrection, and is given later philosophical justification in St Thomas Aquinas' anti-dualist Aristotelian reworking of Christian doctrine. Notoriously, dualism resurfaces in a particularly virulent philosophical form in the seventeenth-century epistemology of Descartes hand in glove with an empirical scientific methodology that seriously raises the prospect of total (godlike) human control of nature. Much modern literature and art, again reviving ancient myths, may be appreciated as a reaction to such developments, and the Romantic revival of the Prometheus myth is especially noteworthy in this connection. For although the main Promethean theme of free defiance of a tyrant god (or demiurge) appealed to the Romantic imagination, its ambivalence did not go unnoticed by the leaders of that great poetic movement. Thus, in one key re-working of the Promethean theme – Mary Shelley's Gothic shocker *Frankenstein* – we have a cautionary tale of the fruits of *hubris* that has significant affinities with the Faust story, and that clearly continues to have contemporary resonance in an age of nuclear power and genetic engineering. Thus, although the stories of Faust and Frankenstein and the Genesis, Prometheus and the gnostic narratives to which they are indebted are not literally true, they clearly provide insight into normative questions of the highest human significance that are also unsusceptible to any non-question-begging scientific resolution. It would also seem to follow not only that a grasp of such issues must be part of any significant RE, but that some understanding of religious and theological issues is also a significant requirement of any meaningful literary education.

To be sure, some will insist that all of this is just so much evasion, and that there must be more to religious meaning and truth than this: for what has this non-literal narrative significance ultimately to say on the pressing questions of the faithful about whether there is actually a God or an afterlife? The short answer is that it probably says everything that can be said. Once more, the trouble with such concerns may be that they are seeking answers in the wrong places. Traditional theological arguments for the existence of God of the kind still studied by students of theology and philosophy are often presented as formal proofs open to refutation by the detection of equally formal fallacies, and in the course of a relatively recent mid-twentieth century revival of philosophical theology, leading analytical philosophers were still arguing as though the case for or against God might be decided by something like empirical methods (see, for example, Flew and MacIntyre 1955). But to deploy the grammar of theological 'arguments' for God as first or final cause is already to have shifted into a different epistemic key from any such argument, and barring some naïve conception of God as just some great Nobodaddy in the sky, notions of divine causation are not reducible to the efficient causes of modern science. Kant was, of course, the first great modern philosopher to show how arguments for morality and religion need to be distinguished from mathematical and empirical scientific proofs (Kant 1967), but we have lately observed how the more recent defence by MacIntyre and others of the inherently narratival form of normative discourse also reinforces the claim that final cause explanations are indispensable to any understanding of the moral self. On this view, however, to speak religiously or theologically of creation as the result of God's agency, is precisely to claim that that such creation cannot be entirely reduced to efficient causation.

Thus, on any conception of divine and/or human personhood as purposive agency, it seems that not only such great God-fearing faiths as Judaism, Islam and Christianity, but even such major non-theistic religions as Buddhism, could hardly avoid the expression of spiritual and moral norms, ideals and aspirations in narratival terms. However, in so far as such narrative is not reducible to the causal categories of natural and social science, it is also not to be expected that the spiritual and moral realities in terms of which human agents have sought self-understanding are either so reducible. From this viewpoint, it is hardly surprising that themes of evergreen philosophical and theological concern about the nature of soul and body, good and evil, destiny and freedom, have found their most vivid and enduring expression and depiction in the non-literal metaphors, analogies and allegories of such great religious and other cultural narratives as Genesis, Prometheus and Faust. For ancient followers of Eleusian, Orphic and other mystery religions, the stories of Persephone, Orpheus and Dionysus were finely wrought metaphors for the soul's experience of embodiment designed to introduce initiates to an order of spiritual and moral reality transcendent of ordinary empirical-rational awareness. Moreover, it is crucial to appreciate the no less affective than cognitive character of such engagement. In this light, the emotional dimensions of moral and spiritual reality are best addressed and/ or accessed through the symbolic and metaphorical resources of great art which has the power not just to inform minds but also to move hearts. In this vein, it is clear that the faith of countless millions of Christians has been precisely driven, less by theological arguments than by that profoundly moving experience of divine love for creation conveyed by the Gospel story.

When all is said and done, any serious and responsible RE inevitably runs the risk that many people will judge such narratives – not least the Christian story – to be little more than fairy tales. But from the plausible perspective that – far from being nonsensical – fairy tales embody deep wisdom about ourselves and our world, it is arguably one important task of religious and other educators to reclaim the view that science is not the last word on human wisdom – at least with respect to some key human questions – and that there are indeed significant philosophical, theological, literary, artistic and other sources of human knowledge and understanding. From this viewpoint, it may be instructive to close with a brief reflection on Iris Murdoch's remarkable late work *Metaphysics as a Guide to Morals* (1993). In that work, it is clear that while Murdoch doggedly resists any Judeo-Christian concept of a personal God, she nevertheless holds that there is a transcendent dimension to human self-understanding – in the absence of which, indeed, little sense is to be made of our moral lives. In the event, although her work remains free of a Judeo-Christian deity, it may be doubted whether it is entirely devoid of a religious or non-secular dimension. One might express this by saying that whereas Christianity inclines to an image of divine transcendence in terms of a craftsman God, for Murdoch what is transcendent is not so much the craftsman but the standards of excellence to which the successful craftsman aspires. Thus, listening to J.S. Bach one may have the sense that the B Minor Mass is great by virtue of the composer's fidelity to artistic standards that are not entirely of his own making: that, more generally, any failures of art or moral virtue are ultimately hard to grasp as other than failures to achieve standards that are not entirely of our own making. Murdoch, in short, offers a transcendent – if not a religious – view of the sources of normativity that seems Platonic rather than Christian. Any such view may also be just so much sophistry and delusion: but I believe that there are deep philosophical, normative and/or metaphysical reasons for holding that it is not.

References

Anscombe, G.E.M. (1981) 'Transubstantiation'. In *Ethics, Religion and Politics: Collected Philosophical Papers Volume III*. Oxford, Blackwell.

Augustine, St (1961) *Confessions*. Trans. R.S. Pine-Coffin. Harmondsworth, Penguin.

Butler, E.M. (1948) *The Myth of the Magus*. Cambridge, Cambridge University Press.

Carr, D. (1994a) 'Reason, Meaning and Truth in Religious Narrative: Towards an Epistemic Rationale for Religious and Faith School Education'. *Studies in Christian Ethics*, 17 (1), 38–53.

—— (1994b) 'Taking Narrative Seriously: Exploring the Educational Status of Story and Myth'. In K. Alston (ed.) *Philosophy of Education 2003*. Philosophy of Education Society, University of Illinois at Urbana-Champaign, Urbana, Illinois, pp. 81–9.

Flew, A. and MacIntyre, A. (eds) (1955) *New Essays in Philosophical Theology*. London, SCM Press.

Gribble, J. (ed.) (1967) *Matthew Arnold*. London, Collier-Macmillan.

Kant, I. (1967) *The Critique of Practical Reasoning and Other Works on the Theory of Ethics*. Trans. T.K. Abbott. London, Longmans.

Lyotard, J-F. (1984) *The Post-Modern Condition: A Report on Knowledge*. Trans. G. Bennington and B. Massumi. Manchester, Manchester University Press.

MacIntyre, A.C. (1981) *After Virtue*. Notre Dame, IN, University of Notre Dame Press.

—— (1992) *Three Rival Versions of Moral Enquiry*. Notre Dame, IN, University of Notre Dame Press.

Muir, E. (1960) *Collected Poems*. London, Faber and Faber.

Murdoch, I. (1993) *Metaphysics as a Guide to Morals*. Harmondsworth, Penguin.

Russell, B. (1968) *Problems of Philosophy*. Oxford, Oxford University Press.

Wittgenstein, L. (1967) *Zettel*. Oxford, Blackwell.

Young, J.O. (2001) *Art and Knowledge*. London, Routledge.

Chapter 13

Religious Education through the Language of Religion

Iris Yob

Abstract

The principle of the separation of church and state is a strong theme running through US legal and political life with the effect that while it is permissible to teach about religion in the public (i.e., state supported) schools, many teachers are reluctant to do so. Faiths could be approached as various ways of making meaning. Like all ways of meaning making (scientific, aesthetic, historic and so on), religions employ symbolic language. Religious symbols refer, denote, represent or express meaning, literally or metaphorically, so that religious experience can be communicated, expressed and developed. In considering a Religious Education curriculum, the concept of religious symbolic language has much to offer. First, it supports religion as a legitimate form of knowledge and hence a rightful object of study. Second, a comparative study of the symbols of religion across times, cultures and faiths reveals a resonance that adds richness and meaning to them. Third, approaching religious study through the symbolic language that religions typically employ is much truer to the subject matter than many other approaches to RE.

In the United States, Religious Education (RE) is construed in two distinctly different ways, reflecting a long history of negotiation between church and state. RE that takes place within state-supported institutions, known as public schools, is at most education *about* religion. In private schools, specifically those supported by religious organizations, it is likely to be education *for* religion. While the distinction between the two can never be determined in the final sense and is influenced by changing political, social and religious forces, a long-standing history of constitutional and political debate has attempted to maintain what is commonly referred to as the 'wall of separation between church and state'.

Although the distinction between education *for* and education *about* religion is carefully parsed, one item in particular lies on common ground that permits a genuine study of religion for either purpose. If religion is seen as a way of understanding the world and whatever might lie beyond it, it is important to study how that understanding is constructed, expressed and communicated. What language does religion speak, what is this language about, and how is it used to make meaning? These seem to be eminently important questions for both religious and non-religious school systems to address. In the case of the religious school, a study of the language of religion would seem to be an important aid to understanding what one is about when one is being religious. In the case of the non-religious school, a study of the language of religion is important because so many use that language in the world in which we live and which we must negotiate as community members, neighbours and citizens.

The tension over RE (usually known as RI) in the schools was present in the US from the beginning. In his last annual report to the legislature, Thomas Mann, founder of the common schools in Massachusetts in 1842, spoke directly to the fear that these institutions would be characterized by irreligious tendencies. He reminded the legislators that Massachusetts, unlike Great Britain and many other European countries, was not under the control of an Established Church that among other things ordered the education of the young. While taxes to support free schools for all the children of the Commonwealth were not to be used in support of parochial or church-sponsored schools, nevertheless he admitted it was unconscionable, and even counter-productive to the good of society, to operate the common schools without sound Christian instruction (Cremin 1957, p. 102).

The strongly Protestant tone in the public schools came under fire when a large population of Irish immigrants arrived in New York City. As early as 1805, The Society for establishing a Free School in the City of New York had been incorporated. Founded by Quakers, it was purposefully non-sectarian to reach the poor and had the support of the city and state. However, by mid-century, controversies began to multiply with challenges mounted by other religious organizations seeking government funds to support free schools, with the consequence that the New York City legislature ruled that public funds were to be used only for schools that were free, open to all, and non-sectarian. In the 1820s and 1830s, many new immigrants had arrived in the young city, and by 1855 'more than half the city's residents were foreign-born, and more than half of those were Irish' (Ravitch 2000, p. 27). Hostility from the largely Protestant Americans against the new Catholic Irish poor provided the context for the 'unbridgeable cultural gulf' between the Public School Society with its Quaker and Protestant roots and the Catholic clergy, especially given the challenge of providing equal educational opportunity in the immigrant poor neighbourhoods and the more stable middle class Protestant neighbourhoods (Ravitch 2000, p. 33). Despite the efforts and claims made by the Public School Society, Catholics still saw the schools as 'deist, sectarian, and anti-Catholic'. The textbooks used were judged to be 'most malevolent and foul attacks' on Catholicism, and objections were lodged over the daily reading of the King James Bible (Ravitch 2000, p. 45). Exposing the Protestantism of the common school, so interwoven in school activities and the lives of teachers, administrators and textbook writers, brought shock and denial, political manoeuvering and street rioting, and eventually new legislation and a new Board of Education by the 1860s. The public schools in New York City and indeed throughout the country continue to wrestle with new challenges at the arrival of new waves of immigrants, notably Italian, German and Jewish, and more recently, Muslim and Asian, and issues surrounding poverty and equal opportunity for all.

Identifying sectarian influences in the public schools, however, has now moved largely to the courts for determination where the limits and possibilities of religion in the schools continue to be argued. The most recent decision (Zelman *vs* Simmons-

Harris *et al.*, 2002), for instance, upheld tuition support for parents choosing to send their children to private religious schools in a school district that gives parents free choice of schools for their children.

Meanwhile, the study of religion, even in the sense of study *about* religion, in public schools has remained a possibility but one hardly ever taken up. A move by high schools on Cape Cod, Massachusetts to include a semester-long course on world history which would include a study of world religions was a departure noteworthy enough to warrant an editorial in the *Cape Cod Times* (31 May 2006, A12). A study (Zam and Stone, 2006) reports that 60 per cent of K-12 public school teachers in a nationwide sample affirms that knowing about religion is necessary for understanding and living with diversity and nearly all of the group agreed that there was a need to consider the study of religion in the curriculum, yet 94 per cent of the same group admitted that they would not teach about religion and less than one-third would even consider talking about religion with their students so litigious has the issue become. In this context, a fresh look at how religious knowledge can be shared might give new impetus to including religious studies in the curriculum.

Religious Symbolic Language

If the basic unit of thought is the symbol and language is seen as a system of symbols arranged in ways that give meaning, then all modes of thought – scientific, artistic, religious – are basically built as symbol systems. One of the most useful symbol theories is that of Nelson Goodman. Exploring symbolic systems as 'ways of world-making', his philosophical contribution connects with other theories that have been significant in educational thought. For instance, his work resonates with that of Jerome Bruner who unpacked the idea of the 'structure of the disciplines' as a means of authentically teaching the various subjects of the school curriculum. Bruner argued that each discipline has its own way of organizing, creating and representing what is known and of building new knowledge, the implication being that teachers should not so much teach their students the facts established within a discipline but how to think within that discipline; that is, how to think like a scientist, an artist, a historian, and presumably, a religionist (Bruner 1960, ch. 2).

What then is a symbol and a symbol system or language? – Important questions for those who would teach the body of collected human knowledge and prepare students to make their contributions to future knowledge. In original societies, symbols are to be found wherever the unusual, striking, powerful, effective, superior or exceptional are found. Sun, moon, stars, trees, rocks, mountains, water, fire, wind, changing seasons, birth, death, marriage, tools, ropes, feasts, mother, father, animals and times are filled with meaningfulness, while rituals, accompanied and explained by myths, attend virtually every activity. No clear line is drawn between sacred and secular.

For modern Westerners, material symbols continue to play a central role although in religious worship the spoken and written word has assumed important roles as well. Believers are now more distanced from their symbols, in the sense that they regard them less superstitiously, more readily distinguish between their religious and non-religious uses, and deliberately submit them to philosophical analysis and scientific verification.

Some symbols have been remarkably tenacious in the history of religion across centuries and cultures. The African who exclaims over an arresting stone: 'Ha, are you there?' and carries it off believing it to be potent; the ancient tribes of central India, who set a burial monolith over the grave to fasten down the troubled soul of the dead; the pre-Islamic Arabs who venerated certain stones calling them 'the house of God'; the Hebrews who tell of Moses striking the rock to provide a fountain of water in the desert for the pilgrims; and the statement of Jesus that 'upon this rock I will build my church' are each employing stones symbolically in religious understanding (Eliade 1958, ch. IV), although in strikingly different ways but with resonant meanings. A variety of things – objects, times, places, words, pictures, movements, sounds and gestures – can be symbolic, that is, can refer. Since reference is the common function of the great variety of symbols, there are different kinds of reference at work in symbolic languages.

Literal and Non-Literal Symbols

In simplest terms, symbols may be categorized as referring literally or metaphorically. Literal reference 'applies to those cases, such as naming, predication, description, where a word or string of words applies to one thing, event, and so on, or to many' (Goodman 1984, p. 55). So in the context of traditional Christian theology, 'Peter' refers literally to the disciple of Jesus and 'disciple' literally refers to each of the twelve identified as among the original followers of Jesus. When the church is referred to a 'light set on a hill', the phrase is being employed in an odd or unusual way – it sorts out various things including the church but not lights on hills; it denotes the church, but does so metaphorically. A great deal of difference among and even within particular faiths rests on the degree to which believers acknowledge a symbolic reference to be metaphorical or literal, with the more fundamentalist faiths ascribing to a more literalist interpretation of its grounding symbols.

In case one should think that metaphor is a simple matter of comparing one thing with another, however, Goodman describes the relationship rather as a matter of 'teaching an old word new tricks'. Better yet, since a referent does not function alone but comes with a set of prior applications, both literal and figurative, it is a matter of 'a whole apparatus of organization taking over new territory' (Goodman 1976, p. 73). In technical terms, Goodman describes the metaphoric process as a 'transfer of schema' (that is, a set of categories or a system of concepts) from a familiar setting to a novel one. Guided by the networks of literal and metaphorical understandings of its past usage and the present context in which it is applied, we use the schema to organize the new realm along the same lines as the old. The transfer from familiar to novel can surprise even the metaphor-maker, but once brought about, it invites contemplation and exploration. Herein lays metaphor's emotive and cognitive power.

Denotation

Labels can be employed to denote, either literally or metaphorically, people, pla~ events, processes and so on. 'Jesus' denotes a particular person literally and 'Good Shepherd' denotes him metaphorically; 'Ten Commandments' denotes the Law literally, 'the schoolmaster to bring us to Christ' denotes it metaphorically. Although some denotata are more precise than others, denotation is the naming, narrating, describing, predicative function of symbols (Goodman and Elgin 1988, p. 34).

Denotative symbols are not only basic to any schema, but denotation may also be allusive and complex. Anthropologist Victor Turner illustrates what he calls a kind of 'folk etymologizing' that plays a key role in the religious understanding of the Mdembu people in northwest Zambia. These people name the elements of their rituals *ku-jikijila*, a word that literally denotes 'to blaze a trail' and with the exercise of a practised ingenuity, also refers to a similar word, *chijikijilu*, which in turn literally denotes 'beacon'. By denoting at once 'to blaze a trail' and 'beacon', the label for ritual elements figuratively suggests that rituals connect the known world of the senses to the unknown, invisible realm of the spirits. In so doing, *ku-jikjila* conveys the notion of a structured and ordered world over against the unstructured and chaotic, an indication of the complexity of the cosmological understandings of the Ndembu people, all captured in a word (Turner 1977, p. 15).

Representation

It is clear that verbal denotation has not been the sole, nor even the most predominant, form of reference in religious understanding. As Miles indicates, even contemporary Christianity, which is characterized as the 'religion of the Word', has not always been so heavily dependent on language. In her study of early, pre-Renaissance and Reformation Christianity, she concludes that visual imagery has played an important, and at times the major, role in religious cognition at least in the experience of the ordinary worshipper. She explains that people had before them daily the image of the cathedral, the statuary, the paintings and liturgical presentations. While the priests, with their backs to the congregation and speaking softly in a foreign tongue conducted the services, the viewer stood as a member of an 'interpreting congregation' within a particular architecture, surrounded by the graphic arts, listening to the chants and watching the priests act out before them what they saw in the paintings, stained glass windows and vaulted ceilings about them. And given the explanation at the time of sight as the sending of a ray from the eye to make active contact with what is observed, these worshippers believed that when the priest raised the host for all to see, their eyes literally touched divinity (Miles 1985, pp. 8–10).

While partly dependent on its physical features of sound, colour, movement, shape and tone, representation is not limited to or even confused with imitation or mere resemblance. It is a symbolic relationship, that is, a representation stands for, or refers to something. Its power lies in the fact that it can provide access to realms of objects and ideas otherwise elusive or directly inaccessible to the senses. Representative symbolic languages need to be learned just as verbal languages do

(Goodman 1976, pp. 34–9) and most belief systems have employed the services of teachers – imams, priests, shamans, elders and wise women – to induct the young into understanding.

Exemplification

At times, an object is used as a symbol because, by literally possessing certain characteristics, it can readily serve as a model or sample of something else (Goodman 1976, pp. 52–7; 1978, pp. 63–70; Goodman and Elgin 1988, pp. 19–20). Stones have been a recurring symbol in the history of religion; exhibiting the qualities of strength and endurance, they have been used as symbols of powers that are either literally strong and enduring or can be figuratively described as such in character, personality or efficacy. In totem societies, it has been remarked that the animal becomes at once a symbol of power in that it possesses special potencies such as strength, speed and keen perceptions, as well as a model for the tribe which in a sense submerges itself in the animal's being and personality (van de Leeuw 1938, pp. 75–82). The Christian faith builds from the life of Jesus in a similar way, recognizing certain potencies of courage, love, sacrifice and mercy, and accepting this life as the Way in which to walk.

As exemplars, heroes have had a prominent place in religious myth and history. Characteristically, they go away, suffer and return with something better. Messianic stories in religious faiths follow this pattern and the epic journeys are reflected and typified in the pilgrimages of lesser mortals. Moses in the desert, Abraham travelling to a far place, Ruth leaving Moab, Jonah in Ninevah, Daniel in exile, Esther in the palace of Ahasuerus, John the Baptist in the wilderness, Martin Luther King Jr in a Birmingham jail, and even the character Solo in *Star Wars* have made their journeys and returned with salvific power. The lives of heroes may exemplify the transitions in life from immaturity to maturity. Their stories show what to expect and how to meet it. By their readiness, courage and persistence they indicate what is worthwhile (Campbell with Moyers 1988, ch. V). They also provide the foundation for theological constructions around salvation and redemption.

Exemplification, Goodman suggests, is seldom given much attention, but it is an important and widely used means for understanding in non-verbal languages. This is certainly true of religious symbolism. One referential element in many of the characters and events, the parables and stories, the layout of sacred sites and the strict performance of rituals is that they exemplify the actions of the gods, the desirable behaviour of believers, or the features of a particular religious understanding of the cosmos or some part of it.

Expression

At times, for the initiated, a symbol figuratively possesses characteristics that make it particularly apt as a symbol. Grey colours, for instance, are said to be sad. Not only colours, but shapes, movements, perspective and all the elements that go into a painting, architectural space or some other visual art, even apart from the actual subject matter, can express sadness, joy, alarm, awe or some other quality.

Dillenberger describes how the elements of George Segal's contemporary sculpture 'Abraham and Isaac' are employed to express particular understandings such as the primal generation gap and the moral problem of the older generation being 'in charge'. For example, she points out that the paunchy figure of Abraham expresses the generative power appropriate to a patriarch; his clenched left fist expresses his horror at the deed he is about to perform; the relatively stronger and taller figure of Isaac, kneeling and pleading is a figure of a young man's psychical weakness in the presence of his father (Dillenberger 1986, pp. 105–124). Works of art typically employ expressive symbols in this manner.

In *Death Set to Music*, Paul Minear examines how four masterworks express various meanings of death in human experience. As he takes the works apart movement by movement, it is apparent that the message of the music depends significantly on expressive symbols. To illustrate with one small example, we can look at his discussion of the second movement of Brahms' *A German Requiem* and the declaration:

> the grass withers and the flower falls but
> the word of the Lord abides forever.

Central in this statement is what he calls 'one of the most decisive "buts" in all music'. From the mournful words of the first phrase there is an abrupt change to the positive affirmation of the second phrase, a transition that is expressed equally in the musical qualities as in the words. The first phrase is sung as a dirge – slowly, in the lower voices – but at the 'but' the tempo and mood quicken and brighten. He attributes the 'brightness' of the mood to the more animated and exuberant voices of the higher ranges taking over from the sombre tones of the voices in the lower pitches, the coming into play of the whole orchestra and the interplay of a fugue. The combined effect of words and music in this context is the sober recognition of the transience of life even in the course of one summer's wait for the later rains contrasted with the endless patience and permanence of God (Minear 1987, pp. 70–71). The change in musical tone does as much or more to express the hope of this declaration as the words alone can do.

The *aum* chant of Buddhist monks, when properly pronounced, contains all the vowels. It is said to be a four-syllable word, where the fourth syllable is silence. It is a word without denotation. In the symbol, these characteristics are a figurative display of a number of truths important in Buddhist understanding: the resounding oneness of being, the recurring cycle of birth and dissolution, the spiritual need for silence after sound, the essentially wordless meaning of mystery (Campbell with Moyers 1988, pp. 230–31).

Similarly, sequences such as the snake's annual shedding of its skin, the waxing and waning of the moon, the succession of seasons, planting and reaping, immersion into and emerging out of cleansing waters have each served as symbols, exemplifying the cycle of death followed by new life, redemption and salvation, despair and hope. Bowed heads and bent knees in a religious service have in many traditions expressed impotence, humility and contrition before a god (Van der Leeuw 1938, p. 341), and the opulence of many places of worship expresses the worth of one's God.

The ordered positioning of the images of rulers, saints, apostles, demons, angels, the Virgin and Christ in medieval churches and the respective places reserved for prominent and common people expressed the ecclesiastical, social and spiritual hierarchy in which the worshippers were oriented. In contrast, the iconoclasm of the Protestant Reformation, with its whitewashed walls and people mingling as equals in the congregation, was a startling re-presentation and re-expression of the disposal of such hierarchies and substitution of a theology of equality before God (Miles 1985, ch. V).

Re-enactment

Symbols can also refer by re-enacting, a term Scheffler employs to describe the meaning-making function of ritual. The rituals celebrated within religions often refer to some important moment in the past, thus connecting the present group with the power and meaning of the original event. Scheffler also points out another kind of reference that occurs during a ritual performance: a reference to performances of the same ritual by other groups at other times or in other places (Scheffler 1986, p. 65). So the primitive initiation rites which symbolize some cosmic event in myth-based societies also refer to the previous initiation ceremonies of the tribe; the observance by a Jewish congregation of *Yom Kippur* re-enacts the observance of these same services by other Jewish congregations in other places across centuries of *diaspora* to the original Hebrew congregations, as the Eucharist connects Christians with other worshippers throughout Christendom right back to the original Last Supper. Scheffler also notes that this relationship – the repetition of an act which exemplifies or imitates other similar acts, albeit allusively – builds up a history of such performances, and a religious tradition and community is developed (Schleffer 1986, pp. 66–7).

St Francis recognized the effectiveness of this kind of symbolism. In his Rule of 1221, he enjoined the brothers to ignore coins that they may find, dispose of their goods, and not engage in regular business enterprises, but to survive by begging, passing indiscriminately from door to door. Francis suggested that their combined lack of material wealth was not only an imitation of Christ's poverty but was also intended to establish a *communitas*, a sense of belonging to a group on the edge of mainstream society.

Re-enactment is then a significant form of religious symbolism, helping to provide not only identity, but also continuity and connection within a religious community, a significance that could be enhanced in times of crisis. In another sense, not only rituals but other symbolic forms can fulfil a similar role. We see this for instance in the recently acknowledged art-works of Australian aborigines. The telling of the stories of the ancestors in song, dance and painting is passed down from generation to generation by the guardians, members of the tribe who are thought to inherit ownership of them. Although the art of these hunters and gatherers is seldom permanent, often being drawn in the sand or even in ochres on their bodies, the 'dreamings' as these artworks are called must be remembered and reproduced with exactness to maintain the 'truth' they contain. Through them, each new generation is connected to the tribe.

One of the most powerful religious symbols has been the circle. It has appeared in primitive rituals as a means of demarcating a sacred space. The layout of Native American villages was circular to represent the surrounding horizon. We have inherited from Sumerian mythology the circle with its four cardinal points and 360 degrees based on the perceived number of days in the year. Chinese and Aztec cosmology pictured a circle about the nation that made it the 'Kingdom of the Centre'. Circles have appeared in the dome-shaped temples of India, in paleolithic cave paintings, the calendar stones of the Aztecs, the visions of the prophet Ezekiel who saw wheels within wheels, the haloes painted around the heads of holy figures, ring ceremonies including those of the present wedding service, the *mandala* of Eastern religions, Tibetan sand paintings and in the way we speak of the family circle. Circles make reference to sacred completeness, totality and the cycle of life (Campbell with Moyers 1988, pp. 214–17). It is possible that when religious groups employ the circle symbol they can have an increased sense not only of present community but also with those who preceded them and with some imaginative reflections with others of other faiths and the broader sweep of humanity for whom also the circle carries meaning. Given the pervading sense of isolation and loneliness, or imperialism and self-aggrandizement of modern peoples, re-enactive reference could serve to bring people together both locally and globally, suggesting a potentially significant role for shared religious symbolism (McFague 1987). For this to occur, however, a religious group needs to realize that the symbol is shared, identify the common meanings, and since religions can both divide and unite, be prepared to release some of their own particular claim on the symbol.

Multiple Reference

In many symbol systems the relationship between symbol and symbolized is often complex, ambiguous and suggestive. Some symbols are effective because they do suggest a multiplicity of interpretations, literal and metaphorical. The greater our store of relevant knowledge, Goodman and Elgin assure us, the greater our resources for understanding what these symbols represent (Goodman and Elgin 1988, pp. 113–20).

Miles recalls a discussion of an eighth-century painted icon in Santa Maria in Trastevere in Rome. The painting depicts Mary seated on an imperial purple cushion, stiff with jewels, crowned with a bejeweled coronet, and a huge nimbus radiating about her. The reigning pope of the day, John VII, is depicted at her feet. For the original viewers, in all likelihood the painting represented the legitimacy of the pope as the channel and interpreter of the divine will on earth. The message intended by its donor was most likely political, emphasizing his direct access to the Virgin and his immense power. In terms of visual content alone, however, it could also represent for a viewer the splendour of the Virgin and the total abasement of the highest earthly spiritual power. To one modern critic, it represents the domination, oppression and self-aggrandizement of the Church. Miles wonders whether it may also have expressed to women of the eighth century an assurance that something of the presence and power of the feminine has been an important part in the development of Christian understanding (Miles 1985, pp. 30–31).

Stories as histories, myths, legends or parables often lend themselves to multiple interpretations. Spiegel's research on the history of the Abraham and Isaac story, the *Akedah*, and Dillenberger's analysis of sculptures of this story and the embellishments and glosses that have been added to explicate the original account and Noddings' appalled condemnation of the story for its influence on how the notion of family is conceived (Noddings 1984, pp. 43–4), reveal how its central theme – unspeakable command and rescue – has assumed different significances at different times. Various tellings of the story have represented the character of Abraham, of Isaac and of God. Parents, who during the fearful sieges of the Crusades sacrificed their own families rather than apostatize, saw themselves re-enacting the tradition that originated with the old patriarch and his compliant son. Others have found in the story an example of sacrifice worthy of emulation, of promised rescue and redemption, of the primal generation gap, of Messianic sacrifice and of the moderation of justice by mercy. For still others, the story expresses the drama that accompanies a testing of faith (Spiegel 1967).

Implications for RE

In considering a RE curriculum, the concept of religious symbolic language has much to offer. First, it supports religion as a legitimate form of knowledge and hence a rightful object of study. Its ways of conceptualizing and expressing meaning follow the same logical patterns and symbol processes – denotation, representation, exemplification, expression and re-enactment, both literal and metaphoric – as other forms of knowing, are embedded in their own histories of practice, and are cognitively accessible once one learns the keys to unlocking them. Even science, often thrown up in contrast to religion as a way of making meaning to the disparagement of religion, employs similar symbolic tools to create and express theories, ideas and scientific truths (e.g. Yob 1992).

Second, a comparative study of the symbols of religion across times, cultures and faiths reveals a resonance that adds richness and meaning to them. Stones, seasons, water, food, messianic figures, and the host of other symbols, combined with gestures, apparel and sacred spaces, embedded in stories, expressed in art, architecture and music, and re-enacted in rituals at sacred times reappear with similar significance and similar meanings albeit as variations on a theme, and gather gloss upon gloss. Their significance can be intuited by the very young and yet their full exploration can challenge the mature scholar. The work of Mircea Eliade and Joseph Campbell, among many others, can provide curricular materials for study for all ages. Courses of study could be developed thematically rather than faith by faith to illustrate the resonance among the symbols employed and the collective and rich meaning they provide when taken together.

Third, and very importantly, approaching a study *about religion* or *for religion* through the symbolic language that religions typically employ is much truer to the subject matter than many other approaches to RE. Traditionally, in public schools, social studies classes have been charged with a study of world religions where religion is studied as a historical, socio-cultural phenomenon. Within the social sciences, it is not studied as a way of making meaning in its own right, not as a study of religion as religion. An examination of religious symbolic language, exploring how the religions develop and express meaning, would give students a better understanding of what religion is really about. The symbols, incidentally, not only carry cognitive meaning but also are infused with emotional and moral value. For believers, they open up understandings about the cosmos, a people's origin and destiny, and the individual's place in the grand scheme of things. They speak of awe, fear, hope, duty and order. They suffuse believers' lives with meaning at the most significant moments – birth, coming of age, marriage, new beginnings, loss, death. In other words, such an approach would lend itself more readily to an authentic study of religion that is after all more than a matter of dates, founders and propositional beliefs. And just as such a study is more authentic in non-religious settings, so too it can be more meaningful to students in religious settings, where an education for religion must embrace more than the catechism that might appeal solely to the mind without engaging the heart as well.

References

Bruner, J. (1960) *The Process of Education*. Cambridge, MA, Harvard University Press.

Campbell, J. with Moyers, B. (1988) *The Power of Myth*, ed. Betty Sue Flowers. New York, Doubleday.

Cremin, L.A. (ed.) (1957) *The Republic and the School: Horace Mann on the Education of Free Men*. New York, Teachers College Press.

Dillenberger, J. (1986) 'George Segal's "Abraham and Isaac": Some Iconographic Reflections'. In *Art, Creativity, and the Sacred: An Anthology in Religion*. Ed. D. Apostolos-Cappadona. New York, Crossroad, pp. 105–124.

Eliade, M. (1958) *Patterns in Comparative Religion*. Trans. Rosemary Sheed. New York, New American Library.

Goodman, N. (1976) *Languages of Art: An Approach to a Theory of Symbols*. Indianapolis, Hackett.

—— (1978) *Ways of Worldmaking*. Indianapolis, Hackett.

—— (1984) *Of Minds and Other Matters*. Cambridge, MA, Harvard University Press.

—— and Elgin, C. (1988) *Reconstruction in Philosophy and Other Arts and Sciences*. Indianapolis, Hackett.

McFague, S. (1987) *Models of God: Theology for an Ecological, Nuclear Age*. Philadelphia, Fortress Press.

Miles, M. (1985) *Image as Insight: Understanding in Western Christianity and Secular Culture*. Cambridge MA, Harvard University Press.

Minear, P. (1987) *Death Set to Music*. Atlanta, John Knox Press.

Noddings, N. (1984) *Caring: A Feminine Approach to Ethics and Moral Education*. Berkeley, University of California Press.

Ravitch, D. (2000) *The Great School Wars: A History of the New York City Public Schools*. Baltimore, Johns Hopkins University Press.

Scheffler, I. (1986) *Inquiries: Philosophical Studies of Language, Science and Learning*. Indianapolis, Hackett.

Spiegel, S. (1967) *The Last Trial: On the Legends and Lore of the Command to Abraham to Offer Isaac as a Sacrifice: The Akedah*. Trans. J. Goldin, New York, Pantheon Books.

Turner, V. (1977) *The Ritual Process: Structure and Anti-Structure*. Ithaca, NY, Cornell University Press.

Van der Leeuw, G. (1938) *Religion in Essence and Manifestation*. Trans J.E. Turner. New York, Macmillan.

Yob, I.M. (1992) 'Religious Metaphor and Scientific Model: Grounds for Comparison'. *Religious Studies*, 28, 475–85.

Zam, G.A. and Stone, G.E. (2006) 'Social Studies Teacher Educators: A Survey of Attitudes toward Religion in the Curriculum'. *Religion and Education*, Winter, 90–105.

Chapter 14

Religious Education and Liberal Nurture

Andrew Wright

Abstract

Should nurture have a place in the common, state sponsored schools in England and Wales and if so, what character should it adopt? Some argue that secular liberal approaches to education eschew, or at least minimise, the place of nurture in formal schooling in an attempt to safeguard the freedom of students. This view is rejected and it is argued that nurture constitutes a necessary foundation for all educational activities. Contemporary Religious Education in common state schools deliberately nurtures pupils into a distinctively secular liberal understanding of religion. Upon what theological grounds should Christians respond to this strategy of nurturing children into a secular liberal system of beliefs and values?

Introduction

The standard dictionary definitions of 'nurture' tend to combine two interlinked meanings: first, the provision of food and nourishment, second the rearing, training and formation of children. Throughout the chapter I take as read a number of assumptions about nurture: that it is an intentional activity; that it can be provided for implicitly through the deliberate organisation of the child's environment, and explicitly through intentional instruction, encouragement and guidance; that it can involve both the positive gifting of selected cultural goods and the negative withholding of others; that the domestic life of the family provides the primary context for nurture, with formal schooling providing a significant secondary context; that nurture within formal schooling is normally focused and systematic in intention, and generally utilises a broad range of pedagogical strategies; that nurture impacts on the whole child in terms of his or her ability to feel, think and act, and as such cannot be limited to a process of pre-cognitive formation applicable only to the early years of schooling; that, judged in terms of its ability to achieve its intended outcomes, nurture can be both successful and unsuccessful; and, finally, that the teleological goals of the nurturing process can be both appropriate and inappropriate (both Christians and terrorists nurture their children).

The Eclipse of Nurture?

Certain strands of contemporary educational discourse betray a latent suspicion of nurture, most visibly in postmodern claims that the induction of children into a specific cultural tradition constitutes nothing less than an exercise in the administration of raw power (Parker 1997; cf. Wright 2004, pp. 141–3). Such claims are predicated on that 'most invisible, because it is the most pervasive of all modern goods, unconstrained freedom' (Taylor 1992, p. 489). The philosophical roots of this position can be traced back at least as far as Descartes, whose hermeneutic of suspicion brought about the dislocation of the individual from their cultural heritage and undermined relational accounts of personal identity. Following Descartes, identity came to be predicated on the freedom to exist in splendid isolation from any socio-cultural constraints:

> If you have a basket of apples, some of which (as you know) are bad and will spoil and poison the rest, you have no other means than to empty your basket completely and then take and test the apples one by one, in order to put the good ones back in your basket and throw away those that are not. (Descartes 1970, p. xxi)

Modernity sought to preserve autonomy through three, not necessarily complementary, strategies: (1) rational appeals to the court of reason and the subsequent acceptance of received tradition on the grounds of merit rather than imposed authority; (2) romantic appeals to humanity in its pristine natural state, as yet uncontaminated by the corrupting influence of society; (3) liberal appeals to the twin virtues of freedom of belief and tolerance of the beliefs of others.

(1) Rational appeals to the court of reason are imbedded in a particular brand of liberal education whose primary concern is for the development of a disciplined mind. A well-formed mind, according to Newman, will acquire

> a habit of order and system, a habit of referring every accession of knowledge to what we already know, and of adjusting the one to the other . . . [and] the actual acceptance and use of certain principles as centres of thought, around which our knowledge grows and is located. (Newman 1982, p. 378)

A crucial distinction needs to be made at this juncture: for Newman the cultivation of mind could only take place by immersing students in received intellectual traditions, whereas for Descartes it must always begin with a blank slate. It is in this latter sense that the appeal to reason provides a counter to nurture: by empowering students to think autonomously, it was deemed possible to protect them from the imposition of regimes of power masquerading as knowledge. Rather than merely accepting the received opinions of others, students must learn to assess critically any and all claims to knowledge, including those of the communities within which they are being reared.

(2) Romantic appeals to humanity in its pristine natural state have their roots in the tradition of child-centred education initiated by Rousseau. He believed that the process of nurturing children into the prevailing norms of society would inevitably corrupt the minds of students; though everything that comes from God is good, everything degenerates in the hands of humankind (Rousseau 1986, p. 5). Rousseau's

denial of original sin and consequent appeal to the natural goodness of the 'noble savage' led to his advocacy of a negative education predicated 'not in teaching virtue or truth, but in preserving the heart from vice and from the spirit of error' (p. 57). Darling identifies four core aspects of such negative education: unlimited scope for play; freedom to learn in an environment devoid of external constraints; the introduction of stimuli only if appropriate to the child's natural being; and the replacement of direct teaching and instruction with encouragement to the child to think things through on the basis of her natural reason (Darling 1985).

(3) Liberal appeals to the twin virtues of freedom and tolerance have their roots in the educational thought of Locke. His *Thoughts Concerning Education* embrace a high view of the power and effectiveness of education: 'of all the men we meet with, nine parts of ten are what they are, good or evil, useful or not, by their education' (1989, p. 83). Further – and in apparent contradiction to the flow of the present argument – he clearly understands education as a form of nurture, cautioning that great care must be taken in 'forming children's minds, and giving them that seasoning early, which shall influence their lives always after' (p. 103). It is clear that for Locke nurture is justifiable provided it results in the emergence of a well-rounded liberal citizen: the archetypal bourgeoisie gentleman in possession of 'a sound mind in a sound body' and in full ownership of the virtues of freedom and tolerance (p. 83). This suggests a certain level of ambiguity amongst advocates of the claim that modern education has overseen the eclipse of nurture: nurture, it appears, is acceptable provided it results in the habit of autonomy.

All three strategies are currently advocated within contemporary RE, as taught in state schools in the UK. (1) Students are encouraged to reason about religion, albeit in a manner that reinforces prevailing relativistic ideology and tends to result in a thoroughgoing agnosticism (Thompson 2004a, p. 149). (2) Students are taught that the ultimate criterion for truth is that of their own spiritual desires and preferences (Wright 1998). (3) Students learn in the context of a value-system that advocates the intrinsic value of pluralism and the fundamental importance of the twin virtues of freedom and tolerance (Cooling 1994). For many the conclusion to be drawn from all this is clear: in the name of freedom contemporary education has systematically rejected the task of inducting children into, and nurturing them within, any specific tradition of beliefs and values.

The Inevitability of Nurture

Strategies designed to preserve the autonomy of children are firmly in place in contemporary education. What is not clear, however, is that such strategies constitute a rejection of nurture *per se*; on the contrary, the persistence of nurturing strategies in Locke's pedagogy suggests that the dichotomy between education-as-nurture and education-for-autonomy is a false one. In this section I argue that nurture is an inevitable and necessary foundation of all educational activities, and consequently that strategies designed to establish individual autonomy actually function as a means of nurturing children within a secular liberal worldview.

It is impossible to establish a neutral 'god's-eye' perspective on the world: we are necessarily embedded within the traditions in which we are brought up, and which mould us into the people we are. Contra Descartes, it is impossible to empty our basket of apples and start the pursuit of knowledge afresh. According to Gadamer, whenever we seek to develop our knowledge we always start out from our prior commitments and beliefs, which constitute the necessary fore-structure of our understanding (Gadamer 1979). The questions we ask are dependent on our prior assumptions and beliefs: 'a person who is trying to understand a text is always performing an act of projection' (p. 237). The inevitability of such pre-understanding leads Gadamer to rehabilitate the notion of prejudice, understood not as some blinkered knee-jerk reaction, but as reflective pre-judgement and pre-supposition. It follows that faith seeking understanding takes precedence over understanding seeking faith: 'Long before we understand ourselves through the process of self-examination, we understand ourselves in a self-evident way in the family, society and state in which we live' (p. 245). This enables Gadamer to recognise that 'the fundamental prejudice of the Enlightenment is the prejudice against prejudice itself, which deprives tradition of its power' (p. 239).

Newman's notion of 'illative sense' has affinities with Gadamer's argument (Newman, 1979, pp. 270–72). Knowledge is not grounded in indubitable proof, but in informed assent to reasonable beliefs. To be effective, such assent requires a right state of heart and mind. Hence knowledge is bound up with personal temperament: we believe on the basis of judgements that flow from our holistic engagement with the world we indwell. By illative sense, Newman means 'the capacity to appraise the force of the evidence and to identify the point at which it suffices to warrant a firm conviction' (Dulles 2002, p. 40). Abstract reasoning and empirical verification cannot by themselves form the basis of our beliefs and commitments. According to Newman, though arguments from probability can never exclude the possibility of error, this is no warrant for scepticism. Probability is not opposed to certitude, since arguments from probability can generate firm conclusions that we are entirely justified in assenting to with whole-hearted commitment. Hence I can reasonably assent to the certain knowledge that genocide is evil and Mozart a musical genius, even though I cannot actually rule out the possibility that I may be mistaken. Our assent to our beliefs springs from 'a process of informal reasoning in which the mind works spontaneously and unreflectively' (Dulles 2002, p. 41).

The implication of the positions of Gadamer and Newman is clear: when secular liberals give assent to the virtues of reason, freedom and tolerance they do so on the basis of their faith in a distinctively modern worldview brought into being by the Enlightenment. Consequently when they use these virtues as the basis for an educational programme designed to preserve individual autonomy by avoiding the imposition of any received tradition, what are actually doing is nurturing children into a modern liberal way of being in the world.

Lesslie Newbigin calls on the religious educator to 'expose for examination the fundamental axioms, the prior decisions about what is allowed to count as evidence, which underlie his way of understanding' (Newbigin 1982, p. 99). Research has revealed a clear set of prior faith commitments underlying contemporary non-confessional approaches to RE (Cooling 1994; Hardy 1975, 1976, 1979; Thatcher

1991; Thompson 2004a; Wright 1998, 2004). Hence, Thompson's observation that since 'education must of necessity "confess" something', 'non-confessional religious education is founded on a contradiction' (Thompson 2004b, p. 64). Rather than lacking any prior faith commitment, so-called 'non-confessional' liberal RE actually nurtures children into a clear understanding of the nature of religion and its significance for personal spiritual development. Children are taught to believe whatever they like, provided they tolerate the beliefs of others; to make choices by being truthful to their inner experiences and feelings; and to make up their own minds, rather than have others make them up for them. The principles upon which such teaching is delivered are not normally subject to negotiation; rather they form the implicit bedrock within which children are nurtured. If, as Thompson fears, the outcome of such education is more often than not the confession of agnosticism, then this simply reflects the fact that such agnosticism constitutes the default position of secular liberalism *vis-à-vis* religion.

There is a danger of Christians underestimating the robustness of this liberal reading of religion, and ignoring its attractiveness in many spheres of contemporary society. Alasdair MacIntyre has suggested that the moral discourse of contemporary society is in a state of 'grave state of disorder' (MacIntyre 1985, p. 2). It is tempting to apply his argument to contemporary RE and argue that it presents students with mere 'fragments of a conceptual scheme, parts of which now lack those contexts from which their significance derived' (p. 2). However, though the liberal representation of Christianity is deeply inadequate in terms of the theological self-understanding of Christians, it is at least consistent in terms of its own philosophical self-understanding. It may well draw on fragments of the Christian scheme in a manner that fails to do justice to Christianity, but it moulds such fragments together into a story that many – rightly or wrongly – find far more coherent than the Christian story. Like it or not, the pragmatic virtues of freedom and tolerance appear to many in contemporary society to possess far greater value than the truths of Christianity.

Hence I have reservations about Thompson's claim that though 'some framework of belief and way of seeing the world is necessary', liberal RE consistently fails to provide one (Thompson 2004b, p. 63). The problem for Christians is not that contemporary RE lacks a distinctive framework, but that this framework is not a Christian one. Though from a Christian perspective the prevailing liberal framework is palpably misguided, there is no denying the authority it enjoys within contemporary society. Thompson argues that the primary task of education is to introduce 'pupils to what is considered true and of value in a particular society' (Thompson 2004a, p. 150). Quite so, that is precisely what contemporary RE does when nurturing students within the prevailing secular liberal worldview.

Christian Responses to Liberal Nurture

We have reached the pivotal point of this chapter. I have argued that nurture is necessarily foundational for all educational activities, and that contemporary RE nurtures students in a secular liberal understanding of religion. I now want to go on and address the question as to how Christians ought to respond to this situation.

The main body of Penny Thompson's *Whatever Happened to Religious Education?* chronicles the shift from confessional to non-confessional RE. Her historical account serves as the launch pad for her appeal for a return to explicitly Christian confessionalism in community – as opposed to faith-based – schools in the UK. I am in broad agreement with the basis of Thompson's argument: that education has the task of transmitting the best that a particular society has to offer; that 'learning takes place within traditions which are circumscribed by particular boundaries and undergirded by particular assumptions'; that religious understanding requires teaching within a particular tradition; that 'the task of RE is one of careful introduction into a particular religion'; and that this is 'best carried out by those who have both insight into and a degree of devotion to the faith' (pp. 150–51). I depart from Thompson's analysis when she suggests that these principles demand a return to a form of confessional Christian nurture in which the telling of the Christian story leads to an encounter with the truth of the Gospel, teaching includes an invitation to commitment, and lessons are delivered by committed Christian teachers not afraid to engage in the advocacy of their faith (pp. 153–5). Thompson defends her position on a number of grounds, for example, that confessional teaching is allowed by law, that Christian education can branch out into the teaching of world religions, and that Christian nurture does not disallow critical thinking (pp. 162–4).

The reason for my opposition is not the standard one: I have no problem with the notion of confessional Christian education *per se*, and indeed advocate it strenuously in the context of church schools. My problem lies elsewhere. Thompson insists that education always operates within a cultural context, and as such is necessarily a confessional activity. However when she addresses the nature of so-called 'non-confessional' liberal RE she appears to contradict herself: on the one hand she claims that non-confessionalism is built on the false premise that it is possible to teach without confessing something, and on the other she insists that 'in fact many different types of "confessions" operate in religious education' (Thompson 2004b, p. 61). Either RE 'proceeds on the basis of disguised confessions', or the fact that 'it is based on a radical pluralism which (by definition) can offer no means of resolution' results in a failure to nurture children within any specific tradition (Thompson 2004a). The latter option clearly contradicts Thompson's claim, supported by the first part of this chapter, that confession is an inevitable part of education. Since secular liberalism clearly sponsors confessional forms of education it appears that the problem identified by Thompson lies elsewhere: not in the absence of nurture, but rather in the material substance of the worldview of secular liberalism within which students are currently nurtured. Hence the bedrock of her argument is that radical pluralism is both untrue and incoherent. Though I also believe radical pluralism to be both untrue and incoherent, it seems to me difficult to deny both that it is robustly defended by its advocates and that the vast majority of the British public view it as a coherent worldview and subsequently base their lives on it.

My fear is that Thompson underestimates the impact of secular liberalism on society: like it or not we live in a post-Christian world that has developed a clear and robust understanding of religion which enjoys a broad measure of consent across many sections of society, and into which it seeks to nurture children. This raises the fundamental question of authority, specifically the authority of Christians to impose their particular confession on non-Christian children. It is significant here that the liberal establishment has shown generosity in making specific allowances for religious communities, including Christian communities, to nurture children within their own non-liberal traditions. For many liberals Thompson's proposal will appear to lack such generosity, demanding as it does the right of Christians to oversee the RE not only of Christian children, but also of children outside of the Christian community. The core of the problem is a misreading of the context within which Christian teachers currently find themselves: it is no longer the traditional catechetical context in which the core task was to nurture Christian children within the Christian faith; rather it has developed into a missionary context in which Christian teachers work in a predominantly secular liberal environment.

This issue is well understood by Trevor Cooling, who accepts that Christian teachers in state schools now operate in what is essentially a post-Christian context. As such they must take pluralism seriously, not because it is a Christian value, but because it constitutes a key dimension of the liberal society within which Christian teachers are called to mission. State schooling refuses to 'prescribe one framework for all pupils', but instead has adopted 'the much more restricted function of encouraging pupils, with a variety of frameworks, to develop strategies for functioning as citizens in the plural framework in a way that both maintains the integrity of their fundamental beliefs and promotes community harmony' (Cooling 1994, p. 120).

Cooling argues that in such a situation the 'Christian needs to have good reason to refrain from proclaiming the message of redemption through Christ', and concludes that 'the ethical constraints imposed by schooling in the secular democracy provide such reasons' (p. 149). Thompson accepts that Cooling's missionary model is designed to enable children 'to hear the Gospel in school, and be challenged by it' (Thompson 2004a, p. 147). However she rejects other key tenets of Cooling's position, in particular his advocacy of 'distancing devices which make it clear that no pressure is being put on children to adopt any of the religions put before them' (p. 148). She suggests that his commitment to non-coercion 'seems to be motivated as much by concern for fairness within a society containing many religions, as his evangelical background' (p. 148). Has Cooling allowed his acceptance of the ethical constraints placed upon him by liberalism to undermine his fidelity to the Gospel? In order to answer this question we must address the issue of the appropriate way for Christians to behave when faced with an educational system committed to nurturing children within a secular liberal worldview.

Christian Responsibilities towards Secular Liberalism

In this final section I suggest five theological principles to guide Christian behaviour in secular liberal schools.

1.   Incarnational Engagement

This principle is reflected in Article 16 of the Lutheran Augsburg Confession of 1530. Since, 'all government in the world and all established rule and laws were instituted and ordained by God for the sake of good order', it follows that

> it is right for Christians to hold civil office, to sit as judges, to decide matters by the imperial and other existing laws, to award just punishments, to engage in just wars, to serve as soldiers, to make legal contracts, to hold property, to swear oaths when required by magistrates, to marry, to be given in marriage. (Grane 1987, pp. 166–8)

The Confession guards against a docetic retreat from the world: 'Our churches condemn the Anabaptists who forbid Christians to engage in these civil functions' (p. 166). At the same time, it rejects a misplaced Ebionite identification with the world, insisting that faith must always take precedence over civil duties: 'Christians are necessarily bound to obey their magistrates and laws except when commanded to sin, for then they ought to obey God rather than man' (p. 166).

2.   Humility and Service

Such incarnational engagement must be grounded in humility: Christians are to serve a secular world held in being by God. Acknowledging the 'analogy between divine and human political justice in which the poor are lifted up and the prisoner released', Colin Gunton insists that Christians must strive to establish the universal justice realised in Christ (Gunton 1988, p. 192). However, 'there are necessary differences between the way in which the justice of God is achieved in Christ – by the refusal to exercise coercion – and by the way in which fallen human societies, both those claiming a Christian basis and others, tend to realise it' (p. 192).

The transforming power of God's justice becomes a reality in the world through the crucifixion of Jesus: God conquers not through raw power, but in weakness, humility and servitude. Hence the primary task of Christians 'is not to organise the world, but to be within it as a particular way of being human, a living reminder of the true basis and end of human life' (p. 193). God grants to non-Christians the freedom to live their lives outside of the Kingdom of God; this cannot be undermined by Christian attempts to enforce and police God's rule.

3.   The Common Good

A leading outcome of any incarnational engagement with the world in a spirit of humble servitude is the Christian duty to uphold the common good. This is the clear understanding of the Augsburg Confession: since 'lawful civil ordinances are good works of God, Christians must work to uphold them' (Grane 1987, p. 166). Luther's reading of the Augustinian doctrine of the 'Two Kingdoms' has frequently been read as giving priority to the *civitas Dei*, with Christian commitment to the *civitas terrena* limited only to the need to protect society from a descent into anarchy. However, for Luther the Christian is a citizen of both kingdoms ... Indeed, one must state that the Christian is first a citizen of the kingdom of the world and only then a citizen of the kingdom of God ... Since God is also at work in the temporal government, there is ultimately no conflict, since the divine will is authoritative in both kingdoms and governments. (Lohse 1999, p. 320)

4. Prophetic Challenge

In order to preserve the common good Christians must, where necessary, be critical and prophetic. I have argued elsewhere that one of the key tasks facing Christian teachers is to challenge a closed form of liberalism that works against the common good and seek to recall liberals to their original vision of a liberalism open to non-liberal traditions (Wright 2001). Liberalism in its closed form treats the principles of freedom and tolerance as non-negotiable absolutes that must be protected at all costs. This ignores the fact that freedom and tolerance are significantly underdetermined concepts: freedom can be misused (e.g. the freedom to inject heroin) and there are many things unworthy of tolerance (genocide, child abuse etc.). The result is a benign totalitarianism committed to a thoroughgoing relativism and deaf to voices of alterity and difference. Liberalism in its original soft form views the twin principles of freedom and tolerance as constituting a flexible interim ethic designed to allow conversation to take place between diverse worldviews in a spirit of humble respect: open to a diverse range of truth claims, such liberalism seeks to nurture the human quest for knowledge, wisdom and truth across contrasting and often conflicting world-views.

It is on the basis of such an open liberalism that I have argued that a RE concerned simply to maintain a closed liberal worldview needs to be replaced with a critical RE designed to enable children to engage with the truth claims of the various world faiths. Thompson is quite right to point out that such a critical approach cannot be equated with Christian nurture: my contention that such nurture constitutes part of the *civitas Dei* and as such must be located in Christian churches, homes and schools. RE in our post-Christian state schools constitutes part of the *civitas terrena* and as such must not be misconstrued by Christians as an appropriate location for Christian nurture. Thompson's suggestion that there is an inconsistency between my advocacy of critical thinking within the secular RE classroom and my Trinitarian Christianity fails to recognise the reality of the *civitas terrena* and assumes that secular schools constitute part of the *civitas Dei* (Thompson 2004a, p. 146).

5. Christian Proclamation

What then of the commission to 'go and make disciples of all nations, baptising them in the name of the Father and the Son and the Holy Spirit' (Matthew 28:19)? Here Christians need to combine the 'shrewdness of serpents' with the 'innocence of doves' (Matthew 10:16). Though there are clearly locations in the public sphere where Christians legitimately proclaim the Gospel openly and explicitly without any danger of coercion, my contention is that the secular classroom is not one of them. A Christian may legitimately proclaim the Gospel openly in a secular school *only if first explicitly invited to do so* – not because liberal polity demands it, but because it is required by the Gospel. Having accepted the responsibilities attached to the secular notion of professionalism, Christian teachers are duty bound to adhere to them: as guests in an alien environment they must show appropriate respect and humility. Christians should certainly be open about their beliefs and respond honestly to questions about their faith; but that is different to using their authority as teachers to explicitly and aggressively propagate the Gospel. To do so is to respond inappropriately to the invitation of non-Christians to work alongside them in securing the common good. In this situation the most effective form of proclamation is indirect communication: through the character, virtues and actions of the Christian teacher, and the liberal-sponsored critical engagement with questions of religious truth in the RE classroom.

Conclusion

I have argued that the criticism that secular forms of education are incoherent and unworkable because they reject nurture as the primary basis of education is unfounded: on the contrary, secular liberal schools actively nurture students into a specific worldview. Hence the concern of Christians should not be that nurture *per se* does not take place, but rather that liberal schools adopt robust nurturing strategies designed to induct children into a variety of forms of agnosticism and theological relativism. The Christian responsibility in this situation is not to seek to re-impose forms of Christian nurture, since such a strategy will, given the current make-up of society, inevitably be coercive and hence run counter to the Christian Gospel. Rather the Christian task is fivefold: to maintain an incarnational presence in secular schools; to serve secular society in a spirit of humility; to seek to maintain the common good in accordance with the will of God; to challenge liberal schools whenever their educational strategies mitigate against students' dignity and well-being; to proclaim the Gospel robustly – directly when invited to do so, and indirectly at all other times.

References

Cooling, T. (1994) *A Christian Vision for State Education: Reflections on the Theology of Education*. London, SPCK.

Darling, J. (1985) 'Understanding and Religion in Rousseau's *Emile*'. *British Journal of Educational Studies*, 33 (1), 20–34.

Descartes, R. (1970) *Philosophical Writings*. London, Nelson's University Paperbacks.

Dulles, A. (2002) *Newman*. London, Continuum.

Gadamer, H.-G. (1979) *Truth and Method*. London, Sheed and Ward.

Grane, L. (1987) *The Augsburg Confession: A Commentary*. Minneapolis, MN: Augsburg.

Gunton, C.E. (1988) *The Actuality of Atonement: A Study of Metaphor, Rationality and the Christian Tradition*. Edinburgh, T. & T. Clark, 1988.

Hardy, D.W. (1975) 'Teaching Religion: A Theological Critique'. *Learning for Living*, 15 (1), 10–16.

—— (1976) 'The Implications of Pluralism for Religious Education'. *Learning for Living*, 16 (2), 55–62.

—— (1979) 'Truth in Religious Education: Further Reflections on the Implications of Pluralism'. *British Journal of Religious Education*, 1 (3), 102–119.

Locke, J. (1989) *Some Thoughts Concerning Education*. Oxford, Clarendon Press.

Lohse, B. (1999) *Martin Luther's Theology: Its Historical and Systematic Development*. Edinburgh, T. & T. Clark.

MacIntyre, A. (1985) *After Virtue: A Study in Moral Theory*. London, Duckworth.

Newbigin, L. (1982) 'Teaching Religion in a Secular Plural Society'. In J. Hull (ed.) *New Directions in Religious Education*. Basingstoke, Falmer Press, pp. 97–107.

Newman, J.H. (1979) *An Essay in Aid of A Grammar of Assent*. Notre Dame, IN, University of Notre Dame Press.

—— (1982) *The Idea of a University Defined and Illustrated*. Notre Dame, IN, University of Notre Dame Press.

Parker, S. (1977) *Reflective Teaching in the Postmodern World: A Manifesto for Education in Postmodernity*. Buckingham, Open University Press.

Rousseau, J.-J. (1986) *Émile*. London, Dent.

Taylor, C. (1992) *Sources of the Self: The Making of the Modern Identity*. Cambridge, Cambridge University Press.

Thatcher, A. (1991) 'A Critique of Inwardness in Religious Education'. *British Journal of Religious Education*, 14 (1), 22–7.

Thompson, P. (2004a) *Whatever Happened to Religious Education?* Cambridge, Lutterworth Press.

—— (2004b) 'Whose Confession? Whose Tradition?' *British Journal of Religious Education*, 26 (1), 61–72.

Wright, A. (1998) *Spiritual Pedagogy: A Survey, Critique and Reconstruction of Contemporary Spiritual Education in England and Wales*. Abingdon, Culham College Institute.

—— (2001) 'Religious Education, Religious Literacy and Democratic Citizenship'. In L.J. Francis, J. Astley and M. Robbins (eds) *The Fourth R for the Third Millennium: Education in Religion and Values for the Global Future*. Dublin: Lindisfarne, pp. 201–219.

—— (2004) *Religion, Education and Post-Modernity*. London, RoutledgeFalmer.

<h1>Chapter 15</h1>

<h1>Crossing the Divide?</h1>

Jeff Astley

Abstract

The divide (which seems to have become a part of educational orthodoxy) between a 'confessional' education into religion, on the one hand, and a 'non-confessional' education about religion, on the other, is not unbridgeable. The role of empathy in understanding religion, and the place of affect more generally, both in religion and in religious communication, calls into question the distinction between the descriptive elucidation and the passionate adoption of religion. 'All decent religious education possesses the potential of being religiously transformative, simply by displaying the transformative stories, ideals, concepts, doctrines, spiritual practices, worship, loves and lives of religion ... In studying transforming ideas one lays oneself open to the possibility of transformation.' Religious Education should not immunize its students against the possibility of such a religious response.

Much of the debate over the proper form that RE should take in schools assumes a clear distinction between a 'confessional' RE that is described as nurture, formation or education-into-religion, on the one hand, and a 'non-confessional' education-about-religion, on the other. This is routinely related to the contrast between participant- and observer-understandings, sometimes conceptualized in terms of the difference between the *religious understanding* of the religiously committed and the student's 'relatively detached' *understanding [of] religion* (Cox 1983).

Focusing on Feeling

Both forms of understanding admit of degree: understanding is 'not an all-or-nothing-at-all matter' (Smart 1986, p. 224). This is particularly significant in the case of understanding the affections, where the distinction outlined above appears more blurred than it does for our understanding of cognitions. I have argued elsewhere that we can only understand feeling-states 'in so far as we have them, or something very like them, ourselves', and therefore that learning to understand (say) Christianity empathetically must include some development of:

> those feelings (with, of course, reflection on them) that are also components of Christian attitudes, emotions, experiences and evaluations, and concomitants of Christian beliefs and action. The fuller understanding of Christianity being aimed at, the 'wider' and 'deeper' these feelings need to be. (Astley 1994a, pp. 93, 96–7)

ence, the learning outcomes that constitute successful learning about the affective component of a religion overlap with those of learning that religion, and the 'taste' of religious emotion that is necessary for empathetic understanding is an ingredient in the same dish as the one enjoyed during a full meal. Where these learning outcomes result from the phenomenologist of religion's 'imaginative rehearsal' of another's feelings ('a kind of mimicking'), Ninian Smart argues both (a) that the 'bracketed make-belief' that is involved in this process is easier 'if you half-believe and think that considerable insight is to be derived from the tradition that you mimic', and (b) that 'the flavour of the mimicking is likely to be sweet' – that is, to involve sympathy ('feeling with') and not just empathy (Smart 1973, p. 37).

However, my concern to give due weight to the affective goes wider than this. Emphasizing knowledge-claims is an important feature of school – and, indeed, church – RE (Rudge 2000, p. 94), because 'beliefs are peculiarly open to reflection and debate: to argument, criticism and development' (Astley 1996, p. 61). Yet there is far more to religion than its cognitive dimension, and an exclusive focus on the cognitive is in danger of badly misconstruing the nature of religion and, by extension, its typical forms of communication and adoption.

Affect is of paramount significance in religion not only in its own right, but also as a key component, contributory cause or close accompaniment of all authentic religious attributes – including religious knowledge itself (Astley 1994b, ch. 6). As John Cottingham has put it, religion only has significance for people if 'a certain mode of receptivity is already in place', one that includes 'a certain kind of emotional dynamic' that is transformative of experience (Cottingham 2005, pp. 83, 85). Therefore, 'we entirely fail to capture what is involved in someone's adoption or rejection of a religious worldview if we suppose we can extract a pure cognitive juice from the mush of emotional or figurative coloration, and then establish whether or not the subject is prepared to swallow it' (p. 80).

The significance of this feeling dimension is often underplayed in those educational analyses that prioritize 'encouraging young people to make [religious] decisions autonomously', and their doing so 'on the basis of a reasonable scrutiny of available evidence' (Jackson 2004, pp. 27–8; see also pp. 34, 36, 51).[1] Dispassionate intellectual processes of evidence sifting and weighing are very unlike what religious decision-making is like on the ground, except within very limited areas (e.g. about the authorship of biblical books). Some writers on religion and RE are so eager to underscore the importance of the cognitive truth-claims of religion, that they summarily dismiss the significance of religious emotion and the subjective appropriation of religion, characterizing those who dwell on these elements as 'romanticist', 'experiential-expressive', 'anti-realist' or 'post-modern'. I shall quote from a number of authors whose work falls under these categories,[2] believing that many of their insights should be taken seriously even by those who retain a more

---

1 Although Jackson himself later criticizes 'neo-modernist' rationalist accounts of religious and spiritual education that concentrate on conceptual clarification, criticism and restatement to the neglect of the affective dimension (p. 85), his earlier remarks suggest that he is working with a rather different construal of religion from the one I wish to develop.

2 Reworking material previously published in Astley (2004b).

traditional religious ontology and epistemology. In particular, these authors' nuanced analyses of the grammar of religion, and of the nature of religious spirituality and religious truth, are often profound. Religious insight comes from surprising sources; even the heretics may have something to teach us (see Astley 2004a).

Seeing the Point of Religion

The writers that I flirt with here criticize excessively cognitive readings of religion and its communication, supporting accounts that place more emphasis on religion's affective and lifestyle dimensions. They insist that religion is (at least in part) what religion does. Theologically, their position is informed more by a soteriological framework than by the more cognitive perspective of a doctrine of revelation. It understands religious beliefs primarily as *beliefs-in*: attitudinal states that generate active commitments. We may wish to argue (against their more radical voices) that cognitive religious *beliefs-that* are components of, or are implied by, such states. But we should agree with them that, *religiously speaking*, this latter species of belief is less significant than the attitudes, emotions and practices that surround, support and permeate religious statements and concepts. Even the concept of God can function non-religiously; it is only when it is responded to that it becomes a religious concept. 'The devils also believe [that there is one God], and tremble' (James 2:19b); but it is only in their trembling that there is anything remotely religious about their believing (and even that is not enough to turn them from their devilry).

Induction into a spirituality or religion by means of confessional RE forms us in a variety of different ways, including how to feel religiously. In this process we are taught what the proper spiritual attitudes are that we should adopt, and we learn to embrace them. In a word, we learn to tremble. This feature is essential to a full religious understanding, which is 'not just a matter of words alone' but involves redirecting one's passions. 'Without such things as fear, contrition and increasing love of God, the concept [of "God"] has not been fully understood' (Martin 1994, pp. 188, 190). Attitudes, emotions and life-changing actions are integral to the idea of religious belief. Dewi Phillips asks, 'What would it mean to say that one believed in God without this involving any affective state in one's life? Even if sense could be made of these "beliefs" divorced from active responses, *what would be particularly religious about them*?' (Phillips 1993, p. 112, my emphasis; cf. pp. 118–19 and also Malcolm 1977; Caputo 2001, pp. 114–17; Jones, 2002, pp. 73–7).

The point of religion lies primarily in its spiritual power. Thus religious concepts should not be interpreted as neutral portrayals of transcendent realities and processes, which we coolly adopt or drop depending on the extent to which they cohere with our framework of 'truth-claims'. They are *effective concepts* that lead to a sense of spiritual wholeness and salvation. They are contained in beliefs that have been framed to drive our spiritual and moral lives – doctrines to live and die for. Most religious concepts are saturated with religious affect. Within Christianity, for example, the doctrine of creation is inextricably linked with feelings of dependence and gratitude; the concept of God's presence with awe and the flavour of grace; and claims about the resurrection with a sense of meaning and hope. Hence, the clarification of these religious concepts within the church's religious teaching is not some sort of austere intellectual exercise, but a process that is intended both to define and to generate spiritual attitudes, insight and response.

As we come to understand religion properly, in its own terms, we are changed by it; because religious concepts *work*. A full (confessional) RE and a full religious understanding is therefore salvific and life-giving.

Gareth Moore claims that religious conversion includes 'conversion of language'. It is a matter of learning a new way of speaking (i.e. of religious understanding) as part of learning a new way of life, and religious language gets its meaning from 'a determination to do certain things and not to do others, to adopt certain attitudes and avoid others' (Moore 1988, p. 131). There isn't just a causal relationship between conceptual understanding and religious response; religious concepts and practices are also internally related – a true religious life being partly constituted by true religious concepts.

Despite the apparent implications of much of their work, neither Moore nor Phillips regarded themselves as expressivists or non-realists in religion. I do not intend to address this controversial point, believing that we should take seriously many of their insights independently of such positions. This is particularly the case when they ask us to consider what 'reality', 'existence', 'truth', 'fact', 'belief', 'prove' and 'objective' amount to *within religion*, for this should generate a debate about the point and purpose of religion. So I am not claiming that religion is to be understood as wholly non-cognitive or expressive, nor that notions of fact or truth have no place in its analysis. I too believe that the question of truth is 'at the heart of spirituality' and that our spiritual lives have to be 'attuned to the way things actually are' (Wright 1998, p. 92; 2000, pp. 107–111). But there are features of the idea of a religious or spiritual fact and a religious or spiritual truth that are peculiar to religion and spirituality. We should therefore not conflate them with other, more mundane understandings of fact and truth – particularly those that undergird science and history, or even non-religious metaphysical systems. Religions certainly contain and imply many pure (non-evaluative) historical, empirical, common-sense and meta-empirical truth-claims; but are such claims truly distinctive of religion? Don't *spiritual claims* lie at its heart? These assert spiritual, affective, self-involving and evaluative truths that cannot be reduced to other – more purely 'objective' and 'realist' – categories. 'There are certain kinds of truth such that to try to grasp them purely intellectually is to avoid them' (Cottingham 2005, p. 11).

Ignoring this dimension of religion in a panic at the expressivist rhetoric of writers such as Phillips can easily blind us to the significance of normative claims about what is truly religious. It is easier than many think to miss the point of religion: to fail to grasp what the religious perspective really means, what it is 'getting at' – and thus fail to 'get it'. Don Cupitt, although an explicit and vocal non-realist, is nevertheless right to complain that 'in our faculties of theology students are trained to get it all wrong'; and religious studies is not going to help them to get it right (Cupitt 2000, p. 22). The real significance of religion sometimes lies sufficiently deep below its surface meaning that the observer who studies it from the outside can often be wholly misled. (As insiders can; witness the Gospel accounts of Jesus' disciples.)

Phillips maintains that religious beliefs are not explanations, but religious or spiritual perspectives, judgements, evaluations, commitments and expressions. (We may wish to say 'not only'.) Hence religious questions about the existence of God are not ('not primarily') theoretical questions. 'Job asks for an *explanation* of creation,' Phillips writes, 'but is given a *song* of creation' (Phillips 2001, p. 78), for God is found *in* praise, thanksgiving, confession, petition.[3] To wonder about God's existence *within* the practice of religion is to wonder about prayer and praise, Phillips insists; it is 'to wonder whether there is anything in all that' (p. 98). On the issue of locating (and mislocating) the category of 'the spiritual' in religion, Phillips writes:

> We do not first assent to the belief that nature is majestic or that the forest is a dreadful place, and then decide to react in certain ways. Rather, our reactions to nature as majestic, or reacting with dread to the forest, are primitive instances of concept-formation in this context … Animism, the intellectualism [R.R.] Marett opposed, would say that primitives danced because they thought it would bring the rains. Rather, they danced at the coming of the rain. The intellectualised postulating of rain spirits misses the spirit in the rain. (Phillips 2001, p. 195; cf. 1993, pp. 116–19)

RE may also miss the spiritual, if in rather different ways.

Crossing to Commitment

For Hanan Alexander, the point of spiritual education is 'not to objectify the good but to "subjectify" it, to enable the student to commit himself to it, become one with it, so that its ways become his … [that is] to become an insider, to live inside a particular vision of the good life' (Alexander 2001, p. 192). Academic study, as in non-confessional RE, intends no more than a clarification of spiritual practice or tradition. A full spiritual education that educates *into* faith must transcend this 'outsider' learning, so as to include the 'insider' engagement that leads to the adoption of the spiritual perspective. It therefore requires not only 'intelligence' but also 'passion' (p. 193).

Although he is sometimes criticized for not knowing the difference between understanding a religious belief and adopting it, Phillips acknowledges the distinction. Because religious doctrines, worship, rituals, and so on, are connected with practices other than those that are *specifically* religious, he believes that 'it is

---

3   Those who criticize the speech of Yahweh from the whirlwind for not providing an adequate intellectual explanation for the problem of evil are both naively optimistic about the possibility of any 'adequate theodicy', and less wise than Job about what constitutes an 'answer' in religion (see Phillips 1993, pp. 154, 160, 166–9 and Phillips 2004). Other religious writers who are rarely charged with unorthodoxy seem to agree: 'It is sheer nonsense to speak of the Christian religion as offering a solution of the problem of evil' (MacKinnon 1968, p. 92); 'To want to escape the "night" and the costly struggles with doubt and vacuity is to seek another God from the one who speaks in and as Jesus crucified' (Williams 1979, p. 179).

possible to convey the meaning of religious language to someone unfamiliar with it'
(Phillips 1970, p. 230).

> True, religious believers call obedience to God a form of understanding. It would follow
> that anyone who did not practise such obedience in his life, lacked *that* understanding.
> But a philosopher can understand what I have just said about religious understanding and
> give an account of how obedience to God differs from other kinds of obedience, without
> being a believer himself, that is, in this context, without being obedient to God. (Phillips
> 1986, p. 12)

In a more recent text, Phillips labels this elucidation of religious perspectives the
'hermeneutics of contemplation'. Its task is merely 'to elucidate, without advocacy,
what it is like to see the world in this way … what is involved in speaking in this
way' (Phillips 2001, p. 53). It is logically independent of the intention that learners
should *adopt* these perspectives or ways of talking for themselves, by responding to
God. 'To possess such understanding is not itself to talk to God. The latter involves
bending the knee. Someone may understand what prayer is, but still be unable to
pray, or even want to pray' (p. 200).

I wonder, however, whether this is not too neat and tidy a distinction. In particular,
I doubt whether one can make so clean a cut within the joint of the potential *learning
outcomes* of these two different types of RE. In the same book, Phillips writes:

> Does … philosophical contemplation [entail] actually being able to engage in the various
> reactions we have talked about? That would be going too far, but it would be odd if one
> were able to give attention to them without *any* such response having ever entered one's
> soul. On the other hand, to contemplate is not the same as to appropriate personally. But
> it is to be able to see in the rituals and practices which people find majestic, terrible, or
> sinister, that human life can be like that. (p. 182)

Elsewhere he has written that (non-confessional) RE should not be in the hands of
the religiously 'tone deaf' (1970, pp. 166–7), but should be taught by those who are
able to take religion seriously, to see something in it, to respect it.

Ludwig Wittgenstein distinguished two forms or stages of religious learning (cf.
Astley 2002, ch. 2):

> A religious belief could only be something like a passionate commitment to a system of
> reference … It's passionately seizing hold of *this* interpretation. Instruction in a religious
> faith, therefore, would have to take the form of a portrayal, a description, of that system
> of reference, while at the same time being an appeal to conscience. And this combination
> would have the result in the pupil himself, of his own accord, passionately taking hold of
> the system of reference. (Wittgenstein 1980, p. 64)

We may equate Wittgenstein's first mode of religious learning with *learning
about a faith*. It has a third-person accent; it is 'grammar-like and something
like an account that we can get from others who have been there long before us'.
The religious knowledge of the believer, however, 'must always move towards a
present-tense, first-person mood', since knowledge of God 'has to have the form of

personal appropriation built in' (Holmer 1978, pp. 24–5). The initial learning is now transformed in the mouth, mind and heart of the believer into the learning *of faith*.

Wittgenstein offers the key to this second mode, style or stage of religious learning. It is no detached, dispassionate adoption of religious beliefs, undertaken after cool enquiry on the basis of clinical critical reflection, but a passionate embrace. It involves the learners 'speaking for themselves', 'taking sides', 'plighting troths', 'trusting' and acting on trust. It therefore shares many of the qualities of a value commitment. 'Coming to God is not a change of opinion, but a change of direction; a reorientation of one's whole life' (Phillips 1988, p. 118). We shall never *fully* understand religious concepts unless we feel their accompanying affects ourselves, and are disposed to behave in a manner appropriate to what we have learned. 'To understand a religious expression supposes that a passion will also follow the learning', as 'we let the categories of religion gain their dominance in our daily life' (Holmer 1978, pp. 66, 71).

Religious commitment is akin to falling in love, and thus has few objective criteria that others may share. 'A declaration of love is a personal matter ... because the person who makes it does not thereby commit himself to supposing that anyone who fails to love what he does has somehow gone wrong' (Frankfurt 1988, p. 92; cf. Astley 1994b, pp. 228–41). Because the 'truth' about our beloved is of this personal nature – something about what *we* are and do – we may say that it is inevitably 'subjective'. Authentic loving and authentic faith are matters of each to her or his own. 'Instruction in a religious faith' can give us some understanding of religious concepts, but frequently this has as little depth as a second-hand, conceptual understanding of love. One may 'learn the language of love and never be in love. [One] might recognize it in others, ... or ... use it in feigning love' (Rhees 1969, p. 124). But this is very different from truly learning what love is by being in love.

We may learn about and come to 'know' many people, but embrace and then really come to know one person much more intimately. It is the same with religion. And here too there is always the risk that things might go further. 'Respect' can lead to 'response'; taking others seriously is a step towards becoming serious about them. Therefore those who are not religiously tone deaf (and these are the only ones who can even begin to understand properly the religion they are studying) are always going to be 'at risk' when engaged in such a study. We might imagine them as mountaineers who have ascended to the edge of a narrow ravine, and now peer across to a landscape they have so far only observed from afar. They are in the right position to cross the divide, if only they have the heart for it. This is one way (the way?) in which an understanding of religion can lead to religious understanding, through a conversion of heart and head together – 'a very radical form of learning from Christianity' (Cooling 1996, p. 177).[4] In this way, the gulf is bridged.

Exploring a religious tradition properly (deeply) can change people. Observing empathetically its rituals, music and other practices and expressions, and waiting on its powerful, self-involving concepts and beliefs, can have a profound effect on

---

4   For Michael Grimmitt, 'learning from religion' involves no more than that pupils should evaluate their understanding of religion in personal terms and their self-understanding in religious terms (Grimmitt 1987, pp.165, 168, 203, 211, 225–6, 241; 2000, p. 15).

the learner. These things possess the power to transform. Religious traditions only survive because of the spiritual power inherent within them; that is their *point*. Do we really want our pupils to miss the point?

Yet some rejoice that these potent forces can easily be tamed within the classroom, for example when students are taught by those who have little sense of the power of religion, or when direct access to its depths is avoided – perhaps by substituting a superficial examination of the (frequently half-hearted) religious responses of religion's purported 'adherents'. Even an in-depth study of the religiosity of Jeff Astley is never going to be an adequate substitute for engagement with the power of the narratives, symbols, teachings, parables, scriptures, prayers, liturgies, doctrines and visions of cruciform living that make up the Christian way.

The same arguments may be made, of course, for all the 'living religions'. Religion can always be domesticated and brought to heel. But if its power *is* released, no amount of clucking over the squeaky-clean professional intentions of the teacher is going to keep the divide divided.

The Mediation of Religious Disclosure

This analysis may be taken further. Fergus Kerr has warned us that RE could prove to be a form of *confrontational* learning: it 'does not take place in a vacuum … [but] as a challenge to the values and practices that the learner already has, whatever they may be' (Kerr 1998, pp. 77–8). Andrew Wright has written of the particular form that the 'risky and challenging process' of a transformative education may take when it allows for an encounter with the transcendent other. In Rudolf Otto's words, this other is radically other – the dreadful yet alluring '*Mystery* inexpressible and above all creatures' (Otto 1925, pp. 12–13; Wright 2004, pp. 208–214).

In one of my earliest papers (Astley 1981) I claimed that some people come to experience God by first coming to know (i.e. to understand) the concept of God, because learning the meaning of 'God' puts them into the position where they can come to discover God – or, if you prefer, to be discovered by God. This is something even more radical than the passionate embrace of religious appropriation: it is old-fashioned 'religious experience', the human corollary of divine revelation. My argument was that an understanding of the complex of concepts that makes up 'the meaning of God' may itself be a necessary, although surely never a sufficient, condition for discerning God.

This is not just a matter of being able to 'recognize' God as God, as I am able to recognize Jim when I learn that he is bald and has a hooked nose; for in the latter case I have been able to see Jim all along. But in religious cognition we might sometimes have to know what to look for before we can 'see' it at all. Or, to switch to an auditory metaphor, we need to know what the 'authentic voice' of God is like, before we can hear it for ourselves. A similar cognitive situation holds when one has to explain to someone what he is looking for, or should be listening for, before he can see a pattern in an ambiguous puzzle-picture, or pick out a specific bird's song within the dawn chorus. Perhaps understanding theistic language is our way of putting ourselves linguistically into a position to receive God's self-revelation.

Is this, in fact, the norm? Generally speaking, people do not experience a God who is otherwise totally unknown to them; they come to know a God who fits the concept of God that they have already acquired at second-hand (compare Ramsey 1971, pp. 215–16; 1973, pp. 64–5 and Franks Davis 1989, pp. 159–65).

Part of the explanation for this may be broadly psychological rather than purely epistemological, if it is the case that some people can only come to an awareness of God if they are favourably disposed towards the image of God. Richard Hanson offers a frank confession of the way in which the attribute of *fascinans* of the *mysterium tremendum* can affect someone's religious belief:

> I want to believe in God and I do believe in God because I cannot resist the attraction which such belief holds for me … We choose God, not out of a stern sense of duty nor in a spirit of cool calculation of expediency, but because God makes himself sweet to us … The motive-power of Christian belief is the attraction of God's love. (Hanson 1973, pp. 1–2, 8)

To open ourselves to the compulsive attractiveness of the concept of God, by positively and empathetically seeking to understand it, is to put ourselves freely into a position to receive the religious intuition-revelation. Some at least must understand in order to believe, not only so that they can believe in something understandable but also because for them the understanding catalyses or evokes the experience that leads to belief. This may be what happens when people are converted by reading the Bible, or even by listening to sermons. Might it also happen to those who receive RE?

An Inadequate Conclusion

Not all RE will deliver such a radical form of religious knowledge. But all decent RE possesses the potential of being religiously transformative, simply by displaying the transformative stories, ideals, concepts, doctrines, spiritual practices, worship, loves and lives of religion. A good description of any spiritually powerful and effective concept, vision or framework can transform the lives of those who have come to understand it, if only they are allowed to come close enough to it. In studying transforming ideas one lays oneself open to the possibility of transformation. And sometimes, particularly in religion, to know something properly – deeply, thoroughly – *is* to love it. A deep understanding will then evoke a passionate embrace and a release of spiritual power (and then, perhaps, something *more*).

Of course, one must already have been *somewhat* 'transformed' in order empathetically to understand some of these transforming concepts at all. But this is where we came in, with a claim about the importance of having had certain feelings in order to understand religion, for which feeling is so central. Again, the better the education and the understanding, the more likely and more authentic the religious response.

The debate over nurture often focuses on the teacher's intentions. Not only is this a somewhat negative criterion of demarcation between the forms of RE, but the claim that in non-confessional RE the professional teacher '*should not intend* to evoke any religious commitment' is also sometimes misconstrued as 'she *should intend* that the pupils *do not* come to any religious commitment'. But good RE ought never to immunize its students against the potential spiritual effects of understanding the concepts of a religious faith. We know, however, that bad RE – while doubtless intending to make us more 'familiar with' and 'better informed about' the faiths – can so misrepresent a religion that we miss its point entirely. I fear that this is sometimes also true of religious nurture. It is inexcusable in either context.

References

Alexander, H.A. (2001) *Reclaiming Goodness: Education and the Spiritual Quest*. Notre Dame, IN, University of Notre Dame Press.

Astley, J. (1981) 'The Idea of God, the Reality of God and Religious Education'. *Theology*, LXXXIV (698), 115–20.

—— (1994a) 'The Place of Understanding in Christian Education and Education about Christianity'. *British Journal of Religious Education*, 16 (2), 90–101. Reprinted in Astley and Francis (1994), pp. 105–117.

—— (1994b) *The Philosophy of Christian Religious Education*. Birmingham, AL, Religious Education Press.

—— (1996) 'Theology for the Untheological? Theology, Philosophy and the Classroom'. In Astley and Francis (1996), pp. 60–77.

—— (2002) *Ordinary Theology: Looking, Listening and Learning in Theology*. Aldershot, Ashgate.

—— (2004a) 'Religious Non-Realism and Spiritual Truth'. In G. Hyman (ed.), *New Directions in Philosophical Theology: Essays in Honour of Don Cupitt*. Aldershot, Ashgate, pp. 19–33.

—— (2004b) 'What is Religion and Whose Faith is it Anyway? Some Issues concerning the Nature and Normativity of Religion, and the Risks of Religious Education'. In H. Lombaerts and D. Pollefeyt (eds) *Hermeneutics and Religious Education*. Leuven, Leuven University Press, pp. 399–416.

—— and Francis, L.J. (eds) (1994) *Critical Perspectives on Christian Education: A Reader on the Aims, Principles and Philosophy of Christian Education*. Leominster, Gracewing.

—— and Francis, L.J. (eds) (1996) *Christian Theology and Religious Education: Connections and Contradictions*. London, SPCK.

Caputo, J.D. (2001) *On Religion*. London, Routledge.

Cooling, T. (1996) 'Education is the Point of RE – not Religion? Theological Reflections on the SCAA Model Syllabuses'. In Astley and Francis (1996), pp. 164–83.

Cottingham, J. (2005) *The Spiritual Dimension: Religion, Philosophy, and Human Vocation*. Cambridge, Cambridge University Press.

Cox, E. (1983) 'Understanding Religion and Religious Understanding'. *British Journal of Religious Education*, 6 (1), 3–7.

Cupitt, D. (2000) *Philosophy's Own Religion*. London, SCM Press.

Frankfurt, H.G. (1988) *The Importance of What We Care About.* Cambridge, Cambridge University Press.

Franks Davis, C. (1989) *The Evidential Force of Religious Experience.* Oxford, Clarendon Press.

Grimmitt, M. (1987) *Religious Education and Human Development.* Great Wakering, McCrimmons.

—— (ed.) (2000) *Pedagogies of Religious Education: Case Studies in the Research and Development of Good Pedagogic Practice in RE.* Great Wakering, McCrimmons.

Hanson, R.P.C. (1973) *The Attractiveness of God.* London, SPCK.

Holmer, P.L. (1978) *The Grammar of Faith.* San Francisco, Harper & Row.

Jackson, R. (2004) *Rethinking Religious Education and Plurality: Issues in Diversity and Pedagogy.* London, RoutledgeFalmer.

Jones, S. (2002) 'Graced Practices: Excellence and Freedom in the Christian Life'. In M. Volf and D.C. Bass (eds) *Practicing Theology: Beliefs and Practices in Christian Life.* Grand Rapids, Eerdmans, pp. 51–77.

Kerr, F. (1998) 'Truth in Religion: Wittgensteinian Considerations'. In D. Carr (ed.) *Education, Knowledge and Truth: Beyond the Postmodern Impasse.* London, Routledge, pp. 68–79.

MacKinnon, D. (1968) *Borderlands of Theology.* London, Lutterworth Press.

Malcolm, N. (1977) 'The Groundlessness of Belief'. In S.C. Brown (ed.) *Reason and Religion.* Ithaca, NY, Cornell University Press, pp. 143–57.

Martin, D.M. (1994) 'Learning to Become a Christian'. In Astley and Francis (1994), pp. 184–201.

Moore, G. (1988) *Believing in God: A Philosophical Essay.* Edinburgh, T. & T. Clark.

Otto, R. (1925) *The Idea of the Holy: An Inquiry into the Non-Rational Factor in the Idea of the Divine and its Relation to the Rational.* ET London, Oxford University Press.

Phillips, D.Z. (1970) *Faith and Philosophical Enquiry.* London, Routledge & Kegan Paul.

—— (1986) *Belief, Change and Forms of Life.* London, Macmillan.

—— (1988) *Faith after Foundationalism.* London, Routledge.

—— (1993) *Wittgenstein and Religion.* Basingstoke, Macmillan.

—— (2001) *Religion and the Hermeneutics of Contemplation.* Cambridge, Cambridge University Press.

—— (2004) *The Problem of Evil and the Problem of God.* London, SCM Press.

Ramsey, I.T. (ed.) (1971) *Words about God: The Philosophy of Religion.* London, SCM Press.

—— (1973) *Models for Divine Activity.* London, SCM Press.

Rhees, R. (1969) *Without Answers.* London, Routledge & Kegan Paul.

Rudge, J. (2000) 'The Westhill Project: Religious Education as Maturing Pupils' Patterns of Belief and Behaviour'. In Grimmitt (2000), pp. 88–111.

Smart, N. (1973) *The Science of Religion and the Sociology of Knowledge.* Princeton, Princeton University Press.

—— (1986) *Concept and Empathy.* London, Macmillan.

Williams, R. (1979) *The Wound of Knowledge: Christian Spirituality from the New Testament to St John of the Cross.* London, Darton, Longman & Todd.

Wittgenstein, L. (1980) *Culture and Value.* Ed. G.H. von Wright. ET Oxford, Blackwell.

Wright, A. (1998) *Spiritual Pedagogy.* Culham, Culham College Institute.

—— (2000) *Spirituality and Education.* London, RoutledgeFalmer.

—— (2004) *Religion, Education and Post-Modernity.* London, RoutledgeFalmer.

Afterword

M.C. Felderhof

This 'Afterword' was to have been written by the late Professor Terence McLaughlin, whose premature and sudden death has come as a shock to all who knew him. I cannot hope to replace his philosophical sense and acuity that could help us see through the morass of contemporary educational life with the well-judged fairness, balance and wisdom that marked his work. He is sorely missed.

The preceding chapters are the outcomes of deliberations between (a) educationalists, (b) theologians and (c) philosophers, representing the three major disciplines that have a direct bearing on Religious Education (RE). They point to necessary corrections that should be made in RE from these three perspectives. There is a need for:

1. greater attention to the language of religion if children are to access the depth of religious life and the realities this form of life seeks to communicate (Carr, Yob);
2. greater attention to religious doctrine and reasoning if children are to develop judgement and to engage truly and tolerantly with others who think differently (Watson, Houston) but also the acknowledgement of the proper limits to the demand for justifications (Lloyd);
3. greater attention to context: historical, social, and intellectual culture that have the power to shape and distort the task of educating the young in religious matters (Fleming, Maple, Thompson, Sullivan);
4. greater clarity and honesty about some educational expectations from RE (Kay) and the actual impact of contemporary multi-faith RE (Barnes, Wright);
5. greater clarity and honesty about the religious outcomes of RE (Astley) and the implications this might have for schooling (Thiessen).

Such changes should be made if RE is really to improve in school. But academics cannot simply impose the changes even if there was a widespread agreement and consensus about them in the wider RE profession. Ordinary community schools in a secular, plural society raise practical issues of how the changes would be received and accepted by the general public.[1] A political dimension needs to be embraced. I propose to take the discussion forward by considering the process through which these changes are to be realised. How can one go about devising a form of RE for the young, appropriate to our time and place, which will actually be supported? My recommendations arise in part from my experience as the drafting secretary

---

1   Elmer Thiessen provides one solution, but the withdrawal of RE into faith schools cannot be the whole solution for the majority of the population. It would either leave many pupils without any RE whatsoever in non-faith schools or it would divide the school population wholly on religious grounds which would probably not be politically acceptable in the UK.

of the Birmingham Agreed Syllabus Conference seeking to review and revise the RE syllabus for this large multi-faith city in Britain. The work is dominated by the practicalities of guiding and helping RE teachers in delivering RE to pupils in the different phases of education and in very diverse schools and engaging the other major stakeholders in education. The various meetings of the conference and its committees have convinced me of how important this engagement with the wider community actually is to RE.

Those with a serious stake in education include pupils, parents, local communities (including the faith communities), business, the state and the wider society. Any practical solutions must take into account their legitimate interests and concerns. Indeed, they must all contribute in some way to bring about the solutions. In a democratic society professionals are duty bound both to acknowledge this and to facilitate these contributions. Accusations of imposing, coercing, indoctrinating fall too readily from the lips (and pens) of RE theorists, which makes it all the more imperative that educational professionals form genuine partnerships with other stakeholders if they are not to be subject to the same reprimands.

In this regard educational law in England and Wales is particularly helpful, for it insists that an RE syllabus must be agreed and stipulates the process through which this agreement is to emerge and between whom it is to be made. In addition, the law does not envisage a static situation but requires the Agreed Syllabus to be reviewed every five years. RE is *in via*. In essence the teaching profession, on a basis of equality, must regularly negotiate with the Churches, other religious faith groups and elected councillors or their representatives to establish what should be taught. This can be a protracted process. Discussions for the 1975 Birmingham Agreed Syllabus for Religious Education began in 1970 and involved a referral to the courts; so no one can be in any doubt about how genuine and vigorous these discussions can be! Discussions for the 1995 Birmingham syllabus began in 1992 whilst the latest review, which began in the spring of 2005, was only drawn to a conclusion in June 2007 with the adoption of a new agreed syllabus by the City Council.

The necessity for developing an Agreed Syllabus locally has two very valuable consequences. Firstly, the complex process of agreement directly addresses the crisis of authority from which teachers generally and RE teachers in particular suffer in the postmodern world. Postmodernism attacked the grand narratives that provided the basic beliefs from which teaching could proceed. The radical questioning entailed in this attack may well be appropriately unsettling in Higher Education but has proved to be disastrous for school teaching. Without some consensus on what is largely deemed true and valuable, school teachers could no longer teach with confidence but offered instead to 'manage learning', abdicating much of their previously assumed responsibility to pupils. Little could be taught with any authority and what is taught is subjected to a hermeneutical suspicion that cynically tars every claim with accusations of some personal, class or other interest. Working out, and arriving at, a social agreement on what is to be taught in RE may not finally resolve the intellectual questions but can at least provide a basis for practice in the classroom, giving direction and authority to the teacher.

The growth of religious pluralism in society due to immigration and globalisation simply served to exacerbate the incipient relativism of postmodernism. But through a process of communally agreeing, the teacher is provided with a socially authoritative underpinning[2] so essential if they are to start teaching the young, nurturing their nascent cognitive, affective and conative capacities, and transmitting the resources of previous generations. Without some authorised content one cannot develop a pupil's analytical and critical skills just as one cannot nurture musicality without teaching some piece of music. Naturally as children grow in maturity they will be expected to take a greater and greater degree of responsibility for their judgements in religious matters, for choosing to what they will attend and for their creative contributions to the life of faith. Nevertheless, the starting point of the pupil is always the shared communal life and its intellectual capital, not some Cartesian blank sheet. The capacity of pupils to exercise their judgement will rest in large part on the traditions and conceptual apparatus they have been given, and they will do so with reference to the community in which they live, avoiding the irresponsibility of privatisation and individualism. They are answerable to the community and will use its language and its symbolic systems to arrive at the meaning of their life. The community in turn exercises its responsibilities by collectively identifying the curriculum.

Secondly, the process of agreement creates a social context of dialogue. If in a religiously plural society we expect young people to engage in dialogue and to identify the sense and values of our personal and collective communal life, then those conditions must first be created in the wider local community. Interaction of the representatives of the political and religious communities with the professional educators is therefore vital if schooling is to reflect and serve the young people of the community and if schooling is not to become a source of social isolation and alienation. The dialogue between the representatives and educationalists also presupposes that there are inter-religious discussions, dialogue and, to some extent at least, a shared life. Ghettoised communities will inevitably undermine the educational endeavour. Politicians can do a great deal to facilitate this inter-religious dialogue between faiths or they can aggravate relations through neglect or by disproportionately privileging some at the expense of others or by ignoring historic and cultural traditions. They may even deliberately create inter-religious tensions for short-term political ends (Papastephanou 2005). Only an agenda of dialogue and agreement can be religiously and educationally constructive.

The outcome of the process of agreement must not be prejudged nor professionally prescribed or proscribed without genuine consultation. It may be that the professional educators regard schools as their domain and that they are in the vanguard of the educational enterprise but it is the community that directly or indirectly employs them and it is parents who entrust them with their offspring. This presumes an element of accountability and the process of coming to agreement is an important means of rendering an account. Professionals are not accountable to some vaguely defined liberal educational philosophy – though they might use this philosophy to commend to the other stakeholders the wisdom of what they propose – for there are serious educational considerations. This observation is occasioned by the not infrequent censures overheard in meetings that this or that practice or expectation is

---

2   The need to bolster the authority of teachers with a socially agreed syllabus was recognised as early as the 1920s. I owe this observation to Penny Thompson.

not acceptable on 'educational grounds'. But unless these grounds are stated, argued and accepted by the wider community they will be received as a professional will-to-power. Professional educators may believe they know best about what should be done in RE but these beliefs need to be reasoned and justified in the community, in the *agora*. Socrates was prepared to die and not to escape into exile when the community wrongly found him guilty because he recognised the authority of the *polis* even when he disagreed with it. Today, we may not expect educators to offer up their lives but we might expect them to recognise the authority of the community.

Education law in England and Wales is helpful in another practical way of resolving the dilemmas facing RE. It has defined the overarching aims of schooling. It states that the curriculum for a maintained school must be:

a balanced and broadly based curriculum which –
1.	promotes the spiritual, moral, cultural, mental and physical development *of pupils* at the school and *of society*;[3] and
2.	prepares such pupils for the opportunities, responsibilities, and experiences of adult life (ERA 1988).

This reminds RE professionals and religious communities alike that the real foci of the educational agenda are the pupil *and* society. In law, the interests of (religious) institutions and the demands of fields of study are clearly subordinate to the needs of pupils and society. This is not always in evidence in multi-faith RE where religions are not unusually treated as some kind of hypostatised entities that must each be treated equitably as objects of study (Felderhof 2005), and as such it is religions that come to have centre stage in education. Of the two attainment targets often set for RE, for example, in the Non-statutory National Framework for RE (QCA 2004), 'Learning about religion' comes first. From there it is a small step to see religions as separately identifiable, contending parties in which each must have its fair share of the curriculum and of curriculum time. They may be supposed then to enter into some kind of beauty contest in which pupils are invited to state their preference. Or they are imagined as presenting a nonsensical choice between the Christian god, Jewish god, Muslim god, and Hindu god or no god at all. 'Confessional' RE with its singular vision is rejected not because it corrupts the youth (because that would have to be demonstrated) but because it is monopolistic, excluding other parties from the beauty parade; the confessed insights into truth and value are also rejected not because they are shown to be false and worthless but because the mere existence of other possibilities renders them doubtful. All these confusions, with religions in neat boxes, arise because the primary educational focus is religions.

In reaction, the most recent thinking in Birmingham has placed the attainment target 'Learning from faith' first in order to acknowledge that it is the pupils and society which the educational process is to develop. With the spiritual and moral development of pupils firmly in view, the process of agreement centred on the dispositions to which all religious traditions, together with teachers and community representatives, believed pupils might reasonably aspire. It remained for the religious traditions to specify what, where and how in their ample resources they believed they

3	Emphasis mine.

could promote these dispositions. This puts the matter in the right order. Religious traditions do not exist in self-contained boxes or as ends in themselves. They set out to promote human flourishing, which most traditions believe can only be achieved through a relationship to what is transcendent. Religions are no longer contending parties in search of adherents but traditions with a common agenda. Each anticipates to contribute and each seeks to augment (or possibly challenge) the insights of the other. Teachers are encouraged to note and to build on the traditions from which the children in the classroom come on the principle of inclusion. There is no pressure to cover as many traditions as possible; rather, the goal is to broaden and deepen the spiritual and moral insights pupils may gain from their encounter with faith.

The cultivation of dispositions in pupils will have cognitive, affective and conative dimensions and is contextualised in a community that is in a state of conversation, to which schools and pupils contribute. There are educational and pedagogical factors to consider but these are not separated from religious concerns, more often than not they are mutually interdependent. To illustrate: religions encourage attentiveness to the 'Other' and to others; learning also demands a disciplined attention. Without this disposition of attentiveness and without love, education could be self-serving and self-indulgent, religious faith idolatrous. If anyone doubts the need for religious traditions to contribute to this dispositional development of children and to make an input into the education of children, one only needs to examine the 'Every Child Matters' outcomes framework in Britain. It is against this framework that broader educational targets and indicators are now set, evidence gathered and judgments made (Ofsted 2005).

The 'Every Child Matters' vision is as thin as its grammar. It enjoins five phrases, perhaps 'mottos', or possibly commands to the young (but why are the young addressed in this way and not the professionals?): 'Be Healthy', 'Stay Safe', 'Enjoy and Achieve', 'Make a Positive Contribution', 'Achieve Economic Well-Being'! These phrases do not go beyond a vision of society and human beings as self-absorbed individuals relating to others on the basis of mutual self-interest. To command health, achieve economic well-being and oblige safety is about as paradoxical as it is empty to invite the young to enjoy and achieve without specifying what, or to enjoin them to make a positive contribution without any indications of what is regarded as positive or to what enterprise. One wants to say there is more to life; certainly religious martyrs witnessed to a very different kingdom, they ignored health, safety, enjoyment; St Francis abandoned economic well-being. Poor deluded souls!

RE could do better.

References

ERA (1988) *Education Reform Act* <http://www.opsi.gov.uk/acts/acts1988/Ukpga_19880040_en_1.htm>.

Felderhof, M.C. (2005) 'RE: Religions, Equality and Curriculum Time'. *Journal of Beliefs and Values*, 26 (2), 201–214.

Ofsted (2005) *Inspection of Children's Services: Key Judgements and Illustrative Evidence*. London, DfES.

Papastephanou, M. (2005) 'Religious Teaching and the Political Context: The Case of Cyprus'. *Journal of Beliefs and Values*, 26 (2), 139–56.

Qualfications and Curriculum Authority (QCA) (2004) *Religious Education, The Non-Statutory National Framework*. London, QCA.

Index